Vintage Films

Other books by Bosley Crowther

THE LION'S SHARE: The Story of an Entertainment Empire
HOLLYWOOD RAJAH: The Life and Times of Louis B. Mayer
THE GREAT FILMS: Fifty Golden Years of Motion Pictures

VINTAGE FILMS

by BOSLEY CROWTHER

author of *The Great Films*

G.P. PUTNAM'S SONS · NEW YORK

To Tommy, Abe and Howard,
cherished co-workers and
companions in the old Screen
Department of the New York Times,
this book is dedicated with
affection and gratitude

SBN:399–11637–0
Library of Congress Cataloging in Publication Data

Crowther, Bosley.
    Vintage films.

    Includes index.
      1.   Moving-picture plays—History and criticism.
I.   Title.
PN1995.C76   1977   791.43'7   76-19038

PRINTED IN THE UNITED STATES OF AMERICA

CONTENTS

INTRODUCTION

In choosing the title for this compendium of what I call "vintage sound films," I was mindful of the striking similarities between rare old movies and rare old wines. Each domain confronts us with an infinite range of suitable candidates for individual proclivities and tastes. There are wines that are noble, robust, delicate, shimmering, or shy and there are films that are powerful, overwhelming, exquisite, dramatic, or droll. These are discriminations which have to be arbitrarily made, presumably by persons who have experience and competence in the fields. Wines and movies can improve or deteriorate with age, and what may seem a superior achievement at the time of its incipience may turn out to be something quite different with the passage of time. The hundreds of variations in content and quality in each range make it injudicious and even perilous for anybody to be didactic in proposing what is best.

Therefore I do not offer this selection of fifty "vintage" films as pinnacles of achievement in motion pictures since the beginning of sound. I am offering here a pick of old (and a few recent) pictures, some famous and familiar, some not, which I have seen and reseen in my former capacity as motion picture critic for *The New York Times* and more recently as an ongoing student and observer of new and old films, as outstanding achievements by screen artists that have stood the test of time and merit continuing presentation for the pleasures and enlightenment they can afford.

Not for one moment am I saying that this comparative handful of films is an exclusive representation of the finest movies made in the era of sound. A few years ago, I published a selection of rereviews of what I discreetly called *The Great Films*: fifty motion pic-

tures which I felt displayed the range of achievement from *The Birth of a Nation* in 1915 on. Thirty-seven of the films in that selection were made with the complement of sound. Obviously, I am not including those thirty-seven films in this book. But, for purposes of self-protection, I am indicating them, whenever mentioned, with an asterisk.

Further, when I laid out this volume, I intended that it should include 100 films, and I made a selection of that many as I moved on with the job. But then it became apparent to my publisher and to me that I could not do justice to 100 pictures within the physical limitations of one book. So fifty that would have been included on an equal footing with those that are here will have to await presentation in a second volume which we intend to bring out next year.

Naturally, readers will wonder on what basis—by what criteria—I have picked the entries for this volume from the scores of potential ones. The answer is that I have followed, as far as possible, the criteria laid down in my introduction to *The Great Films*: I have tried to distinguish first the breakthroughs, those films that have opened new ground, not just in techniques of expression (the use of music per se would be one of those) but in the dramatic subjects chosen (such as gangsterism) and the social aspects that have been exposed. I have sought those films in which content has been so interestingly and artfully combined with cinematic ingenuity and dexterity—or, to put it in one word, *style*—that the result has been a striking motion picture. And, above all, I have picked ones that still live as meaningful and fascinating movies. That is to say, true "vintage" films.

Inevitably, my choices do betray a certain amount

of personal taste. All reactions to movies are subjective, just as they are to wine. One cannot divorce one's own feelings, intelligence, and familiarity from the contents and style of presentation of that which is being seen. My own predilections as a critic—and I have been well aware of them—have been toward material, entertainment, that has something to say. A wine connoisseur would call it body. That may be apparent here.

One final word on a matter that continues to cause me deep concern: the excessive exposure and debasement of some fine old films on TV. The good that is done by the medium in generously presenting old films and making its viewers acquainted with the vast storehouse of treasures of the theatrical screen (exemplified by the stations of the Public Broadcast Service nationwide) is too often offset, if not obliterated by the shamelessly inconsiderate ways in which some great ones are cut and so intruded with frequent commercials that the flow and full effect of them are lost. We cannot do more than deplore this, but keep it in mind as you read this book.

On the other hand, let us be thankful that there are more and more theaters, not just in New York City but around the country which, I am told, are running revival programs of all sorts of interesting old films. Along with the excellent programs that are offered by the Film Department of the Museum of Modern Art, the programs played by the Carnegie Hall Cinema and the Bleecker Street Cinema in New York are intelligently selected and presented. I am most grateful to them for making available to me for reseeing many of the films that are covered in this book.

B. C.

THE BROADWAY MELODY

1929

It may seem a curious departure from my stated intentions for this book that the first film considered in it is by no means a deathless work of art or withering social commentary or even of exceptional cinema skill. Its major claim to recognition by today's sophisticated movie buffs—or to wistful recollection by older and sentimental fans—is the fact that it is a true original, breakthrough film, a first in a major category of cinema creativity and enterprise. It is *The Broadway Melody* and it is here because it was the screen's inaugural musical comedy.

That is a formidable distinction, for the musical, or song and dance, film has extended a standing invitation to the imagination and artistry of ambitious moviemakers ever since the introduction of sound. Unlike other categories of movies, such as drama, outdoor adventure, and slapstick farce, which had already been well established and developed on the silent screen, it came into being only with the addition of audibility, and thus gained accreditation as a genre after 1928. But it swept on to stature and favor quite as powerful as those of any other type by virtue of the human taste for music and the unique flexibility and suitability of the cinema medium.

How such a phoenix could have risen may be a bit difficult to conceive when one now observes the comparative crudity of *The Broadway Melody*. But do not forget, this was the first one, this was the film that broke the ice, and it came forth in February, 1929, less than three years after the inventors and enterprisers made their first public squeaks with sound.

At the time it was released, the moviemakers were on the end of a diving board, pushed along by the startling discovery that the newly perfected novelty of sound was a sensational hit with the public. They were faced with the necessity of finding conceivable ways of fitting atmosphere music, sound effects, and even spoken dialogue to films that theretofore had been as silent as the inside of Tutankhamen's tomb. Their efforts were rendered more uncertain by the fact that some studio brains were of the opinion that this new gimmick would be a passing fad and that there wasn't much point in struggling to master it. Little did they sense that they were stumbling on the edge of what

Queenie (Anita Page) offers cold comfort to her sister and fellow performer, Hank (Bessie Love), from whom she has stolen the affections of Eddie (Charles King).

Eddie (Charles King) leads the chorus line in a rehearsal for one of the novel musical numbers in *The Broadway Melody.*

9

The screen's first big musical production number done in color, "The Wedding of the Painted Doll," from the original *The Broadway Melody*.

was to be a total revolution in the very nature of cinema.

Of course, the first step imagined for the utilization of sound, after two public demonstrations in 1926 of the practicality and attraction of the new invention called Vitaphone, was simply to attach "canned music" to films that were already made or were in the final stages of production. Aesthetically this amounted to no more than the mere substitution of mechanical music for that of the familiar orchestra—or the more commonplace piano—that played accompaniments of background music for silent films. Sound effects also were added to give a tingle of verisimilitude.

The consequence was several pictures—the Warners' *Don Juan* was the first—offered, indeed, on the program with those initial Vitaphone shorts, which had synchronized music scores, all of them much more attractive to the public than their dramatic contents justified. Then the dam was burst on the evening of October 5, 1927, when the Warners opened in New York a silent film which did have in it a couple of scenes in which dialogue was scratchily spoken and two sentimental songs were sung by the popular stage star Al Jolson in the role of a rabbi's son. The film was *The Jazz Singer,* and although it was of no dramatic

worth—was, indeed, a mawkish pretense twice removed from the Yiddish stage—it was a sensation. The mechanical apparatus of sound thus punched a hole in the silent film's armor and released the voices of the characters on the screen.

Although the critical reaction to this achievement at the time was lukewarm, it soon became apparent that the basic achievement here was the potency of having the sentiments of the characters not only visually enacted but audibly conveyed. The voice coming out to the audience, which had already become involved with the illusion of the character's emotions, now made these feelings seem more real. It added a new corporeality to the image of the person on the screen.

For all the critical indifference toward the possibilities of sound, the huge success of *The Jazz Singer* all over the country changed their minds. Quickly the studios not only started adding synchronized musical scores onto most of their finished pictures, but added, too, dubbed dialogue on prints that went to theaters which had wisely equipped themselves for sound. They dubbed these additions "goat glands" and ostentatiously advertised these transplants as "part-talking" pictures.

So the challenge now was to discover not just how

to lick the problems of recording sound, which called for intense ingenuity and engineering skill, but to learn how to write dialogue pictures and direct them—in short, how to talk. All of the studios in Hollywood were engaged in this frenzied race.

Because the felicities of music as an accessory of sound were so obvious and attractive, it was quite natural that Hollywood should now become music-minded, should go overboard in setting up music departments and musicians in the studios and figuring out ways to use music to articulate story ideas. And I find it appropriately prophetic that the first to actually come through with a musically motivated movie was Metro-Goldwyn-Mayer. That was—to get back to our subject—*The Broadway Melody.*

How it came into being was characteristic of the elementary trials and errors of the period, and it is profitable to recall the circumstances of the production, for the enlightenment and amusement it affords.

Already pending at Metro when sound appeared de rigueur was a run-of-the-mill silent-film story—a backstage drama, as such were called—about a couple of singing and dancing sisters who came to New York to seek their fortune on the stage and, incidentally, to seek a reunion with the theatrical boyfriend of one. It was ready to go as a silent when Irving Thalberg, the precocious young man who was the creative head of production at the studio, decided it should be the company's first all-talking film and that, because of its subject and environment, it could do with a complement of songs.

This presented a question: who should write the songs, since the studio at that time had not yet added an in-house music staff? Someone suggested two tune-smiths who were then doing a vaudeville act at a place called the Orange Grove Theater in Los Angeles. They were called in by Thalberg and invited to write some songs to suit the script. He was so casual about it he didn't even remember their names. He called them "the real estate man and the piano player." They were Nacio Herb Brown and Arthur Freed. (Freed later became the most successful and famous producer of a long line of outstanding musicals at Metro-Goldwyn-Mayer.)

Their first number was called *The Broadway Melody,* a typical Tin Pan Alley jingle which was written to be a composition of the boyfriend in the story, who was offering it for sale at the start. They then did one which they thought appropriate for a chorus dance routine—something obviously novel in movies. It was

"The Wedding of the Painted Doll." A third was a romantic love song, "You Were Meant for Me."

Meanwhile, before they were finished, Thalberg agreed to listen to a batch of music supposedly written for the picture by a little Broadway hustler named Billy Rose. Rose showed up for the audition with a full orchestra to render his repertoire, and Thalberg was so impressed by the volume he almost opted for those songs. However, he told Brown and Freed he would still give them a chance, so they arranged to present their numbers on a radio broadcast over Los Angeles station KFI. The ingenious maneuver was successful. Thalberg decided to use their songs. Thus the first original score written for a movie musical, some songs of which are still hummed today (and one that was destined to become a classic of American pop music), was first presented to the public as an audition on radio.

The rest is history of an order that is almost laughably baroque. Harry Beaumont, a minor director who was as callow as the fellows who wrote the script (Norman Houston and Jimmy Gleason), was chosen to wield the megaphone, and he put the whole picture together in a little over a month. That was then no

The irresistible Queenie (Anita Page) is pursued by a wealthy philanderer.

massive achievement when one considers the simplicity of the script and the meager demands made on the actors. All they had to do was sing—and talk.

The dramatic line of the story turned upon the classic cliché of the boyfriend of one of the sisters falling in love with the other one, thus exposing another broken heart to match the myriad lights on old Broadway. Charles King was this faithless fellow, who was really quite decent about it all and, indeed, gave fair warning of the perils of disappointment in the words of his opening song—to wit, that eternal resilience and cheerfulness were essential in those who wished to scale the heights of Broadway. Anita Page was the prettier sister to whom his adoring eyes turned, and the one who was left to nurse her heartbreak and carry on with another partner was the then highly popular Bessie Love.

No, it was a less than awesome story (the details of which we can forgo), and the acting was so stilted and artless it seems today a parody of amateurs. The dialogue was ponderous and witless, like the sodden subtitles in silent films; the sets were tacky, the chorus girls were hefty, and they were dressed in atrociously unchic costumes. As for the musical comedy structure—well, that was ponderous too, but now we can discover the embryo significance of this film. For it was in the obvious gropings for effective and felicitous ways to make interesting transitions from comparatively naturalistic scenes to the cinematic latitude of numbers woven out of music and dance that the seed was sown.

To be sure, for the most part, the numbers were spotted in the way it was done on the stage—on dialogue cues, the performers went into their appropriate routines. The opening song, for instance, was sung by Mr. King at an audition for a music publisher (whom Mr. Gleason played). The central romantic number, "You Were Meant for Me," was sung by Mr. King in a private tryout for a dreamy Miss Page. And a long-forgotten sparkle in the picture—a minstrel-type song called "Truthful Parson Brown," done by four incidental fellows with three guitars and a mandolin—was spotted as an instrumental rendering at a party to please some swells.

But there were tentative and tempting touches of cinematic techniques that would be expanded and used—eventually to the limits of boredom—in later musical films, such as the camera being swung as a sort of roving bull's-eye and finally brought in for a smashing closeup of noisily tap-dancing feet in what was supposed to be a stage production number, to the orchestrated music of "The Broadway Melody." And the big smash number of the picture was an elaborately costumed affair designed to simulate the wedding of a fanciful doll bride and groom, embellished with several cinematic fancies of the camera moving back and in, suggesting original observation, and photographed in color. Yes, after shooting the number in the conventional black and white, Thalberg thought it so good that he ordered it reshot completely in a color process that was then but rarely used, thus initiating another convention that was to become a sine qua non in musical films.

The whole thing may be called pretentious or childish or tacky in this day when our cinema aesthetes incline to treat such antiques with campy, patronizing, or sophisticated disdain. It was an imaginative and thrilling experience for the audiences of its time, and it won the newly inaugurated Oscar as the outstanding film of a very important and historic year.

ANNA CHRISTIE

1930

"All-talking!" That was the catchword used to advertise the early sound movies. And all talk was mostly what they were, especially the straight dramas. With the camera condemned by technical problems to be incarcerated within a huge, immovable booth, and with the microphone hung like a gibbet above the actors' heads, the chances for easy, random movement on the set were circumscribed, and any scenes that had to be made in the actual outdoors were usually shot with silent camera. Sound and dialogue, if needed, were later added. Until cameras and mikes were perfected, the opportunities for making cinema were slight.

That is why few of the straight dramas that were made in the first few years of sound were significant as *motion* pictures or are often recollected today. Most of them, with a few exceptions, were little more than photographed plays, with the actors arranged for conversations in tediously long, static scenes. Even the rigid stage convention of breaking the drama into acts was observed, with slow dissolves clearly betraying the intervals where the curtain was down in the play.

Thus one might feel hard put in trying to decide which of the early straight dramas deserve to be remembered in this book. Might it be the Warners' *Disraeli*, with George Arliss in the title role, giving precisely the same performance that he gave on the stage? Or should it be Samuel Goldwyn's *Bulldog Drummond*, with Ronald Colman as star, or King Vidor's *Hallelujah*, which was really more of an outdoor spectacle? My choice settles down to the production made from Eugene O'Neill's play *Anna Christie*, with Clarence Brown as director and Greta Garbo as its luminous star.

I don't feel this choice is capricious or influenced by sentiment just because the play was written by one of America's foremost dramatists and happened to be the vehicle for Garbo's first sound film—an event of some grave anxiety which was heralded, when ready to be released, with booming advertisements announcing "Garbo Speaks!" I feel that, for all its imperfections—its confinement within a couple of sets, its crude dramatic exposition, its structure in long scenes

The sick, man-hating Anna Christie (Greta Garbo) shows up in a New York waterfront saloon to meet her barge-captain father whom she hasn't seen in years.

of straight dialogue, and the fact that, after all, it was really no more than a three-character face-off film—it did have a salty realism, a rare touch of vagrant poetry, and a strong performance by Garbo that proved her an actress, not just a glamorous star.

The drama itself was elementary—a surprising thing to say of something that was lifted almost straight-up from a highly respected O'Neill play. It opened in the cabin of a coal barge tied up on New York's East River waterfront, with a crusty old boozer (Marie Dressler) listening to a wheezy gramophone and awaiting the arrival of the coal-barge captain (George F. Marion) with whom, when he did return, she repaired (through the discreet Ladies' Entrance) to a nearby waterfront saloon. Thereafter the action of the picture, save for a couple of lively sequences—one good one at Coney Island and another on the deck of the barge—was confined within those two areas.

"Gimme a vhiskey, ginger ale on the side—an' don' be stingy, baby." Anna braces herself with a suitable refreshment. These were the first, and immortal, words Greta Garbo spoke on the screen.

Anna (Greta Garbo) makes friends with Marthy (Marie Dressler), her father's bibulous companion, to discuss the situation.

Imagine that—a barge and a saloon! This for a film with Garbo, the superstar of the day!

But this studied departure from the ornate—and the casting of Garbo in the role of a sickly prostitute from Minneapolis, daughter of the captain of the barge, whom she hadn't seen since she was a small child and to whom she now came as an orphan of the storm— was more than audacious; it was canny, for it gave

Garbo a chance to play a character of distinct and striking contrast to those she had played in silent films, and one that justified her Swedish accent, whenever it happened to pop through.

And pop through it did, very clearly, in her opening scene, when she came through the door of the Ladies' Entrance, lugging an old suitcase, took her stand beside a table where sat the boozing Marthy, and ordered herself a drink.

"Gimme a vhiskey," she muttered hoarsely to the waiter. "Ginger ale on the side. An' don' be stingy, baby." Those were the first words Garbo spoke, in a voice both deep and husky—and they became immortal. For several years thereafter they were repeated ad infinitum in countless speakeasies and cocktail bars by all the smart young ladies who wanted to show how hep they were.

And her next line was equally popular. To the sarcastic waiter's crack "Shall I serve it in a pail?" Garbo answered bluntly, "Dot suits me down to de groun'."

This was the way the ailing Anna came upon the scene, disclosing herself to Marthy, in a long stretch of dialogue, but remaining a pure child to her father when he joined the ladies in the back room. And it was this unsullied image of her that the old retired Swedish seaman chose to keep until the nature of Anna's profession had to be revealed.

That came when a big Irish sailor, hauled aboard the barge in a storm off the coast of New England, fell in love with Anna and allowed that he wanted to marry her—a prospect that her father rebuffed because he didn't want her to hook up with a "sailor fellow" who might be taken by "dat ol' dabil sea." Being a grateful daughter and also loath to deceive the suitor, Matt, she frankly told him and her father what she had been, which led to the usual reactions of shock and outrage in the men, a period of drunken indecisions, and then reconciliations and a happy end.

Actually, the sum of the drama was just a tussle between the two men for the possession of Anna, in whom each saw, in his way, the symbol of a comforting sanctuary from the turmoil of the sea. And Anna, in turn, was forced to struggle between her new regard for these two men and her ingrained disgust and suspicion toward the male sex and indeed toward all mankind.

It was a black-and-white role that Garbo adumbrated with many intriguing shades of dark concealment and dazzling revelation—the cold unsureness and hostility in her face and voice when she hesitantly entered, the hint of memories and hopes when she met and embraced her rugged father, the initial antipathy and then the growing urge toward Matt as they saw more and more of each other (on that trip to Coney Island, particularly), and finally her flood of feminine ardor when she felt for sure she was in love. It was not a great role, but within it Garbo made come alive the embittered and lonesome woman possessed of a reservoir of feelings.

Charles Bickford, young and powerful, was impressive as Matt—a great roaring braggart of an Irishman with a vast, deep-down need to be controlled; and George F. Marion as the old father was an amusing and touching O'Neill type. Miss Dressler, during the time she was in it, before her Marthy saw she was superfluous and bowed out, went a long way toward chewing up the scenery with her tipsy-old-guzzler act.

Clarence Brown's direction, while betraying the restrictions of the camera and the play (which had been made as a silent five years earlier, with Anna played by Blanche Sweet), did some interesting things with movement and boldly naturalistic scenery, drenching the whole thing in a vapor of waterfront atmosphere. The scene of Garbo in oilskins, for instance, reviving the half-drowned Matt with a healthy slug of whiskey and a few encouraging words, had something more than stagecraft. In its cutting from face to face it began to grasp the potentials of close-up talking cinema. And there was one absolutely stunning pan shot of lower Manhattan and the East River, taken from atop the far tower of the Brooklyn Bridge, that gave a full sense of the drama framed within its genuine ambience.

Today *Anna Christie* is an antique—a clear example of an early sound film—but it still has humanity and flavor and the beauty of Garbo's ageless face.

Matt (Charles Bickford) and Anna (Greta Garbo) reveal their burgeoning love to her jealous and disapproving father (George C. Marion).

Anna confronts her father (George C. Marion) on the deck of the barge to decide what to do with Matt (Charles Bickford), a sailor rescued from the sea off New England.

An astonished Rico (Edward G. Robinson) is winged in a surprise attack by rivals.

LITTLE CAESAR

1931

By far the most conspicuous agitation in motion pictures caused by the introduction of sound, outside of the spectacular musical song-and-dance film, was the vitalization it gave to the so-called gangster film, making this a brand-new breed of movie in comparison to the standard crime melodramas of the silent years. Where the latter had been mostly thrillers about train robbers, burglars, and slick-haired crooks, many adapted from well-known stage plays and mimed with obvious theatricality, the gangsters that came out blazing from 1930 on were shattering simulations of the current crime scene and criminal characters ripped directly from the news of the day.

Their explosive vigor and popularity were due to the conjunction of a social crisis and the new cinematic technique. The gangster had emerged in the 1920s as a modern American bandit type, more brazen, exotic, and sinister than any of the fictional criminals we had known before. Drawn for the most part from the masses of immigrant ethnic groups, and bred to the customs and superstitions of the countries from which they came, these bold and ingenious banditti took advantage of the vacuum caused by Prohibition. They merged into clandestine crime rings, and they cornered the opulent traffic in illegal beer and booze, then fought among themselves in deadly warfare that became progressively more conspicuous in the news.

Slowly the American people and then the world became aware of the hideous nature and the power and social menace of these gangs. Astonishment and morbid curiosity as to their methods and their life-styles grew. Plays and novels were written about them, and the mystery of their freewheeling loomed. Then, on a freezing morning in 1929, a gangland slaughter, which became known as the St. Valentine's Day Massacre, occurred in a Chicago garage. Seven members of a feuding gang were lined against a wall and mowed down by rivals wielding tommy guns. The deed was juicily blazoned in the sensation-hungry press and mutely illustrated with grisly photos of the hapless victims lying crumpled in their blood. This event truly crystallized awareness and shocked and numbed the public with nightmare fears and images of the power and indifference to law and order that rulers of crime had achieved.

It was in this climate of sensation that the movies acquired the force of sound. Silent crime films in the pipelines were at once made to sputter and burp with elemental noises of machine guns and such associated with acts of crime. A few middling films about gangsters came through with stilted dialogue. Then, in January, 1931, the first of the classic gangster pictures—I hesitate now to call them "great" because they all had basic flaws of florid reasoning, but classic they certainly were—came thundering out of the shadows of First National (now Warners) studio and the full wave of this type of movie hit the American screen. It was Mervyn Le Roy's *Little Caesar,* a stark account of a fictitious Chicago hood who bore certain noticeable resemblances to several of the more notorious kingpins in crime, including the lordly Al Capone. And it made its title player, Edward G. Robinson, a star of the first magnitude.

This wasn't the first gangster role Mr. Robinson had played. He had been, within the year, in two incipient exercises that are charitably overlooked. But this was the first in which a tough script, based on a novel by W. R. Burnett, and the brilliant direction of the thirty-year-old Mr. Le Roy allowed him to generate the image of a relentlessly power-hungry hood, shooting and

Rico (Edward G. Robinson) at right, threatens impulsively to draw on a gang superior while his immediate boss, Little Arnie (Maurice Black), counsels caution.

Rico (Edward G. Robinson), on his way to gangland power, calmly oversees a conventional stickup in the classic gangster film *Little Caesar.*

shoving his way to the top level of gangsterdom and then being brought down hard.

Frankly, *Little Caesar* did not have the facets and the psychological scope of the next classic gangster picture, *The Public Enemy,* * which came along only six months later with James Cagney in the title role. Robinson's thug, unlike Cagney's, leaped out at the start fully armed, as a hardened small-town hoodlum intent on going places. With a pal, a cheap nightclub professional dancer who occasionally joined him in small stickups, he took off for Chicago and the tempting opportunities of the big time. There, with the brass of a beginner and the daring of a defuser of bombs, he

wedged himself into a lower level in the empire of the shadowy Big Boss and started his campaign of jawing and clawing his way to the top.

Robinson's Rico—"Little Caesar," as he was tauntingly dubbed—conveyed the impression—the conviction indeed—of being relentlessly vicious, impatient, trigger-happy, and dangerous from the start. He snarled and mocked Little Arnie, his first immediate boss, in a voice that had the rasp and timbre of gravel crushing glass. He swiftly shot down a tardy victim (who turned out to be the police commissioner) on his first important holdup, then casually reported to Arnie, "It went all right, but I had to take care of a guy." He slew a backsliding confederate going to confession on the front steps of a church and then attended the ritual gangster's funeral and pointed with pride to his floral wreath. In such scenes as these Mr. Robinson revealed an individual ego that was monstrously sinister.

And at no point did he let his Little Caesar play for sympathy, or build up, as so often happened in gangster pictures, a measure of personal sentiment. He was totally without loyalty and compassion, even toward his only evident friend, the nightclub dancer, who had come to Chicago with him but soon went drifting off in favor of a girl. Only toward the end, when Little Caesar, having gone up the ladder to power, endeavored to wipe out this old buddy to prevent his spilling the beans, did he show the remotest feeling or concern for someone else. And then his disastrous hesitation to do the treacherous job of murdering his pal seemed not so much a matter of emotion as obedience to an author's plot.

What marked Little Caesar was his arrogant vanity, displayed in his smirk and swagger when his gang associates presented him with a watch at a ritual banquet to honor his first successful job, or his preening himself before a mirror as he took on progressively more flashy layers of haberdashery, climaxed when he looked at himself in his first tuxedo and jested at his gaudy image, "All I need is a napkin over my arm."

And it was notable that he had no use for women. "Love!" he exploded with contempt when his pal politely informed him he loved his dancing partner and wanted to go straight. "That's soft stuff," snarled Little Caesar. "You move and it's suicide for both of you."

Unfortunately, the end of the picture was an overloaded cliché. Little Caesar, having failed to kill his old pal and having been informed on by him, was

Rico (Edward G. Robinson) even pulls a gun on his old pal, Joe (Douglas Fairbanks, Jr.), in a crucial stickup of a big private political party in *Little Caesar*.

Rico (Edward G. Robinson), tumbled from power and destitute, goes forth to face his archrival at the climax of *Little Caesar*.

forced to go into hiding and lost control of his mob. Months later, while lying in a flophouse, weakened and bloated by booze, he overheard an old bum reading from a newspaper about the legendary Little Caesar being a fugitive and a coward. "He could dish it out but he couldn't take it," the newspaper story said, applying to himself one of Rico's favorite comments of scorn toward his rivals.

Wildly he leaped from his bed and went storming out into the wintry night to phone his old nemesis, the police sergeant, and boast that he hadn't lost his nerve. Bells rang, policemen scrambled, sirens on police cars wailed, and the cavalcade raced through dark streets to find Rico plowing along through swirling snow. A challenge, a flash of braggadocio from the shabby Rico, and then the cops gunned him down. Only then did the hoodlum show a trace of terror and dismay. "Mother of Mercy," he mumbled incredulously, "is this the end of Rico?" And he died.

But regardless of that ending, which appears more mawkish today than it did in the early 1930s, when a

gangster's death was a grim catharsis in films, *Little Caesar* was an overpowering picture that left its imprint on millions and millions of minds and carried at least the illusion of giving the enigma of the gangster more sharp illumination and clarity. While the characters surrounding Little Caesar, the antihero, were mostly stereotypes, and his pal, played by Douglas Fairbanks, Jr., was quite implausibly smooth and genteel, the conception of Mr. Robinson's Rico was the first to leap to life on the screen and gratify all the voyeurism that a morbidly curious public then had.

It is true that Mr. Cagney's *Public Enemy*, which came only a few months later, was a more in-depth and comprehensive portrayal of a hypothetical gangster and *Scarface*, with Paul Muni, which arrived the following year, was more rounded and explicit in its documentation of the Chicago gangsters and the prototypical Al Capone. But Mr. Robinson's Little Caesar was etched upon the public mind for years and established a name for the Prohibition gangster that lives in the language to this day.

SHE DONE HIM WRONG

1933

Any character as boldly self-assertive as the one that Mae West invariably played in some nine or ten rococo movies during the decade up to 1943 could not escape being discovered lolling luxuriously somewhere in this book, no matter how inconsequential were most of the vehicles on which she lolled. In the case of Miss West, the vehicle—the screenplay—was never the thing; she herself—her authoritative strumpet—was the essence of her dominance on the screen. It became, as we all know, a figure so conformed in the public mind that it was a fixture in American culture and one of the grander sociological accomplishments of American films.

Needless to say, her lusty lady was an unrestrained parody of supervoluptuous seduction and the man-killing potencies of sex. Although this may not have been intended by Miss West—at least, not at first—and certainly it was not detected by some of her more lecherous early fans, it was the thing that made her outstanding and intellectually endurable. After the first shock of seeing her suggestive sensuality on the screen—contained, to be sure, within garments that were as restrictive of sexual freedom as a chastity belt—the very extravagance of her tossing of innuendos both in movements and words was as laughable as the excesses of a gaggle of Keystone Kops.

There was not much to set apart her pictures—to elevate one above the rest as a triumph of grotesque screen humor—so I have chosen the seminal West as the best for contemplation in this book. That was the first film to make her famous—along with the young Cary Grant—*She Done Him Wrong*.

Here the fundamental profile of Westian character and style was introduced to a public which, except for those who had seen it on the stage, had never seen the likes of such audacity as this on the screen. Lolling loftily and grandly on the back seat of a horse-drawn open carriage, dressed in a swath of florid finery, and surrounded by bulging packages of what were obviously more clothes, Miss West made her beaming entrance along a noisily crowded thoroughfare identified

"One of the finest women that ever walked the streets." The diamond-loving Lady Lou (Mae West) in *She Done Him Wrong*.

The voluptuous Lady Lou (Mae West) exercises her charms on a deceptively guileless mission manager (Cary Grant) in *She Done Him Wrong.*

as New York's Bowery in the Gay Nineties. The appearance of such a dazzling image of extravagance and bad taste amid a street full of East Side pushcarts, beer wagons, and immigrants was itself an outspoken suggestion of the incongruity of Miss West's Lady Lou. She was a full-blown example of conspicuous consumption at its worst.

But clearly her neighbors admired her with unrestrained envy and awe.

"Oh, Lou, you're a fine woman!" one poor little lady beamed, taking the hand of the vision as she grandly stepped down from her landau.

Lou responded lightly, "One of the finest that ever walked the streets."

Lou's residence at the moment was a gaudy apartment above the booming beer hall of Gus Jordan, a local political power, whose pride and evident prestige were plainly enhanced by his possession of the belle, who further disposed her favors as a nightly singing and strutting performer in the saloon. But Gus' boastful possession was clearly one of mere eminent domain. A slippery, cigar-smoking rival by the euphonious name of Dan Flynn was frequently roaming around the beer hall, angling up to the bar, passing cigars among the patrons, and openly warning Gus that he was out not only to dispossess him of his saloon and his political power but to take over the intimate favors and the highly commercial assets of Lou.

"You can be had," Lady Lou (Mae West) oozes seductively to the seemingly innocent manager (Cary Grant) of the mission next door to her saloon.

But such a switch, especially of the last-mentioned, was somewhat contingent on Lou's readiness to be detached from a previous suitor by the name of Chick Clark, to whom she still professed to be loyal even though he was doing a long stretch in the jug. Indeed, on a passing visit to him—and to all the inmates howl-

Spider (Dewey Robinson) brings the exhausted Sally (Rochelle Hudson) to the upstairs suite of the saloon singer, Lady Lou (Mae West), who means to befriend the homeless girl.

ing greetings from their cells—she blandly accepted Chick's advisory that she'd better be true to him or else!

However, the evidence was preponderant that Lou was really only true to Lou, to a frankly obsessive love of diamonds, and to her hobby of collecting men. Indeed, she collected both items with equal candor and sangfroid.

"This is just my summer jewelry," she informed a gawking visitor to her room as, to catch their glitter, she held out a hand ablaze with sparklers. "You should see my winter stuff"—the obvious implication being that they were trophies of countless hunting campaigns.

And to a man whom she found attractive, she murmured unctuously, "You can be had," then threw in her now classic come-on, a throaty "Why'n'cha come up and see me sometime?"

At the moment, her apparent prime target was a tall, dark, and handsome young man who was frequently in and out of the beer hall wearing a Salvation Army uniform. He was the manager of a mission next door to the saloon, and what Lou expected from him was obviously not another rock. But he seemed uncommonly wary, not responsive to her temptations at all, which baffled a bit but did not jiggle the smiling confidence of Lou.

Well, with all these things established, the denouement for our heroine came as the consequence of a simple characteristic act of sentiment. A poor little girl whom she befriended when she stumbled despairingly into the saloon by feeding her and turning her over to

Russian Rosie, a chic but shifty friend, was secreted away to white slavery by Rosie, and soon a federal agent called the Hawk was rumored to be snooping around the area trying to unravel the case.

Then Chick broke out of prison and began haunting Lou's bedroom, threatening to do damage to her, and Russian Rosie returned, angrily intending to kill her, but in a tussle over a knife, Lou accidentally put the knife into Rosie, an act which did not serve her cause too well. In the midst of these threatening complications, Lou continued to pop down to the stage and sing such artful ditties as "I Wonder Where My Easy Rider's Gone" (a chant filled with double entendres that fairly staggered audiences at the time), the famous old "Frankie and Johnny," and another wow, "I Like a Man Who Takes His Time."

At the climax, the lurking Chick, in desperation, put a bullet into Dan, thinking he was Lou as he entered her bedroom, and the Hawk showed up to make a pinch, revealing himself to be none other than the Salvation Army lad. (Mr. Grant, incidentally, was adequate, shall we say, in the role.)

So off to the hoosegow it was for the irrepressible Lou, snatched out of the paddy wagon away from the others by the Hawk and, significantly, carried off by him in a hansom cab.

"You're gonna be my prisoner for a *long* time," he archly warned her, then added, ". . . you naughty girl," and she looked at him for a brief pause, then said teasingly, "You'll find out!"

Needless to repeat, the performance of Miss West in this loaded burlesque was a beautiful piece of calculated, precision-timed mockery. Her nimble wit (which was based on her popular stage play *Diamond Lil,* which as with most of her material, was written by her), her gestures, her strut, and her sly pauses, in which she hummed portentously and rolled her eyes, all added up to a hilarious spoof of the famous belles of a bygone day—and, if one wished to stretch it, the lurid vamps of silent films. Actually, her techniques travestied the allurement of sex. Her flesh bulged grossly above her corsets and she walked as though her feet were killing her. Yet, believe it or not, this lady was considered so dangerously indecent at the time by the watchful guardians of Will H. Hays' new rule for morals in films that it was partly to suppress her activity that certain strictures were put into the new Production Code.

Miss West was not suppressed, however. She went on to a succession of films including *I'm No Angel, Belle of the Nineties, Klondike Annie,* and *My Little Chickadee.* In the last-mentioned she pitted her image against that of W. C. Fields, which resulted in an outrageous mismatch of two separately successful caricatures. That practically ruined the nice lady. She did only one other *bad* film after that.

P.S. She did have a small role in *Myra Breckinridge* in 1971. To say it was a shameless exploitation of her old character is more than kind.

MUTINY ON THE BOUNTY

1935

In the long and crowded gallery of memorable portrayals on the screen, none stands out more clearly than that of Charles Laughton's Captain Bligh in Frank Lloyd's *Mutiny on the Bounty*, released in 1935. In this enactment of the most famous naval mutiny in all history, Mr. Laughton gave an inspired performance of the British captain's inhumanity, of despotism beyond all reason, and of incredible cruelty to his crew.

I cannot recall another portrait of a tyrant performing within the limits of his lawful prerogatives, which were those of a sailing ship's master in the late eighteenth century, to match in energy and detail the exhibit that Mr. Laughton gave of the captain of the *Bounty* on its historic voyage in the South Seas. Whether ordering the hideous keelhauling of a poor sailor who had merely besought an extra ration of drinking water, or compelling a master-at-arms to complete the specified flogging of a culprit who had already died beneath the lash, Mr. Laughton was a monument to brutality. Pacing the deck with his jaw jutted forward like a ship's prow and his hands clasped firmly behind his back, he looked the evil embodiment of a monster prepared to destroy. Mr. Laughton's characterization immortalized the name of Bligh far beyond what had been accomplished by the writers of history. Or by James Norman Hall and Charles Nordhoff, from whose three exciting books—*Mutiny on the Bounty*, *Men Against the Sea*, and *Pitcairn's Island*—this splendid film was derived.

And splendid it was back in the 1930s, and today, when compared to a costly remake done in 1962. It had action, romance, adventure, the potent drama of willful men brought face to face—and it had a performance by Clark Gable as Fletcher Christian, the *Bounty*'s first mate, who finally confronted the brutal captain and led the mutiny, that challenged the performance of Mr. Laughton.

It is interesting to note that the conjunction of these two dissimilar stars—Mr. Laughton the civilized Englishman and Mr. Gable the Hollywood tough—was accomplished against the early protests of Mr. Gable, who frankly feared that he would be no match for Mr. Laughton or, indeed, for the stage-trained Franchot

The moment of truth in *Mutiny on the Bounty,* when a defiant Fletcher Christian (Clark Gable) refuses to "sign the ledger" for the alleged theft of some coconuts on command of Captain Bligh (Charles Laughton).

Tone, who was cast to play Mr. Byam, the aristocratic English midshipman who figured strongly in the crisis that occurred. Mr. Gable was afraid that his acting and his undisguisable Americanese would make him look awkward alongside the other men. How self-deceptive, his misgivings were was abundantly clear when the film was released; his Christian was as commanding a character as Bligh.

It was, perhaps, as a concession to Mr. Gable (who had only recently appeared as the hard-boiled newspaper reporter in the comedy *It Happened One Night**) that he was given the advantage of commanding the opening sequence as the officer in charge of a *Bounty* press gang rounding up a crew for the ship in the Portsmouth taverns and streets. In this scene, he had to be aggressive and unrelenting, even to the point of hauling a meek little tradesman away from his newly married wife. This assured everyone that Fletcher Christian was not a softhearted man, but one who did his duty as required.

23

And the need for these capacities was made evident in the scene of sailing day, when Bligh appeared in all his arrogance and ordered a flogging of the man already dead. The appearance of Byam as an amiable fop fresh from a luxurious home presented a complementary counter to Christian's unquestioned masculinity.

The voyage to Tahiti, where the *Bounty* was ordered to pick up a cargo of breadfruit plants to be transported to the West Indies, acquainted us with other members of the crew and provided us with further examples of Bligh's brutalities. There were incidents of flogging, keelhauling, ordering Byam to the top of the mast as punishment for a minor violation, and commanding a sick man into a pulling boat to serve as one of the oarsmen to drag the ship slowly forward when becalmed. All of these incidents, plus indications of the various natures of others in the crew—a timid mess boy (Herbert Mundin), the tippling ship's doctor (Dudley Digges), the pathetic victim of the press gang (Eddie Quillan), an older officer (Donald Crisp)—served as a prelude to the inevitable mutiny.

But before that momentous crisis, there was an idyllic stretch ashore, when the ship was being loaded with the breadfruit and the men were allowed to indulge in the traditional enticements of the South Seas. Christian and Byam "married" native girls (as the titles put it) and lived handsomely as pampered lords. But then came time for departure again under the powerful and even more brutal command of Bligh.

The collision came when Bligh, who had unmercifully clapped some men in irons, attempted to make Christian "sign the ledger" for lifting coconuts to feed them from the ship's stores. When Christian refused to do it and was about to be charged with mutiny, he gathered the malcontents around him and got a real mutiny under way. Bligh and eighteen crewmen who could not accept mutiny, even though they may have been tempted, were put into the ship's longboat and cast adrift with enough stores, presumably, to last

Captain Bligh (Charles Laughton) visits the three cruelly treated prisoners in the *Bounty*'s loathsome brig.

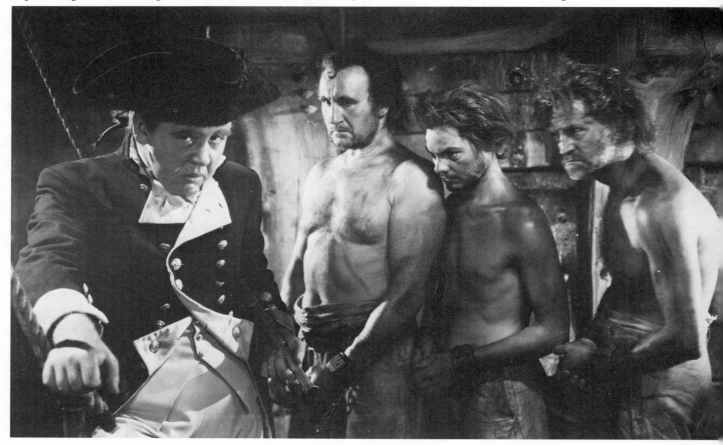

The deposed captain and his company of still loyal seamen are set adrift in the ship's longboat by the triumphant mutineers.

The captured midshipman, Byam (Franchot Tone), who followed Christian in the mutiny, faces a naval court-martial at which he vividly describes Bligh's brutality.

them until a nearby island might be reached. To Bligh's wrathful threats to Christian, the mutiny leader replied, "I'll take my chance against the law; you'll take yours against the sea!" And the last words of Bligh to Christian, shaking an angry fist in the air and screaming across the water, were "I'll live to see all of you hanged from the highest yardarm in England!"

That might have been the terminus of the drama, if history and a skillfully written script had not prolonged the story of interlocking conflicts and adventure to a just, ironic end. The *Bounty*, under the command of Christian, turned back to Tahiti, jettisoning the plants en route, and the longboat, with Bligh in the sternsheets, started west across the empty sea. And it was now, in these perilous circumstances, that another face of the captain was shown—that of a still domineering but courageous and able seafaring man.

In a carefully compacted sequence, the perils and hardships of that historic trip across 3,600 miles of ocean in the open boat were grippingly recounted— the violence of a storm at sea, the stringent rationing of food and water, the snaring of a gull and the giving of its blood, at Bligh's specific order, to a man who

was deathly ill—all was played by Mr. Laughton with impressive fortitude and restraint. It was in this phase that the character took on new dimensions of strength and mystery.

Dissolve next to Christmas in England with snow falling and people singing carols, and then to sun-drenched Tahiti, with the mutineers likewise caroling "God Rest Ye Merry, Gentlemen" and Byam's baby being born to the soft strains of "Star of Wonder" as an obbligato in the musical score. (The music, incidentally, was conventional, not a major contribution to the film.)

Then, in a long subtitle of the sort that was still allowed, it was explained that Bligh, now a national hero for his valiant voyage in the open boat, was given a new ship, the *Pandora*, and sent out to try to find and arrest the mutineers—which was not historically accurate, but it made for a fitting climax to the film. In Tahiti, he found that Christian and most of the mutineers had slipped away in the *Bounty*. But he did find Byam and a couple of others who had refused to accompany the mutineers further. He clapped them in irons and took out after *Bounty*, but went aground on a reef, in sight of the fleeing vessel. And that was the end of the chase.

Back in England again, the noble Byam was tried and condemned for mutiny, but was oddly allowed to deliver a highly rhetorical speech in which he vividly described Bligh's brutalities and justified Christian's deeds. "He's taken that ship beyond maps," he vaunted. "I wonder if he's found his island at last!"

Then the audience was given brief assurance that he most gratifyingly had, with a quick dissolve to the *Bounty* and the mutineers agreeing to beach the ship on Pitcairn Island and stay there forever, with their Tahitian women and their stores. That was the last we saw of Christian, the outstanding hero of the film.

As for Bligh, he was suddenly cold-shouldered after Byam's revelatory speech—a fate that was neither historically accurate nor, in all fairness, deserved by this most magnificently depicted and maligned antihero in prewar films. And Byam, having helped by his comments to bring "a new understanding between officers and men" (as was piously explained in another subti-

tle), was pardoned by the king, though some of his colleagues were hanged, and allowed to sail off into the sunset aboard another ship.

There was no clear penetration of the nature and mentality of Bligh. Neither were there any intimations of the psychological rationales of Christian and his followers, other than that they were reacting to the cruelty of their commander and that they wanted to go back to those Tahitian girls. Audiences didn't ask for explanations in those days before Freud invaded films. It was enough that an action drama was richly written, directed, and played. And this one was, to near perfection. It was munificently produced, with a real sailing ship resembling the *Bounty* as the set for much of the action at sea. Its performers below the three principals were English characters to the core, and Mr. Lloyd's direction was utilitarian and tough.

Yes, *Mutiny on the Bounty* was a great adventure film. And it established for possibly all time in our language the triumvirate of *Bounty*, Christian, and Bligh.

THE THIRTY-NINE STEPS

1935

It may seem a vain endeavor for me to try to say anything new in the way of appreciation or critical comment about Alfred Hitchcock's *The Thirty-nine Steps*. So much has already been written about this most famous of Mr. Hitchcock's early films and certainly the one most reflective of the emerging "Hitchcock style," and so many times has it been rerun in revivals and on TV, that I fear many readers may murmur, on finding it here, "Not *that* again!"

But there are many viable reasons for revisiting it now in the light of Mr. Hitchcock's tremendous output and his ever-growing stature as a filmmaker in the intervening years. There is, for one thing, the matter of his clearly having set a style in suspense melodrama that has been pursued by many others besides himself. (But no one has been able to use it as well as he, since the delicate prescription is uniquely secreted within his brain.)

The creation and pursuit of his brand of suspense—a precipitate succession of bizarre and awesome dangers for an unsuspecting person in what has

Still handcuffed after their escape from espionage agents, Hannay (Robert Donat) and Pamela (Madeleine Carroll) must share a bedroom at a hideaway country inn—a delicate situation played for laughs.

usually looked to be a peaceful world—have encouraged a submissive disposition in the minds of filmgoers over the years to assume that such sudden chain-linked dangers are normally expectable. How many times have you heard someone say, "This is just like a Hitchcock film," thus accepting the lifelike bait of fiction when actually the occurrence cited is just an isolated freak happening? So clever has been Mr. Hitchcock in making the implausible seem plausible

Hannay (Robert Donat) meets the suspicious Pamela (Madeleine Carroll) under the watchful eye of a secret agent.

The respected Scottish laird, Professor Jordan (Godfrey Tearle), reveals himself to Hannay (Robert Donat) to be the desperately sought-after "man with the missing finger" in *The Thirty-nine Steps*.

A typical Hitchcock bruhaha on the stage of a London theater after the climactic shooting of the crucial Memory Man.

and real that he has brainwashed some four generations into a habitual suspension of disbelief. And if that isn't worth some reflection, I don't know what is!

Like virtually all the Hitchcock movies, the few before it and the three dozen since, it began with a plausible setup in a normal environment. A man (only his legs were shown at the outset, which could have been a clue) walked in and took a seat in the midst of a performance in a London music hall. Onstage, a man with a phenomenal memory for all sorts of random things was doing his act answering questions thrown at him from the audience. What could have been more mundane and less apparently fraught with danger than this?

Suddenly a burst of pistol shooting down in front near the stage set off panic in the audience and caused it to stampede. In the midst of this riot of confusion, the man we saw entering at the start found himself pressed against a woman who besought him to take her home with him. Amused and curious, he did so, but when they arrived at his flat he was astonished to find she didn't want to be there for the usually expectable thing but was seeking sanctuary from two desperate fellows who were after her. Indeed, she told him frankly she was a free-lance spy and that she was vying with these fellows to get hold of some highly valuable military plans.

Thus our hospitable fellow, whose name was Hannay, found himself suddenly implicated in a bizarre and dangerous plot. What could he do about it? Go to the police, you might say—which, of course, might be somewhat difficult and uncomfortably dangerous, too.

But then, having decided to sleep on it, he was awakened in the middle of the night by the woman stumbling into his bedroom with a knife stuck deep in her back and gasping a plea that he complete her mission. Go to Scotland, she begged him, to a place circled on a map she held, and look for a man whose little finger on his right hand was severed at the middle joint. This man knew what she was after: the secret of the thirty-nine steps. Then she flopped over dead.

Such was the ominous complication with which the picture began, and such was the point of departure for a succession of wild adventures and close escapes. Getting out of his building in a milkman's borrowed coat and hat, past the two fellows waiting outside, Hannay hurried to Euston Station and boarded the Scotland-bound train. Again you may ask, why didn't he go at once to the police? Quite simple: The police were now a second menace. How could he explain to them the murdered woman in his flat?

On the train to Scotland, he found himself being pursued by a posse of fellows he thought to be police. When they finally tagged him, he led them a chase through the train, tangling comically with dining-car waiters and a pack of snarling dogs in the baggage car, to give them the slip by debarking while the train was passing over the famous Firth of Forth Bridge.

Next, without tedious explanation, he showed up at a lonely farm on a highland moor, where he persuaded the dour, suspicious farmer to let him stay the night. But a glint of recognition from the farmer's compassionate young wife (who had seen a story in the newspaper about the fugitive "murderer"), and then the clattering arrival of the questing police in the night, sent him forth, with the police racing after, for a breathless chase across the moors.

That chase reached a break-loose climax when Mr. Hitchcock had milked it for suspense; then Hannay reached the residence spotted on the map. There, to his total amazement and propulsion into imminent peril, he found the affable laird of the manor to be the man with the finger missing at the joint! An attempt by the laird to shoot him, a miraculous escape (the bullet lodged in a hymnal in the pocket of the overcoat the farmer's wife had given him), and Hannay was next at a sheriff's office, telling his story and seeking an alibi. But the sheriff double-crossed him, called in the police, and again Hannay got away from them, fled in the midst of a parade, and found himself mistaken for a speaker at a political rally nearby.

Such were the touch-and-go adventures that menaced the fugitive trying to avoid the secret agents as well as the police, until he wound up helplessly handcuffed to a beautiful lady in the bedroom of a Scottish inn—and if you want to know how he got *there* you'll have to see a revival of the film! But the point is that Mr. Hitchcock used this charming interlude to relax the suspense for a few minutes and indulge in some witty repartee, in which the couple exchanged minor insults ("the white man's burden," he slyly taunted her), until another menace intruded and they were off to London to straighten things out.

There at the London Palladium, Hannay found the Memory Man again and suddenly he realized that here was the key. At that moment he glimpsed the laird from Scotland, lurking behind the curtains of a balcony box. So, innocently, he threw a question, "What are the thirty-nine steps?" and as the Memory Man started to answer automatically, "The Thirty-nine Steps is the name of an organization of foreign spies collecting information for—" a pistol shot rang out. The Memory Man dropped, and pandemonium again raced through the house. And then, as the Memory Man lay dying, he revealed that he was carrying in his head the highly technical secret plans that were being sought!

Thus ended this breakneck melodrama, with the still strangely manacled hand of Hannay groping for the hand of the pretty lady to whom he had been temporarily bound.

As one can see even from this outline, there was little logic or likelihood in the domino setup of adventures that befell our persistent man. It didn't make sense that a young bachelor visiting London from Canada should allow himself to get into such a situation or that he should continue to pursue a decidedly vague objective at peril of his life all by himself.

But this was precisely the sort of liberty that Mr. Hitchcock indulged in in most of his films. He didn't worry about logic, and certainly not likelihood. Indeed, he went for the *un*likely, the unexpected, the element of surprise, such as the sudden shot in the crowded theater or the discovery that the affable Scottish laird was the man with the missing finger or that the Memory Man had the secret plans.

Indeed, Mr. Hitchcock acknowledged later in his career that the things which activated his dramas, as in this case the secret plans, were details of minor importance. It didn't matter much what they were, so long as they set up objectives which his protagonists had to pursue. He called them the "MacGuffins" in his pictures, the pretexts for the plots.

The way he grabbed audience interest was by mixing with menace and suspense a flow of diverse and colorful characters and spurts of incongruous comedy. Take, for instance, the comic dilemma of Hannay when he found himself dragged into the silly political rally and was compelled to make a speech endorsing one of the candidates whose name he didn't even know while the police (or what he thought were police) were thundering hot on his heels. The characters at this rally, the things Hannay managed to say, and the innocence of the audience when his captors dragged him away, still spouting his exhortation, were not only vastly comical but they were subtle reflections of how unobserving and gullible most people are.

And, of course, Mr. Hitchcock always managed to have the principals in his films played by extremely competent actors who were physically attractive as well. In *The Thirty-nine Steps*, Robert Donat, then a young and charming British star, was excellent as Hannay—debonair, lively, and intense. Madeleine Carroll was the beautiful blonde he encountered, antagonistic when they first clashed but sweetly involved and cooperative after the handcuff episode. And Godfrey Tearle was imposing and archly deceptive as the laird, doubly deceiving the American public because he looked a great deal like Franklin D. Roosevelt at the time.

But the secret of Mr. Hitchcock's method—what we call his style—was the quality of his imagination and the plot inventions that he evolved, plus the excellent timing and urbanity with which he maneuvered them. To be sure, there was a certain formula and pattern in most of his films, and *The Thirty-nine Steps* was in essence a compendium of the lot. But to those who have the notion that "if you've seen one Hitchcock film, you've seen them all," I can only say don't believe it. There are tingling surprises in all.

MR. DEEDS GOES TO TOWN

1936

It seemed that Frank Capra was the man for doing surprising things in the way of inaugurating entertainment in the first decade of sound. Far beyond anyone's expectations, his great trend-setting *It Happened One Night,* * starring Claudette Colbert and Clark Gable, smashed through in 1934 as the first of a brand-new category of witty, romantic comedies. And then, two years later, he came up with an equally riotously successful lark, which had Gary Cooper and Jean Arthur as its darlings—*Mr. Deeds Goes to Town.*

Today we can be condescending in accepting and enjoying both these films as what we might call rather naïve situation comedies. But let us not be too superior or incline to toss them off as frivolous, implausible, and perishable specimens of the prewar fantasies of Hollywood. Although they *were* highly romantic, unlikely evolvements of plots which turned upon twists wherein conjunctions of incongruities happily occurred, they contained soothing implications of egalitarianism and share-the-wealth philosophy that were especially appealing to the audiences of those economically stringent days.

This was in the period when we were still feeling the pinch of the Great Depression, when there was a conspicuous difference between the maximum poor and the minimal rich. The very thought of a poor fellow coming into wealth—or a poor girl, for that matter, which was the classic Cinderella formula—got up so the public could accept it with the least suspension of disbelief, was discovered to be a staple of untold potential on the screen. And it was hit upon and winningly concocted by Mr. Capra and his scriptwriter, Robert Riskin, with *It Happened One Night* and *Mr. Deeds Goes to Town.*

Both of these films, significantly, were based on short stories from *The Saturday Evening Post,* which provided the literary entertainment of the American middle class. And both had been interestingly preceded by a couple of modest little films which likewise turned upon the concept of individuals coming into wealth. The first was *If I Had a Million* (1932), which had several widely varied persons unexpectedly receiving checks for a million dollars each from an ec-

Longfellow Deeds (Gary Cooper) bashfully reveals to the unsuspecting newspaper reporter, Babe Bennett (Jean Arthur), that he has fallen in love with her.

centric multimillionaire who picked their names from the telephone book. And the other was the blissfully romantic *Lady for a Day* (1933), which told of an elderly apple vendor set up in elegant style by a group of Broadway gamblers so she could temporarily carry through a deception about her affluence she had pulled on a daughter who had been in a convent in Europe for many years. Mr. Capra, in fact, was the director of this latter film. So there was a consistency in the succession from it to *It Happened One Night* and then on to *Mr. Deeds Goes to Town.*

The tuba-playing Longfellow Deeds (Gary Cooper), surprised inheritor of a fortune, is given a sendoff by the affectionate citizens of his hometown as he departs for New York City.

At the start of his hectic share-the-wealth program, Longfellow pauses to share a bag lunch with one of his grateful petitioners, while his skeptical public relations man, Cornelius Cobb (Lionel Stander), looks on.

Longfellow (Gary Cooper), held for observation in a psychiatric ward because of his whim to share his wealth, despairs of the whole human race.

Examined by any standards, those of 1936 or today, *Mr. Deeds* had or has to be regarded as pure wishful fantasy. Longfellow Deeds, the lanky hero whom Mr. Cooper so aptly played, was an amiable small-town bumpkin who candidly combined all the platitudinous pieties and virtues of an idealized Boy Scout. He was a bachelor because, as his housekeeper told the lawyers when they suddenly showed up in Mandrake Falls, Vermont, to tell him of his immense inheritance, he was "too fussy" to be married. He dreamed of "saving a lady in distress." He worked at the tallow factory, played the tuba in the local band, and picked up some extra money writing verses for greeting cards. When the lawyers momentously informed him that his uncle had left him incredible wealth, he manifested no emotion, no particular interest, indeed. He just said, "I wonder why he left me all that money. I don't need it." Audiences invariably groaned.

And that's what a disinherited cousin likewise did when Longfellow turned up in New York, bearing basketsful of cakes and cookies from friendly townfolk and his tuba under his arm. "He is," said this darkly envious cousin, "the most naïve fellow I have ever seen," and he slyly began calculating how to grab the inheritance away from him. First, he generously suggested that Longfellow might wish to assign to him a simple power of attorney so he could helpfully take care of all the legal details—as a favor, for no payment, of course. Longfellow declined the invitation, then later remarked quite innocently, "Puzzles me why these people all want to work for nothing." The lawyer's man to whom he made the remark hooted (on behalf of the audience), "Why do mice go where there is cheese?"

Naturally, Longfellow was tagged for an easy mark by clever, conniving New Yorkers who wished to help him unload. They put him in a fashionable mansion (where he sneaked a slide down the grand balustrade), gave him a top-lofty butler who suggested that he wear a "monkey suit," and made him a director—the chairman—of the opera house. But that didn't work, for he figured they were simply trying to get him to defray a budget deficit—a yawning shortage he told them cannily he couldn't understand.

Needless to say, Longfellow was a newspaper celebrity about whom city editors were vying to get stories. One sent around his ace sob sister, Miss Arthur, who craftily put on an act as an exhausted job seeker in front of his mansion one night. Sure enough, he spied her and took her off to a tony restaurant where he generously wined and dined her and had a violinist play for her. Humbly—a bit too much so—she advised him, "I'm really just a nobody," to which he replied with manly virtue, "You were a lady in distress!"

And so, in the company of this nice lady—whom he never suspected, of course—he had a grand fling at sightseeing, paid a long-wished-for visit to Grant's Tomb, where he unburdened himself of a corny apostrophe to the gentleman enshrined: "I see a small-town farmboy becoming a great general . . ." and on and on to the ultimate platitude, "Things like that can only happen in America."

On the mansions of the rich, he commented, "They created a lot of grand palaces here, but they forgot to create the noblemen to go in them"—that to Mary while riding atop a Fifth Avenue bus. He hopped a ride on a passing fire engine. "I always ride the fire

Two little ladies from Mandrake Falls, Vermont, tell the sanity hearing that Longfellow Deeds (Gary Cooper) is definitely considered "pixilated" by all the people back home.

Longfellow (Gary Cooper) is about to hang one on the jaw of his malicious cousin, John Cedar (Douglas Dumbrille), who has questioned his mental competence.

engine," he explained to the astonished firemen, who saw him as a goofy hick, of course. And one night, after walking with Mary in a convenient fog and telling her he was fed up with the phonies in New York and that he was going back home, he gave her a poem he had written just for her, and then he beat it off into the

Longfellow and Babe (Jean Arthur) are romantically reunited after he has been triumphantly cleared at his sensational sanity hearing.

night, clumsily stumbling over a few garbage cans on the curb.

That was too much for Mary. She called him on the telephone, told him frankly that he had been ''making love to a double dose of cyanide,'' and confessed that she was the reporter who had been writing all the stories about him in the scandal sheet. That desolated Longfellow, and the staggered look on his face when Mary laid that bombshell on him was shattering to the audience as well. Fortunately, however, at that moment a ragged man beat his way past the butler at the door of Longfellow's soon-to-be-vacated mansion and confronted him with a wavering pistol and a desperate, heartbreaking tale of having lost his little farm af-

ter twenty years of labor, seen his ''grand little wife'' and his trusting children go hungry, with no prospects for the future, no hope. That gave Longfellow an inspiration. He would set up a private charity to give his fortune away to deserving farmers. He would give each a small farm, a cow, and three years to pay back a loan from him to get them on their feet.

Immediately he was besieged by ragged applicants—hundreds packed into his house and he, in his innocent fashion, tried to take care of them. (I have only recently noted that among them there wasn't a single black!) But at this point, the disaffected cousin seized the opportunity to strike. He got the courts to order that Longfellow be put away and submit to a sanity examination. When the hearing was held in court, with the room packed with curious spectators (including Mary), a pompous psychiatrist gave testimony that Longfellow had a "diseased mind, afflicted with hallucinations of grandeur." Longfellow remained silent and aloof. Another alienist tagged him a "manic depressive." Then two old sisters from Mandrake Falls were brought in to testify that Longfellow was "pixilated." Everybody back home knew, they said, that the "pixies had got him." That was damaging, indeed!

Then Mary got up and unburdened herself of an impassioned speech, telling what a fine fellow and so forth she thought Longfellow was, after which he obviously perked up and quietly told the judge, "You know, I'd like to get in my two cents' worth." Thereupon he began making comments about the unconscious evidences people gave of their mental eccentricities, this in reply to the charge that he himself was a "doodler"—that he made squiggles and whorls on a pad. "The judge here," he said, "is an O-filler. He fills the O's on a page of print. Helps you think." And then he called on the two chattering sisters about that pixilated charge. Who else in Mandrake Falls was pixilated? he asked them. "Why, everyone," they replied, "except us." That finished the case against Longfellow. Everybody howled, and in the general upheaval and confusion he was able to hang a haymaker on his cousin's jaw, then found himself gravitating into Mary's arms. The final comment of the judge was, "You're the sanest man that ever walked into this court."

Well, that was a generous concession. To most of the people who saw the film, Longfellow Deeds was a loony, but a happy and enviable one. He was a freak Prince Charming, some kind of a never-never nut. But as Mr. Cooper played him, with firm and sincere diffidence, he provided a whole generation with a heartening, romantic myth.

Miss Arthur was equally appealing as an all-American girl, clever, enterprising, self-propelling, but as decent as the day was long. And several good character actors filled out the comedy cast.

Today it may seem to some viewers that *Mr. Deeds* was a caricature—a candid lampoon of the pious concept of a grass-roots American. I do not agree with that precisely. I think it was absurd but sincere, preposterously idealistic but as comforting as Grandma's apple pie. Like Mr. Capra's later "social statement" (as he termed it), *Mr. Smith Goes to Washington,* it was an innocent, upright soapbox sermon that there were still good people in the world. And that's not a bad proposition, when you can laugh *with* it, even now.

THE RIVER

"We mined the soil for cotton. . . . Ten million bales down to the Gulf, cotton for the spools of England and France." A Mississippi steamboat comes in for a cargo of the precious produce of the South.

1938

With the possible exception of Robert Flaherty's epic silent film, *Nanook of the North,** made in the early twenties around the regions of Hudson Strait, the most famous American documentary film turned out before World War II was Pare Lorentz's *The River,* released in 1938. This classic consideration of the massive importance and power of the Mississippi in the ecology and economy of the United States was made as a propaganda picture for the Federal Farm Security Administration at the time when the nation was throbbing with the manifold projects and philosophy of President Franklin D. Roosevelt's New Deal. And as such it served its primary purpose of spreading the inspirational word of the need for conservation, rehabilitation, and the construction of new power facilities. It turned out to be so finely writ-

ten, so beautifully executed, and it had such an apt and magnificent original musical score that it gained a worldwide reputation as a great work of screen poetry.

It was not a feature-length picture. It ran for thirty-one minutes, to be exact. But it had the effect and impression upon the eye and mind of being more intensely dramatic than most two-hour-long fictional films. In that thirty-one minutes it compacted a sense of the passage of some two hundred years in the life of the Mississippi and the activities of man along its banks and in the hinterlands of the huge basin which the river and its myriad tributaries constituted. In the end it left one with the feeling that one had made a deep and intimate contact with this great living artery of water, which for ages has just kept rolling along, and that, in its mighty presence, man was greedy, wasteful, and infinitely small.

It began with a simple prologue: "This is the story

of a river, a record of the Mississippi, where it comes from, where it goes, what it has meant to us and what it has cost us.'' And with that it went into a montage of beautiful shots of forested mountains down which tiny rivulets flowed, into small creeks and small rivers, then into larger ones and finally out into the great tributaries, the Missouri, the Ohio, the Arkansas, with shots of farmers plowing fields, and cities and small towns along the banks.

This stunning panorama was accompanied by a narrator's voice which achieved a comprehension of this vastness and its colorfulness in truly elegiac words:

From as far west as Idaho,
Down the glacier peaks of the Rockies:
From as far east as Pennsylvania,
Down from the turkey ridges of the Alleghenies;
Down from Minnesota, twenty-five hundred miles,
The Mississippi River runs to the Gulf . . .
Down the Yellowstone, the Milk, the White and the
    Cheyenne;
The Cannonball, the Musselshell, the James, and
    the Sioux . . .
Carrying every rivulet and brook, creek and rill,
Carrying all the rivers that run down two-thirds of
    the continent,
The Mississippi runs to the Gulf.

Then, with this stirring composition of pictures and strongly evocative names, arousing a mental vista of American pioneers, the film gave a skimming estimation of the damage that ignorance and greed, wastage of the land and timber forests, had done to the massive watershed. Bleak evidence of soil depletion and erosion, of mountainsides being stripped, of cotton and lumber being torn from the heartland to supply the omnivorous factories and mills continued the documentation of what the Mississippi basin had endured, and led into a tremendous comprehension of the great river striking back.

By chance while the camera crews were shooting the footage to be put into the film, there came a great flood on the Mississippi and the dramatic proof of the thesis was at hand. Grim shots of the river rising after torrential rains, signaled by boat and factory whistles and the sirens of the Coast Guard patrol boats putting out onto the swollen stream bent upon fetching survivors off bits of high ground or floating roofs, prefaced an awesome compendium of evidence of the river in

Pare Lorentz, writer and director of *The River*, confers with one of his cameramen, Stacey Woodard (right), while scouting locations in the Great Smoky Mountains of Tennessee.

"Levee patrol: men to Blytheville!" A lonely levee-watcher on patrol along the Mississippi during the disastrous flood of 1937.

"We sent armies down the river to help the engineers fight a battle on a two-thousand-mile front." Repair crews on the flooded Mississippi.

"We cut the top off the Alleghenies and sent it down the river. . . . We left the mountains and the hills slashed and burned, and moved on." Stark evidence of bygone damage to the forests and land in the vast Mississippi watershed.

"Cotton for the spools of Italy and Germany." Loading bales along the Mississippi for shipment to foreign mills.

flood, the frantic efforts of men trying to confine it, and the disastrous damage it caused.

> Three hundred miles we built dikes . . .
> Men and mules, mules and men,
> Natchez to New Orleans . . .

The visual record of this disaster was impressive, and it brought to an overwhelming climax the virtually Biblical admonitions that had gone before. The eloquence of Mr. Lorentz's narrative, spoken in a deep, portentous voice by the actor Thomas Chalmers, and the vividness of Virgil Thomson's musical score, compounded of familiar folk tunes such as "Go Tell Aunt Nancy" and "There'll Be a Hot Time in the Old Town Tonight" peppering its symphonic overview, brought the picture to an emotional peak.

There was the gut impact of it. The remainder—the epilogue—was the pitch, the propagandists' message telling what should be done and how. But even this part was fascinating, and is more so today as a primary documentary forecast of the great push toward conservation and industrial controls that began in the period of the New Deal. Departing from the studiously poetic, Whitmanesque conception and tone of the previous three-quarters of the picture, this section was straight-off and terse, a down-to-earth indication of the wreck-

"Last time we held the levees,
But the old river claimed her valley.
She left stock drowned, houses torn loose,
Farms ruined." A scene in the Mississippi Basin after the great flood of 1937.

age and how it had to be repaired. "Poor land makes poor people, poor people make poor land"—the vicious cycle had to be broken with better housing, better farm techniques, better flood control, and more

"The water comes downhill, spring and fall;
Down from the cut-over mountains,
Down from the plowed-off slopes,
Down every brook and rill, rivulet and creek,
Carrying every drop of water that flows down two-thirds of the continent."

"We had the power to take the valley apart—we have the power to put it together again." TVA's Norris Dam on the Clinch River releasing water contained during the great flood of 1937.

output of electrical power, which would come from the reservoirs backed up by the dams built for flood control. All of these projects were shown. And a big plug for the Tennessee Valley Authority—TVA—was popped in to top it off.

Indeed, the final shot of the picture, which brought it up to the obligatory bang, was that of the floodgates being opened on one of the new TVA dams and water pouring over in rich abundance but clearly under man's wise control.

The River was a historic picture, a model for many documentaries to come, and a training ground for a whole school of documentary makers who were available for major service in World War II. In addition to

Mr. Lorentz and Mr. Thomson, whose later musical participations were few but fine, the alumni of *The River* included Stacy Woodard, Floyd Crosby, and Willard Van Dyke, all cameramen on this project but destined to be top directors on their own.

And although Mr. Lorentz was frustrated by a shortsighted Congress in his ambition to evolve a United States Film Service from his experiences in making government documentaries before the war, his foresight was fully vindicated by the establishment of the crucial film division of the Office of War Information when the war began. He himself made other documentaries and served as an orientation filmmaker for the Air Forces during the war.

The Wicked Witch (Margaret Hamilton), lies in wait to menace Dorothy (Judy Garland) and the Scarecrow (Ray Bolger) as they start for the Emerald City of Oz along the Yellow Brick Road.

THE WIZARD OF OZ

1939

With Walt Disney's first cartoon feature, *Snow White and the Seven Dwarfs,* preempting all the juvenile adoration available in the moviegoing public from Christmas in 1937 on, the young producer-director Mervyn Le Roy decided that he, too, would like to produce something that would grab a bit of the fallout of all that love that was in the air. So he hit upon doing a musical film version of Frank Baum's children's classic, *The Wizard of Oz,* a favorite with American youngsters in the early part of the twentieth century as

had been the Grimm Brothers' fable *Snow White and the Seven Dwarfs.*

Well aware of the sentimental nature of his boss at Metro-Goldwyn-Mayer, the redoubtable and omnipotent Louis B. Mayer, Mr. Le Roy worked on him to approve his obtaining the rights to the Baum book from Samuel Goldwyn, who had tried and abandoned making a film from it. Mayer agreed. But he and the man he appointed to assist Le Roy, Arthur Freed, were against Le Roy's inclination to get Shirley Temple to play the role of Dorothy, the little Kansas farmgirl who traveled to the land of Oz. They recalled that

Out of the woods comes leaping the "ferocious" Cowardly Lion (Bert Lahr) to startle the Scarecrow (Ray Bolger), Dorothy (Judy Garland), and the Tin Woodman (Jack Haley) on their way to see the Wizard of Oz.

Dorothy, awaking back in her Kansas farm home, is surrounded by the mundane counterparts of her fanciful friends in the Land of Oz—Dr. Marvel/the Wizard (Frank Morgan), Hunk/the Scarecrow (Ray Bolger), Hickory/the Tin Woodman (Jack Haley), and Zeke/the Cowardly Lion (Bert Lahr)—along with Uncle Henry (Charley Grapewin) and Aunt Em (Clara Blandik).

Dorothy, backed by her companions, celebrates with the liberated "Winkies," guards of the Wicked Witch's palace, after the Witch has been destroyed.

they had a little actress right there on the M-G-M lot who could handle the role very nicely. She was Judy Garland, who had just made a hit in the series film *Love Finds Andy Hardy,* with Mickey Rooney as the star. And since the moppet, Miss Temple, was not about to be lent to the competition by her studio, Twentieth Century-Fox, Mr. Le Roy had to settle for Judy, which was probably the most fortunate compromise he ever made.

Songwriters Harold Arlen and E. Y. Harburg were assigned to do the musical score and Richard Thorpe was put on as director, but soon after shooting began the rushes indicated he wasn't getting the right spirit

into the film, so he was replaced by Victor Fleming, who in turn was taken off to work on *Gone with the Wind.* * (Such musical-chairs shifting of directors was not uncommon at M-G-M.) King Vidor was called in to finish *The Wizard,* which consisted mostly in wrapping up the opening and closing black-and-white sequences.

When *The Wizard* was released in August, 1939, it was favorably reviewed by the critics, and audiences generously took it to their hearts, but not sufficiently to foretell the tremendous and lasting adoration that was in store for it. In the years that have passed, it has rightly become a top favorite among storybook musical films and has been quite as popular and successful as *Snow White,* to which I feel it is superior in both its story and in technical artistry.

I do not suppose there are many people who haven't seen *The Wizard of Oz,* either as original attendants or as children taken to it in later years. So I don't think it necessary for me to go into much detail as to its story and general characteristics, other than to note that it plausibly established its fantasy—its wondrous happenings—as the figments of a little girl's troubled dreams.

Dorothy, the adopted daughter of a Kansas farm woman, Aunt Em, was obviously lonely and wistful out there on that flat, monotonous farm, with her little Skye terrier, Toto, as her only companion. Aunt Em came down rather hard upon her, a cranky old neighbor lady hated and frequently complained of her dog, and Dr. Marvel, the traveling snake-oil vendor, was the only colorful person in her life. So wistful, indeed, was her longing for some excitement that she put it into a song, the now immortal "Over the Rainbow," in which she wished she could go far away, where troubles melt like lemon drops 'way above the chimney tops.

Then one day there came along a cyclone, a roaring twister that forced everyone into the cyclone cellar. But Dorothy, with Toto, didn't make it in time and went instead into the farmhouse and lay down terrified on her bed. Suddenly there came a violent shivering and the house went swirling off the ground with Dorothy and Toto in it, blissfully asleep.

When it came down, miraculously without damage, and Dorothy and Toto stepped outside, they found they were no longer in the dull Kansas black-and-white farmland but in a dazzlingly Technicolored fairyland which she discovered upon encountering an excited mob of midgets which called themselves

Munchkins that she was in the amazing Land of Oz—just the sort of place that Dorothy had wished she might fly to in her song.

Well, you know what happened thereafter—how Dorothy discovered the house had landed right on top of the Wicked Witch of the East who had been holding the happy little Munchkins prisoners, and all that was left of the cruel witch was a pair of magical red shoes. So with these shoes on her feet and with the guidance of Glinda, the Good Witch of the North, she set off for the Emerald City to see the Wizard of Oz. What she wanted to see him about precisely was how she might arrange to go back home, back to Kansas, which was odd because that was the place she had so much wanted to leave. Before departing, however, she led the Munchkins in a couple of lively songs, "Ding Dong, the Witch Is Dead" and the rollicking "Munchkinland." And, as her farewell to them, she ripped out "Follow the Yellow Brick Road."

Out upon that highway with Toto, she first encountered, standing off in a field, the melancholy scarecrow, who was sad because he didn't have a brain. His was only straw and he so wanted to go see the Wizard to ask for a working one. This amiable rubber-legged fellow, whom Ray Bolger cheerfully played, was perfectly set up for dancing, so Dorothy invited him to come along.

Next they met with a frozen-faced Tin Woodman, who was totally immobilized because his metal joints had rusted. He was freed with a couple of squirts of oil, but he had a depressing problem. He was lacking a heart. So he too was invited to join the excursion, which was now beginning to look like a pilgrimage to Lourdes.

And, lastly, out of the woods came bounding the moth-eaten Cowardly Lion, whose ferocious leaping and roaring was only a show to conceal his cowardice. His wish was to be inspired with courage, to become genuinely *leonine.* This being a reasonable petition and he being a good companion anyhow, as played by the comically squinting, grimacing, and spray-dispensing Bert Lahr, he was allowed to join the expedition, as they set off upon the yellow brick road, arms locked and happily singing "We're Off to See the Wiz-

ard, the Wonderful Wizard of Oz." What happened thereafter you may remember much better than I am able to recount. Though harassed by the broomstick-riding sister of the Wicked Witch who was killed, they finally reached the gates of the Emerald City, tricked their way inside, and discovered that the boon-dispensing Wizard was none other than Dorothy's friend, Dr. Marvel, in a glittering green costume. After some minor complications, he gave them all the favors they wished, and then he spectacularly departed in a gaudy balloon.

Dorothy said farewell to her companions, with a great deal of tearfulness, of course, and was soon waking up in her bed in Kansas with Aunt Em and all the farmhands gathered anxiously around. And great was her joy to discover that the farmhands were her three jolly Oz companions, all just exactly as she'd left them, except that they weren't in their fantasy costumes! Whereupon Dorothy gratefully gave voice to the comforting moral of it all: "If I ever again go looking for my heart's desire, I won't go looking any further than my own backyard!"

I am not sure such advice—to be complacent—has stood the test of time quite as well as has the rest of this delightful and melodious *Wizard of Oz.* It was strictly a Pollyanna preachment which shaped up more as a conventional platitude than as advice to enterprising youngsters in the twentieth century. But the film itself is inspiring, and every time it is shown on TV (which is just about every Thanksgiving), it gratifies young and old.

Miss Garland was magical in it, a bright, apple-cheeked little girl with precisely the right expression of joy and wonder and a voice that truly sang. Her Dorothy was, indeed, the beginning of her great stardom and her fabulous career.

I like to remember the legend that British airmen early on in World War II would take off to meet the Nazi Luftwaffe in the Battle of Britain shouting the rubric of the song, "We're Off to See the Wizard," I cannot say it is true, but it makes a wonderful story and says something about the way this children's film has given gratification and comfort to people all over the world.

The Overland Stage sets out in the early morning over the snow-dusted expanse of John Ford's beloved Monument Valley. This was the first of Mr. Ford's many films to be played in that spectacular area.

STAGECOACH

1939

John Ford's historic *Stagecoach* has rolled across the screen so many times, especially on television, in the long years since it was made, and so much of it has been copied, even by Mr. Ford himself, that I find it slightly embarrassing to place it before you again. But to avoid it here would be outrageous. It was and remains a great film, possibly—all things considered—the greatest all-around Western of all time.

On the face of it, yes, it *was* a Western—a drama set on the frontier with all the trappings of standard Western fiction: the frontier cowtown, the noisy saloon, the stagecoach rolling up with much excitement in the dusty street, open plains stretching off to the horizon, the U.S. Cavalry and Indians. And many of the characters in it were familiars from Western films—a genre, incidentally, which had been waning, with a few exceptions, since the introduction of sound. There was the corrupt and grasping banker, the whore with a heart of gold, the sheriff, the proper cowtown ladies, the gentleman gambler, the doctor addicted to drink, and the fearless outlaw with a price on his head. And, in the manner of all respectable Westerns, it was a romantic fantasy.

But there was a big difference in this one, aside from the fact that it was filled with action, suspense, and excitement. It was a difference that made it emerge as strangely apart and quite superior to the run-of-the-stagecoach Western films and has accounted for its extraordinary popularity and staying power over the years. It was a drama of genuine characters in conflict—not just wooden stereotypes, but flesh-and-blood characters whose confrontations symbolized the differences and prejudices of class, and whose strengths and weaknesses were ultimately tested by the challenge of a common peril. That was the danger of attack by Indians as their stagecoach rolled across the lonely plains. Why the Indians should attack was not quite certain, except that the Indians were supposed to hate the whites, especially when the Indians were on the warpath, and it was their devout business to kill.

There have been some latter-day inclinations to see in *Stagecoach* and other Western films having to do with the collisions of whites and Indians early manifests of broader racial strife, indicating that this controversial issue was most prejudicially treated in American films. There is no question about it. The Indians were usually the villains. But in the instance of

Stagecoach, the Indians were just a reigning menace, nothing more symbolical than that, to jeopardize the journey of the assortment of characters in the coach. It was the crisscrossing dramas of these people that formed the substance of the film.

Interestingly, none was more important than any other, until along toward the end, when the destinies of the whore and the outlaw were allowed to predominate. Dudley Nichols, Ford's favorite screenwriter, who put together the script from a short story, "Stage to Lordsburg," by Ernest Haycox (who evidently was inspired by the drama of a similar journey through Europe in Guy de Maupassant's short novel *Boule de Suif*) assembled the whole thing compactly and precisely as though it were a watch, with a comparable way of moving forward to tick off a passage of time.

Among the passengers who boarded the stage at Tonto for the westward journey shortly after the Civil War were the scarlet woman (Claire Trevor), being run out of town by the plump and righteous wives of the community; the tipsy doctor (Thomas Mitchell), likewise being given the boot because of his bibulous habit; the young and pregnant wife (Louise Platt) of an army officer going to join her husband on a frontier post; an absconding banker (Berton Churchill), a little whiskey salesman (Donald Meek); and the courtly gambler, scapegrace scion of an old Southern family (John Carradine). Up on the box to drive the horses were a comical reinsman (Andy Devine) and, to ride shotgun on this journey, a kindly sheriff (George Bancroft), because it had been learned that Geronimo and a band of Apaches were out there somewhere waiting to strike.

Such was the company that rode forth into the beautiful and awesome expanse of Utah's Monument Valley, a spectacular Western locale that Mr. Ford had only recently discovered and which he used with great affection in this and many of his subsequent Western films. Tailing along for part of the journey was a small troop of U.S. Cavalry under the command of a handsome and efficient young shavetail (Tim Holt). And not far out, the coach was waylaid and joined by an outlaw, the Ringo Kid (John Wayne), who had escaped from prison and wanted a ride to Lordsburg to settle a score with the Plummer gang.

The film was roughly divided into three parts. The first was the get-acquainted phase in which the characters were brought into contact and the lines of their class distinctions were laid. The young, pregnant wife and the gambler rather fancied themselves apart because of their pride in being of the Southern aristocracy. The banker, arrogant and blustering, was interest-

Passengers aboard the Overland Stage are greeted at the waystation, Apache Wells, by the treacherous hosteler, (Chris Martin). They are, from left to right, Hatfield (John Carradine), Buck (Andy Devine), Curly (George Bancroft), Peacock (Donald Meek), Mrs. Mallory (Louise Platt), Dallas (Claire Trevor) and the Ringo Kid (John Wayne).

Dallas (Claire Trevor), the outcast prostitute, and the Ringo Kid (John Wayne) face an uncertain future in the classic *Stagecoach*.

ed only in himself. The doctor was interested mainly in the little liquor salesman, from whose samples case he slyly nipped. And the outlaw and whore fell together in an ostracized class by themselves.

The distinctions were made more evident and strained when they stopped for the midday meal at a way station, and the whore and the outlaw were requested to sit apart, while the banker berated the young lieutenant for planning to leave them before their journey's end. But some thin lines of cordiality were strung that evening when they had to stop at Apache Wells because the young wife was taken in labor, and the whore and the doctor pitched in to help.

This simple, homely little crisis was touchingly staged by Mr. Ford, who managed to make this event symbolic of the leveling of class. Even the whore and the outlaw met in the moonlight after the birth and took a tentative look into the future, if there was to be one for them.

With the small group a trifle more cohesive, the second part of the film was reached—that of the onset of menace, culminated by an Indian attack. The imminence of danger was first spotted by the Ringo Kid, who saw Indian smoke signals rising in the distance when he was about to escape on horseback at dawn but herewith abandoned that intention to stay with the vul-

During the midday dinner stop at Dry Fork, the little whiskey salesman, Peacock (Donald Meek) opts for turning back in the face of a threatened attack by Indians. Seated and standing around the table are the Ringo Kid (John Wayne); the driver, Buck (Andy Devine); Dallas (Claire Trevor); Marshal Curly Wilcox (George Bancroft); Mrs. Mallory (Louise Platt); Cavalry Lieutenant Blanchard (Tim Holt); Hatfield (John Carradine); banker Gatewood (Berton Churchill); Old Soldier (Francis Ford); and Doc Boone (Thomas Mitchell).

nerable coach. And it was made more ominous and suspenseful when they came to a ferry-crossing post and found it burned out, with the ferry disabled, and they had to float the laden coach across. Here Mr. Ford built up the details and used his camera to make the viewer squirm with dread.

And then he hit you with a shocker when, with the stagecoach again on its way, he made a wide sweep with his camera across the perilous plains and panned in sharply to a group of Indian warriors perched belligerently atop a nearby hill. That was a startling introduction that I shall never forget, and with it the climax of *Stagecoach* was precipitately entered upon.

Immediately the tempo was quickened as the driver whipped up his team, the sheriff unlimbered his rifle and gave one to the Ringo Kid, and the passengers were fearfully alerted by an arrow zinging through a window and piercing the little salesman through the heart. And from then on it was hell-for-leather out of a narrow pass and onto an alkali flat, with the Indians racing alongside the thundering coach, raining arrows at it while the sheriff, the Kid, and the male passengers blazed back at them with guns. That was, without any question, the classic horse-opera chase, familiar but made exceptional because the audience had been thoroughly involved. And it went on for several breathless minutes, while various terrifying things occurred, such as the Ringo Kid jumping among the horses and steering them from the wagon tongue after the shouting reinsman had been winged. In calmer retrospection, thoughtful viewers have wondered what good that did (other than to make a vivid detail), just as they have wondered why the Indians didn't shoot the horses and thus bring the coach to a stop. (Mr. Ford long ago answered that one by explaining that the Indians were after the people, not the horses, which they preferred to take alive.)

Anyhow, the battle was a beauty, but the Indians finally appeared about to win—so much so that the gambler was making ready mercifully to shoot the mother and her child—when from a distance came the sound of a bugle, and then the cavalry came sweeping in! The Indians were quickly scattered. The gambler, mortally pierced by an arrow, requested that someone might someday tell his father that. . . . With the sentence incompleted, he died. And that was the end of what was probably the most memorable Western sequence ever filmed.

Regrettably it wasn't the end of the picture, which was carried on into a third phase—that of sorting out the survivors—which was inevitably anticlimactic and too long. The wife and baby were delivered to her husband, the absconding banker was taken into custody (somehow they had got a message from Tonto to Lordsburg that he had made off with the funds), and the Ringo Kid, after going through the ritual of confronting and killing the leader of the Plummer gang, was allowed by the benevolent sheriff to ride off into a hopeful future with the whore.

There is no need to hand out encomiums for performances at this late date. Everyone in the cast was superior under the perfect direction of Mr. Ford. Mr. Wayne, then a small-time cowboy actor, came into prominence with this film, and Miss Trevor, who had passed through a brief stardom, was embarked on a whole new career. The Messrs. Carradine, Meek, and Mitchell, as well as the Messrs. Bancroft and Devine, were transported by *Stagecoach* into a prominence they all then held for many years.

As for Mr. Ford, this picture lofted him to the empyrean of that group of great American directors who were as famous and more lasting than the stars. The poetic gift for using scenery—open spaces, natural features, and sky—that he revealed in *Stagecoach* was complemented by his skill at forming metaphorical concepts with plain, everyday characters. The people in this film were not exceptional—as social beings, that is—but Mr. Ford was able to make us see and feel them as a representation of all mankind beneath the shadow of death. It was a superior achievement that rendered *Stagecoach* a major milestone in American films.

THE GREAT DICTATOR

1940

Surely the most widely talked-about and eagerly awaited film before World War II—with the possible exception of David O. Selznick's *Gone with the Wind*—was Charlie Chaplin's *The Great Dictator*. This was not only because it would be the first film of the beloved comedian since his somewhat erratic *Modern Times,* but because it was accurately reported that Chaplin was going to do a frank and contemptuous lampoon of none other than Adolf Hitler.

The prospect of little Charlot, the most familiar and beloved fantasy character in the world, directing his talent for satire and ridicule against the most dangerously evil man alive loomed as a jest of giant proportions, a transcendent paradox. And it also loomed as a potentially unparalleled example of bad taste. Although it was not known at that time how immense were Hitler's schemes, enough was known to cause people to feel it was no time to joke and especially to make commercial capital of a tyrant of that sort.

Furthermore, the misgivings about the project were complicated by the fact that Chaplin was often rumored and even openly charged with being a "Red." Indeed, his comical contrivance of having the Little Tramp accidentally wave a red flag in front of a group of striking workmen in *Modern Times* was frowned upon by many as a token of his Communist sympathies. And it was rumored by Hollywood columnists that he planned to conclude *The Great Dictator* with an out-and-out socialistic appeal. What earthly reason this presented—or might present—for reproaching his new film is hard to see now, but that gives you an idea of the atmosphere in which it was released.

Actually, Chaplin himself had some worries about going ahead with the film after Hitler's invasion of Po-

Dictator Adenoid Hynkel looks with some bewilderment upon the world he expects to conquer in Charlie Chaplin's classic satiric comedy.

land and the outbreak of war in August, 1939. He brought a halt to production, which he had begun in June, and spent a few weeks in indecision before deciding in September to go ahead. According to one of his biographers, he concluded that "ridicule is a powerful weapon and that laughter is a tonic, a release from pain," which for him was sufficient justification to finish the film as planned.

Let's be thankful he did, for *The Great Dictator* turned out to be a superlative comical satire, with certain flaws, it is true, but altogether a brilliantly audacious piece of Jovian ridicule and mockery. Although some of the critics and first-nighters thought that Chaplin showed insensitivity in some of the scenes representing the suppression of Jews in his mythical totalitarian state and that the handling of such a ticklish subject called for the skills of a Swift or a Voltaire rather than those of the creator of the Little Tramp, the public received the film with high approval and made it a resounding success, discounting the solemn apprehensions that there was no time for comedy.

But there lay the secret of its impact: *The Great Dictator* was no flip buffoonery, no easy, elemental social satire in the manner of Chaplin's earlier films. It was essentially a tragic picture—or tragicomic in the classical sense—and, for all its unquestioned slapstick humor, it had bitter and disquieting overtones. For along with its withering revelations through magnificently inspired mimicry of the overblown conceits, the

Benzini Napolini (Jack Oakie), dictator of Bacteria, gives a not so admiring look at his neurotic counterpart, Adenoid Hynkel (Charlie Chaplin), dictator of Tomania.

Hynkel (Charlie Chaplin), dictator of Tomania, returns the customary salute to a throng of his admiring followers.

gross pretensions, and the dark insanity of an undisciplined and uncontrollable dictator, there were haunting, horrible implications of the desperate fate of the millions of Jews and others whose lives were subject to the barbarism of such a man.

The story line was simple, based on the wild coincidence that the real-life Adolf Hitler looked amazingly like Chaplin's Little Tramp. Introduced by a long flashback sequence of the mad adventures of a German soldier in the First World War—a little fellow who bore a close resemblance to the Little Tramp in Chaplin's earlier *Shoulder Arms*—the story began with this small person returning to his vacant barbershop in the ghetto of an imaginary city (evidently Berlin) after a long hospitalization with amnesia which was caused by an injury in the war. He did not know that his country, called Tomania, was now under the sign of the double-cross, that the soldiers who patrolled the streets were storm troopers, that their business was to repress Jews, and that the all-powerful ruler of To-

mania was one Hynkel, a megalomaniac. Naturally he flared in indignation when the troopers painted "Jew" on his shop, and received a vicious beating when he failed to respond to their "Heil, Hynkel!" by hoisting his hand in the Nazi salute. Of course, the little guy was a twin brother of Chaplin's familiar Little Tramp, except that this one could talk. At last Chaplin had given his character a voice!

The voice of the little barber was rather high-pitched and meek, more or less what one might have imagined the voice of the Little Tramp would be, and it clearly enunciated in English its mostly monosyllabic words. But in the counterpart role of Adenoid Hynkel, who was initially introduced addressing a monster rally of the people of Tomania—a scene that was pointedly recollective of familiar newsreel shots of great mass gatherings addressed by Hitler in Nazi Germany—Chaplin shrieked in a guttural jumble of English-German-Katzenjammer double talk, with violent gestures and facial contortions that were brilliant mi-

50

micry. ''Democratia shtunk!'' he shouted. ''Libertad shtunk!'' he screamed. ''Frei sprachen shtunk!'' (This was politely translated by a commentator's voice on the soundtrack, ''Free speech is objectionable.'')

This lengthy harangue was punctuated by frequent pauses to grimace at the mob, to strut a few steps on the platform, and once to gulp a drink of water from a glass, then repeat the old Chaplin comic business of tossing the rest of the water down his pants. On the platform with him was Garbitsch, his bulbous Minister of War, resplendent in uniform and medals, who split his pants when adjured to ''tighten der belten.'' At the end of this extraordinary tirade, Hynkel was accidentally bumped down a flight of steps by another of his fat lieutenants, Herring, who for that humiliating blunder had all the glittering medals stripped from his chest.

It was in this role of Hynkel that Chaplin was truly at his best, close to the peak of his genius at satiric comedy. It was here that he superbly demonstrated his histrionic virtuosity, his extraordinary powers of ob-

The newly returned Jewish barber (Charlie Chaplin), antithesis to the tyrannical Hynkel, whom he so closely resembles in looks, prepares the hair of his new love, Hannah (Paulette Goddard).

A question of precedence in *The Great Dictator*: Adenoid Hynkel (Charlie Chaplin), the dictator of Tomania, disputes with Benzini Napolini (Jack Oakie), the dictator of Bacteria, as to which shall sit higher in the barber chairs.

servation, and his inventiveness at caricature. To be sure, his performance of the little barber was apt in the old familiar vein, displaying the independence and indomitable spirit of the perennial little man. In his tender devotion to Hannah, an aggressive ghetto girl who, with Paulette Goddard playing her, was practically a duplicate of the girl in *Modern Times*, and in his wonderful dexterity, he was the Chaplin of *The Gold Rush** and *City Lights*.

One scene in which the little barber shaved an elderly Jewish customer entirely in pantomine precisely to the rhythm of Brahms' Hungarian Dance No. 5, conveniently provided by the radio, was unsurpassingly inspired.

But in the role of Hynkel, Chaplin was breaking new ground. He filled the screen with a job of vivisection that is now recorded history. His flabby hand salutes, his sudden lurches into ludicrous attitudes, his fits of rage and facial contortions, his bursts of ecstasy at fatuous flattery—all revealed the absurdity of Hitler's mannerisms and conceits. And he reached heights of metaphorical comment and ironical mockery. Alone in a room of the palace, he did a ballet to the music of Wagner's Prelude to *Lohengrin,* bouncing above his head and pirouetting beneath a huge balloon symbolizing the globe, stroking it, making love to it, and finally clasping it so tightly that it burst, whereupon he broke into tears and buried his face in his arms.

Another brilliant sequence was one in which Hynkel met to bargain with Benzino Napolini, a neighboring dictator, who was boisterously played by Jack Oakie in mockery of Mussolini. The acrobatics by which these two megalomaniacs maneuvered to upstage each other were funny and chilling. The memory of that scene flashed back to many of us a few years later when the news photographs were printed of the assassinated body of Mussolini hanging high from a tree.

The climax of *The Great Dictator* was not as strong as one might have wished, and it was here that Chaplin did give way to that penchant for preaching that flawed his later films. Hynkel was mounting an invasion of a neighboring country (Austerlich), just as the little barber, escaped from prison, was fleeing to the same place. By a characteristically complicated mix-up, Hynkel, in a Tyrolean disguise, was mistaken and captured by prison guards pursuing the barber, and the little fellow encountered a crowd of Austerlichians awaiting their conqueror, who hustled him into a waiting car. "Where are we going?" inquired the little fellow. "You are invading Austerlich," was the reply.

Led to the capital and pushed onto a platform, he was called upon to make a speech, and it was that speech, alas, that brought the picture to an inept and maudlin close. "I'm sorry, but I don't want to be an emperor," the little barber began modestly. "That's not my business. I should like to help everyone—Jew, Gentile, black man, white." And with that the emboldened little fellow launched into a long rhetorical appeal for reason, kindness, and brotherly love. It was totally out of character and context, and the interjected apostrophes to Hannah—"wherever you are, look up!"—accompanied by intercuts of Hannah, previously beaten by storm troopers, raising her head and looking toward the sky, were downright embarrassing. With that sort of rant the picture closed.

I strongly advise anyone seeing this film for the first time to slip out before this final bombast—or, if one should choose to stay, to remember that it was symptomatic of Chaplin's fervor and the passions of the day. He was undeniably a great artist, but he sometimes abused his prerogatives. However, this terminal self-indulgence did not really subtract from the essential enunciation of outrage and condemnation that Chaplin projected in this film. With the help of several expert talents—Oakie, Billy Gilbert as Herring (Göring, of course), Henry Daniell as Garbitsch (Goebbels) and Maurice Moscovish and Bernard Gorcey as ghetto Jews—Chaplin did forge a powerful weapon out of ridicule and a great tonic of laughter that is potent to this day.

THE GREAT MC GINTY

Fortune helps those who help themselves. The champion stuffer of ballot boxes, Dan McGinty (Brian Donlevy), acts upon his guiding principle at a political-machine victory party.

1940

If American motion pictures have turned up a major satirist—someone who has done in this medium, with all its strictures, what Jonathan Swift did in English literature—that someone is Preston Sturges, the writer and director who thrived in the turbulent 1940s, then sadly and inexplicably faded away.

Mr. Sturges had without question the most wonderfully mischievous sense of humor, the most perceptive eye for the absurd, combined with extraordinary talent for making the medium bounce and move, of anyone since Mack Sennett invented slapstick farce. And he had more than that. He used his skill and humor to reveal the social incongruities of his times—the hollowness of hallowed institutions and the fraudulences of manifold stuffed shirts.

But the fantastic thing about him—in his first and most memorable films—was the fact that the bite of his satire and the slash of his farcical wit were never malicious or hurtful. He would make hilarious sport of the crookedness and effrontery of American machine

The political boss (Akim Tamiroff) makes a significant gesture to the bum, Dan McGinty (Brian Donlevy), the phenomenal stuffer of ballot boxes, as he is being introduced by his wardheeler patron (William Demarest).

The Boss (Akim Tamiroff) is charmed by the aggressiveness and impudence of his protégé, Dan McGinty (Brian Donlevy), in *The Great McGinty*.

politics or the pomposities of the wealthy or the humbuggery of Hollywood; and yet he never did so with hate or rancor, nor even with haughty contempt. He generally found their shortcomings amusing, and he always ended with a shrug and a laugh.

For instance, in the first film he directed and for which he also wrote the original script—his classic *The Great McGinty*, released in 1940 with Brian Donlevy starred—Mr. Sturges staggered moviegoers by the audacity and energy with which he gleefully debunked one of the most crucial tenets of American democracy—the dependability of the system on the levels of the municipalities and the states. This was a subject which had never been openly ridiculed in films. Indeed, very few moviemakers had even dared touch on government. Just one year before *The Great McGinty,* Frank Capra had won his acclaim by questioning the undivided honesty of the United States Senate in his *Mr. Smith Goes to Washington.* Mr. Capra did allow there might be certain corruptible Senators submissive to bribery, but he showed how they were finally brought to justice by an idealistic, righteous young appointee who proved that Boy Scout honesty would triumph in the end.

That wasn't the bent of Mr. Sturges. There was no idealism in him. *The Great McGinty* was not the kind of picture to be endorsed by the Rotary Club. In fact, Mr. Sturges had a tough time selling his script for it to Paramount, for which he had recently written the highly successful *If I Were King* and *Remember the Night.* At first, he could not get the nabobs to give him the time of day. Then he lured them out by virtually giving them the finished screenplay on the condition that he be allowed to direct it. That was their way of shutting him up.

When the film was finished, the astonished front office called for several cuts and trims, including some of the most pungent and ribald political-victory celebration sequences. And censors later demanded elision of a familiar quatrain from the old "Frankie and Johnny" ballad which Mr. Sturges used to preface the film:

> This story has no moral,
> This story has no end,
> This story only goes to show
> There ain't no good in men.

"Marriage is the most beautiful setup among the sexes." A slight hitch in the proceedings at the marriage of convenience between Dan McGinty and his secretary, Catherine (Muriel Angelus).

"Lemme at him!" The Boss (Akim Tamiroff) and the new governor, McGinty (Brian Donlevy), disagree on a matter of policy on Inauguration Day.

But there was no need for explication. The film's conclusion was vividly clear, likewise the freshness and vigor of Mr. Sturges' way of handling it.

From the opening sequence in a barroom in a Central American banana port where a cocky bartender was trying to talk a customer out of committing suicide by telling him matter-of-factly how he himself was once the governor of a state, the action jumped in spinning flashback to a brisk, Roman-candle-like account of how this very bartender ascended from a soup line of bums and down-and-outs in an unspecified American city to the eminence he so casually claimed. His method was direct and easy. He simply muscled his way (by stuffing ballot boxes) into a shamelessly corrupt political machine, bossed by a chesty little tyrant who took a fancy to him because of his unbridled gall and knavery, then worked his way up through various jobs, such as collecting "dues" from whorehouse madams and cracking recalcitrant skulls, to getting himself made an alderman, then "reform" mayor, and finally governor.

But trouble began when the boss decided that, to run for mayor, the bucko should have a wife. "Women get the vote now," he confided, "They don't like bachelors." And besides, he reminded McGinty, "Marriage is the most beautiful setup among the sexes." "I know all about it," the bum shot back with a graveled edge of sarcasm in his tone. "My parents was married." A typical Sturges sequitur!

What seemed a convenient and businesslike arrangement was made with McGinty's new secretary, who happened to be a very pretty, respectable young widow and mother of two small kids. And this, alas, turned out to be McGinty's Achilles' heel. After a made-to-order wedding with glum ward heelers perfunctorily tossing rice, and after the bum had been elected and thereby certified to hustle big graft (which he did with no more compunction than he showed in putting the arm on whores), he found himself falling in love with his wife and kids. And, in order to please and impress them, he mistakenly decided to go straight.

"One day," he told his barroom listeners, switching back briefly to them, "I said, I'm strong enough now. Hunh!" he grunted with evident disdain for his folly. "In a pig's ear I was strong enough!"

And therewith began the falling action. Hustled through a montage of shots suggesting his "efficiency" as mayor and his election to the governor's spot, McGinty was shown preparing to assume his new job with a clean slate. But the first one to greet him when he entered his office, sitting slyly in his chair, was the boss, beaming fondly and benignly. "You'll kiss me for this one," he said. "A dam!" An ugly silence from McGinty. The boss continued, "I can see from the expression on your face you don't know what a dam is. A dam," he explained precisely, "is something you put concrete in. You're kind of dumb this morning, aren't you, Dan?"

This did it. A flash of anger and the two rascals were at each other's throats, tumbling like gutter fighters all over the governor's office floor. Sounds of the battle echoed through the state capitol. People came running from all over to gape at the titanic fray. The story was splashed in newspapers. Old scandals were brought to light. And the next thing we knew, from a rush of headlines, McGinty and the boss were in jail, growling and jeering at each other from adjoining cells. But their residence was brief, because a henchman—the one William Demarest played with a sharp edge of skepticism toward all things and with a thoroughly eloquent deadpan—turned up in the uniform of a jailer and bearing the latter's keys. Together the three inseparables made a beautiful Keystone getaway.

With that the action reverted to the smoky bar, with several eavesdroppers now hanging on the bartender's tale. "Why didn't he [the boss] kill you?" one of them asked skeptically. The bartender chuckled reminiscently, "I never could figure that out." "I know why!" the customer shouted. "Because you're a big liar about the whole thing!" The bartender didn't deny it. He just gazed amiably at his audience. Then the camera laconically swung around to discover the now deflated boss and a couple of other of his henchmen toiling benignly in the joint. With that little tickle of enigma the film was brought to a close.

Such was the way with Mr. Sturges. He didn't lecture. He didn't point morals. He didn't even care whether he left us not quite sure he wasn't pulling *our* legs, too. He was as blissfully indifferent to concepts of honor and rectitude as were his political rascals, who had no concepts of those things at all. Certainly, by his evident satisfaction in demonstrating their frank delinquencies, their triumphs, and their blunders, their total ignorance of what was meant by "public weal," he happily left us with the feeling that he thoroughly enjoyed what they did, their arrogant exploitation of an equally corrupt society. As McGinty reminded a madam from whom he was picking up dues, "You *gotta* pay protection. You don't wanna be at the mercy of every guy in a uniform." Or, as the character played by Mr. Demarest put it in one of his wise apothegms, "Ya gotta pay *somebody* to protect you from human greed."

The crux of Mr. Sturges' style was a blend of sophistication and farce. His outrageous situations were not so fanciful and farfetched that they didn't have ugly aspects of documented truth, but he chose to annotate them not with outrage but with pratfalls and punches. And his characters, too, were combinations of sinister rowdies and buffoons. Mr. Donlevy's Dan McGinty was a ruffian with a heart of gelt. Tilted a bit toward the serious, he would have fitted a Robinson or Cagney role. And Akim Tamiroff could have been fearsome as a noxious descendant of Boss Tweed if he hadn't been so shamelessly cheerful and so candidly oozing guile. Mr. Demarest, Thurston Hall, and Harry Rosenthal were among the array of ward heelers who could have switched and been neo-Keystone Kops, while Muriel Angelus in this, her last picture, was charming as the wife.

Mr. Sturges' brand of entertainment was similar to that of René Clair. He loved to *épater les bourgeois*, as the French so charmingly say. He had the feeling for farce of a Chaplin, without the latter's deep compassion and sentiment. He was closer akin to Damon Runyon or to the early Orson Welles. Indeed, it bears remarking that Mr. Welles' great *Citizen Kane** came out just nine months after *The Great McGinty*. It, too, was its youthful creator's first directorial job. It, too, went through problems of stricture in getting to the screen. It, too, was a cynical look at power-hungry American politicos. And Mr. Welles, like Mr. Sturges, became in the next decade a reigning enfant terrible.

Out for a jolly time in the new horseless carriage of Eugene Morgan (Joseph Cotten) in the first phase of *The Magnificent Ambersons*. At left are Lucy Amberson Minifer (Dolores Costello) and Fanny Minifer (Agnes Moorehead), and at right is Jack Amberson (Ray Collins).

THE MAGNIFICENT AMBERSONS

1942

It is generally agreed by students of the cinema that the second film of Orson Welles—made within two years after his classic *Citizen Kane**—was flawed in its final release version and has been further flawed in frequent showings on TV. *The Magnificent Ambersons* was frankly truncated before it left the studio be-

George Amberson Minifer (Tim Holt) resentfully watches as his repressed mother, Lucy (Dolores Costello), meets again her old beau, Eugene Morgan (Joseph Cotten) early in *The Magnificent Ambersons.*

Eugene Morgan (Joseph Cotten) pays a visit to the now destitute Fanny Minifer (Agnes Moorehead) in a home for ladies toward the end of *The Magnificent Ambersons.*

A taut moment in the baronial home of the Ambersons. At the dining table are Jack Amberson (Ray Collins), Eugene Morgan (Joseph Cotten), and the patriarchal Major Amberson (Richard Bennett).

cause the front-office boys were apprehensive that it was going to be a dud after sampling audience reactions at several sneak previews around Los Angeles. They ordered considerable revision, which was left pretty much in the hands of a couple of young film editors (one of whom was Robert Wise, now a distinguished director) because the volatile Mr. Welles had abandoned the film before completion and had gone off to do another job.

Even so, the picture was a masterpiece of bold proportions—an American family saga of stunning scope, set in an unnamed Midwestern city in the period between the century's turn and the First World War. In many ways, especially in its cinematic and architectural styles, and in its assertive presentation of a monstrous central character, it bore a close resemblance to the brilliant *Citizen Kane* and it clearly attested that an artist of colossal potentiality was now astride the medium in the person of Mr. Welles.

The focal character was an inordinately arrogant young man, only son of the unnerved daughter of an aging industrial tycoon, who virtually took over the family when he reached his maturity in the huge, oak-paneled mansion set imperiously atop a hill. He tyrannized over his doting mother, a fading beauty and social paragon, especially after his weakling father strangely sickened and died. He refused to allow this poor lady to keep company with an old beau because he feared that this middle-aged widower, who had achieved some considerable success as the inventor of one of the newfangled horseless carriages, was after the family money—and for psychological reasons more allusive and complex. He defied and abused without mercy a waspish maiden aunt who obviously thought she had a chance at her sister's reunioning old beau. And he even intruded upon the authority and pathetic senility of his ancient grandfather, who was slowly dying—and finally died, surprisingly penniless.

The story which Mr. Welles adapted from a novel by Booth Tarkington was in that vein of reflection upon the nature of America in the period of final transition between the agrarian and industrial eras—a vein that was strongly Chekhovian and had been richly mined by writers such as Willa Cather, Theodore Dreiser, Edna Ferber, and Mr. Tarkington. The general thesis was that the wealthy and politically powerful sectors of the upper class had failed to realize upon their material achievements in humane and cultural ways, had wasted their providential affluence by allowing themselves to become isolated in their great mansions behind the bastions of their wealth, and had lost contact not only with life around them but with their souls.

At his best in *The Magnificent Ambersons*, which was obviously an ironic title, Mr. Welles generated a powerful image of the fatal weaknesses and sterility within the gaunt, drafty residence and the barren hearts of this cheerless family. In structure, the film was eccentric, scenes were generally short and intercut with flashes of comment and gossip passed by townspeople upon the peculiar behavior of the Ambersons in their house on the hill. Occasionally, Mr. Welles himself contributed observations as an off-screen voice. With rare and surprising self-efface-

ment, he did not play a role. The style was pseudodocumentary as it was in *Citizen Kane*. It was a style of staccato narration that he and his Mercury Theater troupe had brilliantly perfected in his period of producing dramas for radio.

And the dialogue was likewise stylistic, both in phrasing and in the way it was tossed off, with lines being casually spoken or even mumbled, not declaimed as so often it was in films, and frequently overlapping so that one character would suddenly cut off another in midsentence, even change the subject perhaps, leaving the viewer with the feeling that the characters were truly talking among themselves, directing their random thoughts to one another and not arranging them for an audience. At times, too, in violent encounters, the characters would literally scream and shout, thus conveying the intensity of their emotions and the abandonment of their pretentious dignity.

Thus the film became a mosaic of intimate and sometimes scandalous glints of the psychological tensions and battles among the Ambersons, with sideline rumors and speculations coming up from the gossips in the town, thus contributing to the viewer's impression of the abnormality and instability of the clan. Whether this aim was calculated in the original plan or whether it worked out as a consequence of cutting for expediency's sake, I am not sure, but I would rather

A dramatic clash on the great staircase of the Ambersons' baronial home between George Amberson Minifer (Tim Holt) and his old-maid aunt, Fanny Minifer (Agnes Moorehead).

imagine it was carefully planned by Mr. Welles. It certainly was a dominant feature of the style of delivery of the whole.

Structurally, the film developed in three phases. The first introduced the family, beginning with a big homecoming party for Georgie, the arrogant son who had just come back from college and was being lionized by his family. At the party were, of course, his beautiful mother; his bitter, sarcastic aunt; his feeble father; the old beau; the latter's daughter, a charming, nubile girl, with whom Georgie became enamored; and a wide swath of people of their class. This phase of introductions and plot arrangement was climaxed by a wonderful scene—perhaps the best in the picture—of a jolly outing through the snow in Morgan's horseless carriage, with people laughing, sleighbells jingling, and a great old tune, "The Man Who Broke the Bank at Monte Carlo," rollicking on the musical track. The gaiety and abandon of this excursion fairly capped the spirit of the idle rich, and a slow iris-in on the backfiring auto going away across a snowy hill with the sounds of laughter and sleighbells fading was a sweet, nostalgic farewell to an age.

The second phase came immediately after, with the camera irising out on the death of Georgie's father, which was the beginning of the stage of family disintegration and of Georgie's taking command, his browbeating of his mother, who meekly submitted to him, and his violent confrontations with Aunt Fanny, who spewed her bitterness and frustration back on him. In this phase, Georgie succeeded in keeping Morgan, the old beau, away from his exhausted mother—though not without a struggle, to be sure—and it was brought to a climax with the mother's death.

Obviously, the third phase was intended to expose and dramatize the irony of disintegration, the anticlimactic death of the old grandfather, preceded by a weird soliloquy in which the old man expressed (to the audience) his dread of passing on to a place where no one was likely to know of the Ambersons or have a privileged spot set aside for him, and the painful adjustment of Georgie and Aunt Fanny to the grim fact of their being destitute. Georgie had to abandon his intention of studying law and he took a job in a high-explosives factory—a "dangerous occupation"—so they could have enough money to live. But it was in this phase of the picture that most of the post-previews cutting was done, and the consequent narrative lapses and non sequitur jumps most clearly showed. Likewise, a labored endeavor to reunite Georgie with the girl after he was injured in an explosion concluded the film with a cliché that did not conform with the preceding theme of fatality.

However, there was so much in this picture that was stunningly perceptive and correct, so many brilliant exposures of character and mood, that I would not want to let this recollection bear too heavily on its flaws. One scene, for instance, of Georgie, who was stolidly played by Tim Holt, confronting Agnes Moorehead's shrill Aunt Fanny on the stairway in the great baronial hall, with the camera shooting from below and then above so that their figures appeared lonely and distorted in that lofty space while they screamed and spewed at each other, was an image of supreme irony. Or just a small scene in which Joseph Cotten as the old beau attempted to call on Georgie's waning mother and was compelled to stand at the foot of the stairs and look up at the unattainable—this was equally eloquent.

Miss Moorehead was the strongest, most dramatic performer in the film, with her dark hints of sexual repression and her bursts of raw hysteria, not to mention her more tender efforts to soften Georgie—this was bravura acting at its best. Mr. Cotten's attractively amiable, understanding, and wistful old beau was likewise a fine and sensitive balance for the sweetness and poignancy of the beautiful Dolores Costello as the mother. And Richard Bennett was appropriate, too, as the old grandfather who bade farewell in true nineteenth-century acting style.

One last word for the credits, which were simply read off at the end by Mr. Welles, concluding with a pointedly humble postscript for himself: "I wrote the script and directed it. My name is Orson Welles."

SULLIVAN'S TRAVELS

1942

You might have thought Preston Sturges was a one-man Stage Door Canteen, the way he dished up a fast succession of superior comedies at the very time this nation was entering the grim period of World War II. Consider this! Only three months after *The Great McGinty* in 1940 (*q.v.*) and his sparkling emergence therewith as a major American satirist, Mr. Sturges brought forth a winning trifle called *Christmas in July* and followed that three months later with a true gem, *The Lady Eve*. This was a sleek and saucy satire on the social naïveté of the nouveau riche, in this case exampled by a dopey but honest and sweet young millionaire (Henry Fonda) who was gulled and eventually wedded by a beautiful lady cardsharper (Barbara Stanwyck). She finally won him by posing as a titled British dame.

Less than one year later, in January, 1942, Mr. Sturges came up with what many think now to have been his most interesting film—one in which he brilliantly expounded with withering satire his derision of the pomposities and excesses of Hollywood and provided some thoughts about the essence of entertainment which could be taken as his own artistic creed. This was *Sullivan's Travels*, a film which I agree was nigh, if not, his best.

On the surface, it seemed no more than a titanic spoof of the greediness and insensitivity of the solons of Hollywood and the silliness and miscomprehension of the "deep-dish" fellows who yearned to turn out message films. Its hero was a well-established director who had enjoyed tremendous success with such pleasant bits of fluff as *So Long Sarong, Hey Hey in the Hay*, and *Ants in Your Plants of 1939*, but who felt that the times for such frivolity were distinctly out of joint. He felt, as did certain other longhairs and pseudointellectuals of the day, that the woes of the world execrated any such blatant levities. He wanted to make an about-face from his fun stuff and come up with a solemn message film, something bold and realistic, something titled *O Brother, Where Art Thou?*

Needless to say, the reactions and rejoinders of the studio brass to this virtually sacrilegious suggestion from one of their top-money boys were less than en-

The successful film comedy director, John L. Sullivan (Joel McCrea), is assisted in dressing for his exploratory foray among the poor and down-and-outs by his valet (Eric Blore).

A familiar way of vagrants for picking up a little money is tried by Sullivan (Joel McCrea) and his companion (Veronica Lake) in the lighter phase of *Sullivan's Travels*.

thusiastic. Their notion of art on the screen was something that showed garbage cans, maybe, but also with "a little sex." A drama on poverty and suffering was as noxious to them as a rotting corpse.

But despite their calamitous misgivings, the hero, Sullivan, was allowed to proceed, to go out into the world and witness Hardship, to learn how the down-and-outers lived, dressed up in a tramp outfit from Wardrobe and with a look of determination in his eyes. But he had to agree to be accompanied by a sleek land-cruiser, furnished with soft beds and a chef, and crammed with photographers and press people to report his fey adventure to the world.

Thus the odyssey started, with Sullivan tramping down the road and the land-cruiser following slowly like a tour bus a few yards behind. But then Mr. Sturges injected one of his typical explosions of slapstick farce, as though to assure the audience that this was all in fun. He had Sullivan hitch a quick ride from a kid in a souped-up car and go racing away, with the land-cruiser racing and careening after him. This was a situation of the sort he employed most tellingly—the huge auto-van rocking wildly, the bull-necked chauffeur struggling frantically with the steering wheel, the press people falling about like tenpins, and the black chef in the galley tumbling fearfully amid his pots and pans. This was a satiric high point, a peak in the comical spoof of the overextravagant life-style and massive bumbles of the Hollywood elite.

On the strength of this near-disastrous foul-up, Sullivan made a deal with the press people to allow him to go it on his own and, without notifying the front office, just meet him in Las Vegas later on. But his undisturbed efforts to make a contact with the People were equally vague (one trick of doing tramp work for a widow became a struggle to maintain his chastity) and the next thing he knew he landed, by inadvertence, back in Hollywood. There, in an all-night lunch wagon, he encountered a jobless extra girl and tried to persuade her to return to her hometown. But she was no fool. She convinced him, after an interlude in his sumptuous home and swimming pool, to let her go with him on his further undaunted See-Life tour.

Again, in his studio tramp outfit (and she in a hash of his old clothes that made her look like a nice child dressed up for Halloween), he gingerly delved a little deeper into hobo camps and havens for the unemployed, riding in smelly old freight cars and sleeping in flophouses. With obvious distaste and revulsion, he looked blankly at this face of poverty, and finally fled from it, back to the land-cruiser, when he and she found themselves fumbling to scrounge some scraps from a garbage can.

As he rather rhetorically put it, "It's as though some force is telling me to get back where you belong! Go back, you phony!" He knew he could not belong.

For a parting, patronizing gesture toward the people he could not join, he decided to go out alone on his last evening and distribute a pile of $5 bills. And it was while doing this, in his costume, that he was knocked out by a slithering tramp and shoved into an empty car on a passing freight, while the tramp grabbed the bills and beat it, only to be run down in the yard and mangled by an oncoming train.

Here the mood changed; the tone of satire gave way to hard reality. Sullivan, groggy and bewildered, crawled out of the car the next day in a distant freight yard, to be confronted by an ugly yard boss who tried to club him, which Sullivan countered by smashing the guard with a rock. Unable to identify himself or explain his helpless situation, Sullivan was hustled through a trial and sentenced to six years' hard labor in a brutal convict camp. Nor were his friends able to reach him, because the body of the tramp, found in the yard, all mangled and unidentifiable, was wearing the pair of sturdy shoes which he previously had stolen from Sullivan. Thus it was assumed and blazoned in newspapers that the Hollywood director had been killed.

So a cruel and degrading new life began for Sullivan in the convict camp among a jungle of scurvy and hopeless men. Here he found himself truly at the bottom of the barrel, experiencing without a chance of relief the sort of existence he had set out to find.

One night, at a special entertainment provided for the prisoners by a black preacher and his congregation at a nearby country church—it was a creaky, flickering showing of an old Mickey Mouse-Pluto cartoon—the vital truth was revealed to Sullivan. These poor, helpless convicts did not cringe from this morsel of sheer entertainment. They hollered with delight and guffawed as they followed Pluto's confusions with unreflecting joy. They were eye-openly grateful for this one little moment of escape.

Needless to say, the director shortly thereafter won release by finding, as he said, the "plot twist" that would attract attention to himself. He ran through the camp proclaiming that he had killed Sullivan! At once

Sullivan (Joel McCrea) and the destitute Hollywood extra (Veronica Lake) whom he has picked up as a traveling companion, queasily sample the food in a charity soup-kitchen.

Battered and shorn of his identity, Sullivan (Joel McCrea) finds himself now a true outcast in a distant freight yard.

he was recovered and whisked back to Hollywood in another Sturges tumult of firecracker press agentry. But when his producers wished to trumpet that he was now ready to do *O Brother, Where Art Thou?* he surprisingly turned the tables.

"I say this with some embarrassment," he told them, mocking an old Hollywood bromide. "I haven't suffered enough to make it."

And when they looked at him with wonder, he came up with the clincher. "There's a lot to be said for making people laugh. It's not much, but it's all we have in this cockeyed caravan."

When I first reviewed *Sullivan's Travels,* I thought the ending a bit too pat. Sullivan's reconversion was not sufficiently well conceived. It was the spot reaction of the character to a shattering experience, not a convincing explication for the audience. It did not refute the axiom that serious drama—message films—had their place. It simply reached an easy conclusion for a still rather immature man, and made a casual surrender to Hollywood's commercial philosophy.

Shortly thereafter, Mr. Sturges explained in an article in *The New York Times,* February 1, 1942: "When I started writing [*Sullivan's Travels*] I had no idea what Sullivan was going to discover. Bit by bit, I took everything away from him—health, fortune, name, pride and liberty. When I got down to there, I found he still had one thing left—the ability to laugh.

The less he had of other things, the more important became laughter. So, as a purveyor of laughs, he regained the dignity of his profession and returned to Hollywood to make laughter. That was Sullivan's conclusion, not mine."

I accepted Mr. Sturges' explanation. But even then—and more so now—I feel he arrived at Sullivan's conclusion because that was substantially his own. He disliked moralizing in movies. He delighted in ambiguities. He preferred to leave us laughing—and guessing. That was precisely his creed. So I now feel that Sullivan's surrender of the purpose with which he started out was only consistent with Mr. Sturges' philosophy, it was a cap to his satiric bent. He was, in a rather subtle fashion, satirizing himself.

Even Joel McCrea's acting of Sullivan—and very skillful acting it was—suggested Mr. Sturges—at least in the early part. He was probably the most attractive hero Mr. Sturges ever conceived. And Veronica Lake, William Demarest, and others were excellent, too.

Actually, what was done in this picture—the mixture of seriousness and farce, the slapstick pursuit of a deep idea—was a beautiful case of Mr. Sturges (a celebrated Hollywood gourmet) professing a distaste for message movies but luxuriously eating his own words. Because, in more ways than he wished to acknowledge, *Sullivan's Travels* was a topnotch message film.

Sam (Dooley Wilson), the amiable pianist in Rick's Casablanca Café Américain, runs through a few of the old tunes for his employer (Humphrey Bogart) and the rival café proprietor, Señor Ferrari (Sydney Greenstreet).

CASABLANCA

1942

Michael Curtiz's *Casablanca* (or Humphrey Bogart's, perhaps we should say) has become such an object of cult worship and such a monumental TV cliché that it may be difficult now to see it and estimate it as a great film. But great it was when it opened, for reasons beyond its artistry, and great it remains when all the camp nonsense and the Bogart idolatry are cut away.

The wonderful things about it were, first, that it told a tale that was laden with romance and adventure within an exotic locale that reeked with the caustic fumes of intrigue and the back-alley stink of world decay; second, its principal character, played by Bogart, was a surefire original, a mordant loner, a soldier of fortune and a closet sentimentalist; third, it was packed with other characters who formed a dazzling international parade; and, fourth, it was hauntingly concerned with a tragic aspect of World War II.

It was this aspect of the desperate gathering of people who were fleeing from Europe, some of them for grim political reasons and some just to get away from war, in the North African city of Casablanca, a Free French checkpoint on their flight to a free world, that gave the story immediate topicality and a clear path to sympathetic hearts. Everyone at that time was sensitive to the plight of those Europeans who were opposed to the Nazis—everyone with a humane heart, that is—and was ready to root with righteous fervor for those who were struggling to get away. It was that same compassion of Americans for the people caught up in the war that caused us to yield with equal fervor to the sentiments of a simultaneous film about the gallantry of British citizens at the time of Dunkirk, William Wyler's *Mrs. Miniver.*

Looking back now, we see that *Casablanca* was as much of a thickly spread romance as was *Mrs. Miniver*—or almost. And it was as isolatedly concerned with a fragmentary, elite group of people as was Mr. Wyler's spongy film. But it had a much tougher fiber to it, it was woven with more substantial threads of personal desperation, selfish motives, and predatory craftiness. And it had that pragmatic Rick in it—the café owner that Bogart played—as a sort of Olympian observer and dispenser of favors at this critical crossroad of the world.

I do not propose in retrospect that Rick was entirely real or, indeed, that his modus operandi was practical or even plausible. His rule as the proprietor and boniface of the most successful bar-casino in town—Rick's Café Américain, where "everybody goes"—was "I stick my neck out for nobody," which was reasonably sensible, and his behavior in the early part of the picture supported his observance of this rule. He would not let potential rowdies or dangerous drunks in the place, he kept a firm hand on the play at the gaming tables, and he maintained a strictly nonpartisan policy in admitting patrons of all political persuasions, even Nazis and the Vichy-oriented French police. (Actually, he did bar the casino to a big Berlin banker, but his crack "I don't mind a parasite; I just object to a cut-rate one" implied that he was more concerned about the fellow's table tactics than about his politics.)

Likewise, Rick maintained good relations—or, let's

"Nobody is going to be arrested, Louis." Rick (Humphrey Bogart) steps in to prevent the chief of Casablanca police (Claude Rains) from interfering with the planned escape of Victor Laszlo (Paul Henreid) and his wife, Ilsa (Ingrid Bergman).

Rick (Humphrey Bogart) sees again his old sweetheart, Ilsa (Ingrid Bergman), from Paris days in his Casablanca nightclub and gambling casino, while the chief of the local police (Claude Rains) and Ilsa's husband, Victor Laszlo (Paul Henreid), observe the delicate reunion.

say, an armed neutrality—with the acerbic and omnipresent captain of the local police, a role that was played with splendid sangfroid by dapper Claude Rains. And he agreed only with reluctance to hold temporarily a couple of stolen so-called letters of transit for a shady little friend (Peter Lorre), who jeopardized Rick's dictum shortly after by getting himself caught and killed. That, as it turned out later, was a pretty long extension of his neck.

And Rick gave other evidence of not being so self-centered and tough. He maintained with evident devotion a black man who played piano in the bar and ran off for Rick's delectation a touching repertory of popular Broadway tunes. He reminisced with evident nostalgia about the old days here and there. And, as Renault, the cop, recalled to him, he had run guns to Ethiopia and fought for the Loyalists in the Spanish Civil War—not exactly consistent with the policy of a man who wanted to keep his neck tucked in. Or were these acts simply debaucheries of his young and foolish past?

In any case, the test came when there dumbfoundingly turned up in his café a great European Resistance leader hoping to get to the United States, and with him a lovely lady who had been Rick's mistress in Paris at the beginning of the war. She wasn't just any old mistress, as we were soon to learn. She was the one, the only, the most romantically remembered lady in his life. She was the one who most warmly swore devotion and then most cruelly broke his heart by failing to keep her promise to flee Paris with him when the Nazis came. She was the one for whom, despite his iceberg exterior, he was carrying a blazing torch.

This we learned later that evening when he sat down alone in his café with a bottle of booze and his companion to play for him the tune that was "*their* song" in the dear, dead days in Paris, the wistful "As Time Goes By." (She had asked Sam, the pianist, to play it when she first came into the café, and Rick had been thunderstruck when he walked in, heard the song, and saw her standing there.) She had tried to be pleasant and congenial at this encounter, but Rick was cold and cruel. Now he was deeply melancholy. "Of all the gin joints in all the towns in all the world," he despairingly muttered, "she walks into mine!"

The flashbacks which followed of the old days, of the two of them doing the Paris rounds, walking beneath the chestnut blossoms, making romantic love (as romantic as the censors then would sanction), she be-

ing mysterious except to say that "there was a man but he is dead now," and Rick toasting her, "Here's looking at you, kid!" generated the amorous afflatus that was the crucial compulsion of the film. For without it—without the thrust of Bogart and the tender passion of Ingrid Bergman in the role of Ilsa, the starry-eyed mistress—the credibility of what followed would have been nil.

For, in subsequent encounters with Ilsa, Rick grudgingly let himself be told that she indeed loved him dearly but the man she thought was dead turned up to require her full assistance. He was the great Resistance leader to whom she had been wed before the war but thought he had been killed. And further along, with desperate intrigues swirling about their heads and a Nazi high official breathing hotly on their necks, Rick saw that the only way this couple—this great man—could be sped on their way was for him really to stick his neck out and give them the letters of transit that he secretly held.

The manipulations by which this was accomplished—the preparing of the couple to flee, the entrapment of Renault with a false promise, the rush to the airport just ahead of the pursuing Nazi official, the killing of the latter and the escape of the couple in a waiting plane, while Rick and Renault walked off together with fatalistic nonchalance—was breathtaking melodrama but very difficult to believe.

However, precise plausibility was not the intent of this film. Its intent and remarkable achievement were its buildup of an overpowering sense of modest people in the shadow of grave perils doing gallant, self-sacrificial things. Rick, an avowed self-server, was the one who did the most—at least in the limited area and the romantic format of the film. He abandoned his self-preserving posture, he gave up his profitable café, and he stayed behind to mount a rear-guard action, all for the principle of freedom and for love. The image of Rick emerging from the shadows of his cynical pose and doing something real for humanity was the greatest satisfaction of the film.

But there were other excitements in it that stirred our blood at the time—the warmth and resolution of Miss Bergman as she stuck by the cause she had embraced, even though she told Rick she still loved *him* and he gratefully acknowledged the assurance with the old toast "Here's looking at you, kid"; the heroic stance of Paul Henreid as the Resistance leader with his back to the wall, rallying the patrons in the café to drown out the Nazis' singing of "Die Wacht am Rhein" with a thundering chant of "La Marseillaise"; the devotion of Dooley Wilson as the pianist, Sam, and the constant crisscross of personal interests represented by diverse characters played by such experts as Sydney Greenstreet, Conrad Veidt, and S. Z. Sakall.

Oh, yes, *Casablanca* was a beauty in the fall of 1942, and it gave us, along with entertainment, a feeling of comfort. The right people were on our side.

Today? Well, it's still a great romance and a memorial to a time and a mood, but the youngsters who see it now seem interested mainly in the Bogart character—in this cool existentialist individual in full control of virtually everything. They dote on his casual mannerisms, his completely self-confident style. Bogart in this particular picture is a metaphor all by himself. And, deep down, I think the young people are touched by its nostalgia, by the eloquent indication that love could come and go—away back then.

At least, the persistence of this picture in revival and on TV is assurance that there's something about it that stays fresh and pure as time goes by.

Captain Delon becomes a last minute accomplice with Rick in arranging for the desperate escape of the Lazlos from the airport at Casablanca. Here he orders a suspicious French military official not to interfere.

The fateful moment of the lynching in *The Ox-Bow Incident*. Left to right, Major Tetley (Frank Conroy), Farnley (Marc Lawrence), Martin (Dana Andrews), the Old Man (Francis Ford), and the Mexican (Anthony Quinn).

THE OX-BOW INCIDENT

1943

Indicative of the confusion *The Ox-Bow Incident* caused when it first came forth as a movie in 1943 was the fact (never publicly mentioned) that it had been finished and kept "in the can" for almost two years before its distributors, Twentieth Century-Fox, worked up the boldness to release it to theaters. Their reasons were characteristic. Its concentration on a cynical account of a Western-frontier necktie party—a lynching—in 1885 was so starkly and brutally enacted

and so relentlessly brought to a downbeat close that its owners were frankly apprehensive as to whether the public would tolerate it. They were also fearful of the damage it might do to the image of one of its key performers, Henry Fonda, who was then a particularly popular star.

So contrary was this picture to the formula of the standard Western film—the virtual law that there were good guys and bad guys and the good guys had to win in the end—that the peril of putting forth a picture in which nobody came out looking good—nobody ex-

The laconic Mexican, condemned with Martin and the Old Man, offers his knife to one of the lynch mob as Ma Grier (Jane Darwell) and Monty Smith (Paul Hurst) look on.

The tag-along cowboy, Gil Carter (Henry Fonda), stands up momentarily to the determined leader of the lynch mob, Major Tetley (Frank Conroy), in *The Ox-Bow Incident*.

cept the three victims of the lynching, and they were dead—was one which a cautious distributor had to take into account. And the caution was justified in this case. *The Ox-Bow Incident,* when first released, failed.

That is not to say it wasn't greeted by sentient critics with loud acclaim. They rightly and appreciatively saw it as an "honest" Western film, one that fairly reflected the ugly weaknesses that certainly prevailed among a Western cowtown's residents uninspired by heroic tendencies. And they liked the leanness and the cold, concentrated artistry with which screenwriter Lamar Trotti and director William Wellman adapted the original novel by Walter Van Tilburg Clark to the screen.

Nothing was superfluous in it, nothing was overdone—not even an easily mawkish detail of a mumbled confession by one of the victims when he knew his time had come. Mr. Trotti, who was also producer, shaped the screenplay to arrive at the point of climactic execution without a single diversion. Well, maybe one—one very small romantic aside was permitted to intrude as the posse was heading up into the hills in search of a band of cattle rustlers who were reported to have killed an outlying ranchman in cold blood and made off with his herd.

This interlude came when the posse met a stagecoach clattering down into the town and discovered a fancy lady who had recently ditched the cowboy whom Fonda played. Now, accompanied by a "husband," she was the momentary butt of some ribald jokes and the cause of some obvious confusion to Fonda. Especially when the "husband" too politely let the dour cowboy know that he was persona non grata, the humiliation was clear, and the interlude did serve to galvanize Fonda's cynicism. (It also served to put the posse more firmly on the trail of the supposedly villainous rustlers, whom the stagecoach driver reported seeing back up the trail.)

For the most part, the progression of the story, from the rallying of a mob in a saloon and the mustering of a sheriff's posse when reports of the rancher's murder came to town, through an ascent of smoldering action to the ultimate lynching episode, was direct and magnificently dovetailed to gain increasing terror and suspense. There was a clean accumulation of details in the beginning phase, when a beetle-browed rabble-rouser urged the townsmen into starting a pursuit and an insolent deputy sheriff defied the orders of a judge

and perfunctorily swore in a posse to take the law into its hands, when a dubious ex-Confederate major arrived stern-visaged to take command, and Mr. Fonda and his sidekick, Henry Morgan, indifferently decided to string along.

Up into the hills went this rabble, howling and making jokes, while three or four levelheaded stragglers— and Mr. Fonda—muttered discontent. The darkness became oppressive; the chill of the night became intense. But when the posse came up to three cowboys, sleeping beside a waning fire, close by a restless herd of cattle, they concluded that these were the murdering rustlers and put them on drumhead trial. No stubborn protest by the leader that he had bought the herd legally (though he had no bill of sale to prove it) affected the vengeful mob. Urged on by the arrogant major, they condemned the men to death and then agreed to wait until morning before hanging them from a tree.

This interlude of waiting—this prolonged suspense, as the three bewildered condemned men slowly realized there was no recourse from the lust of this nasty group—was one of the most disturbing sequences ever seen in a Western film. And it was magnified in horror by a retallying of the mob, insisted upon by one old fellow, to see who were for and who against. A handful—an aging merchant, a black preacher, a couple of seedy cowboys, and finally Mr. Fonda and his pal— stood up against the lynchers, but they were heavily overruled and the triple execution was conducted in the usual grisly way: The horses on which sat the victims, ropes around their necks, were slapped out from under them simultaneously and the bodies left dangling from a tree.

Then a stygian mood of anticlimax, intended and engineered by the measuring of the screenplay and the pacing of the lynchers back to town, settled upon the proceedings when word, minutes late, reached the mob that the rancher had not been murdered, that this lynching had been a gross mistake. The killers gathered back at the bar of the saloon to listen to Mr. Fonda read aloud a letter the leader had penned to his wife in that cold hour before his lynching to try to comfort her. It was, alas, a florid letter and consequently banal. The reading of it by Mr. Fonda was the one regrettable weakness in the film. No words were needed at this point, no painful tugging at the heart. Clearly the shame of the killings, the monstrous crime of taking the lives of innocent men, required no further verification than the knowledge that the deed was done. Nor was a melodramatic epilogue necessary wherein the discredited major, humiliated by the revulsion of his own son at the spectacle of lynching, disappeared into a room and shot himself.

All of this was conventional surrender to sentimentality. But wisely—and fortunately—the horror of the misdeed was allowed to stand. The lineaments of human degradation, hysteria, and hatred had already been seen in that mob, and the shock of these demonstrations had been indelibly conveyed. No cant about "compensating moral value" was injected to soothe the shock. The departure of Mr. Fonda at the fadeout to deliver to the wife a purse of money, raised among the killers, was the sole, ironic recompense.

Mr. Fonda was splendid in his grim role—disgusted, yet unheroically passive to the will of the brute majority. Jane Darwell, who had raised with Mr. Fonda a memorable monument to the courage and resolution of an indomitable mother and son only two years before in the John Ford classic *The Grapes of Wrath,** was here called upon to switch completely and play a

tough old pants-wearing woman screaming for blood. This audacity in casting was courageous, and Miss Darwell did her job without restraint.

Frank Conroy, stiff-backed and haughty as the posturing leader of the mob; Harry Davenport as the white-haired merchant who kept protesting without effect; Leigh Whipper as the incongruous black preacher who also protested plaintively; and Paul Hurst as a nasty, brutish red-neck were all exceedingly good.

But the best was Dana Andrews as the boss of the cattle-herding crew, perhaps—and this is not meant to detract—because he had the most sympathetic role. His progression from surprise and annoyance when first confronted by the mob, through levels of confusion and outraged protest to fear and disbelief was superlative. The cold disgust in his eyes at the climax spoke the final, human judgment on the deed.

Yes, *The Ox-Bow Incident* was a great one—and the heartening thing was that it *was* made, that an aspect of human brutality had been so relentlessly exposed. It was a strong and courageous movie about the prevalence and potency of cowards.

The three innocent victims caught by the lynch mob: the Mexican (Anthony Quinn), Martin (Dana Andrews), and the Old Man (Francis Ford).

MEET ME IN ST. LOUIS

The whole company with stand-ins and extras assembled for the spectacular St. Louis World's Fair finale on a vast MGM sound stage.

1944

Any American moviegoer who was reasonably sentient in the middle 1940s must recall with devotion and joy that superb family period musical picture, *Meet Me in St. Louis,* in which Judy Garland was the star and Leon Ames, Marjorie Main, Mary Astor, the prodigious moppet Margaret O'Brien, and a host of nubile maidens were outstanding in the cast.

For here indeed is the quintessence of the nostalgic white upper-middle-class fiction that extolled in song the beautiful, fanciful trivia of a turn-of-the-century teen-age girl's life in a quaint St. Louis family. There were no problems here, no social issues except how to arrange politely for older sister Ruth to make a firm match with a painfully bashful swain at the other end of an awesome long-distance telephone line; how to maneuver second sister Esther to meet the college boy who had just moved next door and overcome his innocence with a campaign of female stratagems and archly directed songs; how to adjust to the falsehoods that flowed from youngest sister Tootie's lips and prevent

Esther Smith (Judy Garland) all dressed up for the family visit to the Louisiana Purchase Exposition (The St. Louis World's Fair) of 1904.

Family theatricals at the Smith home in St. Louis, with sisters Tootie (Margaret O'Brien) and Esther singing "Skip to My Lou" and "Under the Bamboo Tree," to the accompaniment of brother Lon (Henry H. Daniels, Jr.) on mandolin.

Papa Smith (Leon Ames), standing, for once asserts himself at the family dinner table, astounding Agnes (Joan Carroll), Grandpa (Harry Davenport), Mama (Mary Astor), Rose (Lucille Bremer) and Esther (Judy Garland), in *Meet Me in St. Louis.*

this precocious little rascal from upsetting everyone else's schemes. Toward the end there was the problem of how to counter, all in the course of a bewilderingly crowded Christmas Eve, Papa's momentary impulse to accept a promotion to New York, which would mean moving his lovely family away from St. Louis

on the eve of Esther's pending triumph and the opening of the 1904 World's Fair.

Such was the traffic in this picture, which came out in 1944, just as the nation was enduring the pangs of World War II. And such was the kind of entertainment that was particularly enticing at the time. For instance, running simultaneously on Broadway as a stage play—indeed, it had been running for five years—was a similarly nostalgic look at the doings of a New York family circa the turn of the century. It was *Life with Father* and it ran for three more years. Indeed, it was strongly suspected that the producer Arthur Freed, who had started as a songwriter at Metro-Goldwyn-Mayer with the ground-breaking *The Broadway Melody*, wanted to preempt Warner Brothers, who had snagged the screen rights to that phenomenal play.

With characteristic shrewdness, Mr. Freed got the rights to a series of magazine vignettes, written by Sally Benson, about her girlhood in St. Louis, he got writers to stitch together a screenplay, and he got the still not quite established Vincente Minnelli to be the director of the film. But, particularly, he got Judy Garland, a sparkling star since her triumph in *The Wizard of Oz*, to play the focal female and to sing the eclectically assembled package of songs.

Among these songs everybody remembers "The Trolley Song," that melodically rollicking paean to the thrill of riding an old-time trolley car, crowded with exuberant young people on their way to a picnic at the burgeoning Fairgrounds and chiming in with Judy's lusty solo and the clanging of the foot-stamped trolley bell. And who hasn't heard her sweetly benevolent adjuration to all who may be slightly depressed to have themselves a merry little Christmas, because that's what Judy (or, rather, Esther) meant her temporarily downcast family to do. Irresistible, too, was Esther's chanting out of her upstairs bedroom window on a starry night her adoration for the unresponsive "Boy Next Door."

Likewise clever use was made of period songs such as "Over the Banister Leaning," which was a flowery little duet sung by the two older sisters after a party and they on their way to bed, or "Skip to My Lou," to which the party of bright young guests square danced riotously, or, of course, the title song, which was the original anthem of the long-ago St. Louis Fair.

Obviously Judy was the center of this female-oriented affair. Her breathless enthusiasms, her air of teetering on the brink of womanhood, and her crisply enunciated and bell-like delivery of her songs made her performance in this picture perhaps the key one in her career and raised her to further popularity.

But she was not alone in imparting female magnetism and dominance to the film. Lucille Bremer, a former stage dancer, was enchanting as redheaded sister Ruth. Her willowy, graceful bearing fitted perfectly her femininity. Mary Astor was quietly commanding as the handsome, hard-pressed mother of the brood, and Marjorie Main moved about like a top sergeant as the domineering maid. And Margaret O'Brien as tadpole Tootie might have run away with the show so amusingly mischievous was she. One singular sequence which had her out tricking on a windy Halloween night is possibly the most often remembered and affectionately remarked on in the film.

With such a phalanx of liberated females loose in the household, it was a wonder that any masculine presence was able to make itself realized at all. But Mr. Minnelli skillfully balanced the show. He generously allowed Leon Ames as the respectfully tolerated Papa to get a word in edgewise now and then and even strike one feeble blow for freedom when he tried to engineer the move to New York toward the end. But this was just about the only action of male rebelliousness in the whole film. And, of course, it was overwhelmed by outraged female dissidence. Robert Sully as sister Ruth's shy Yale man and Tom Drake as the Princeton boy next door were handsome and polite but spineless. Male chauvinism made no advancement through them. Once in a while the old Grandpa, played blithely by Harry Davenport, was allowed to emerge from an upstairs bedroom and indulge in some outrageous eccentricity, which contributed to the humor of the picture and the amusement of the ladies, but that was all.

Obviously *Meet Me in St. Louis* was the sexual antithesis to the long-running *Life with Father,* which glorified the paternal autocrat. I don't think the contrast was intended or even commented on, as I recall, because we weren't quite as sensitive to the presence of the war between the sexes as we are today. But the film may have been secretly slanted, after production was under way, to take a slight poke at another male chauvinist image then promoted at Metro-Goldwyn-Mayer. That was the character of Andy Hardy, whom Mickey Rooney played in the memorable Hardy series, a Hollywood phenomenon of the day.

The interesting thing is that Judy had played one of Andy's dominated friends in three of the Hardy pictures prior to *Meet Me in St. Louis.* And I often have remarked that she was here given *her* chance to be a female Andy Hardy—in such a charming way.

And charm, in the end, was the essence of this beautifully organized film—beautifully stage designed, costumed, dance directed, and paced by Mr. Minnelli's sensitive skill. Being concerned with a period, in styles and social attitudes, its fantasies are now as arbitrary and imperishable as though they were captured under glass. And this is the way we should now view it, as a happy celebration of an age, accurate or not as a generality, like the glitter of the St. Louis Fair.

OPEN CITY

Pina (Anna Magnani) receives disturbing news from her Resistance lover, Francesco (Francesco Graudjacquet).

1945

A dozen or so great movies along with the sagas of how they were made truly merit the title of legends in the long history of the screen. But none surpasses Roberto Rossellini's *Open City* (*Roma: Città Aperta*), which he made in the dismal winter of 1944–45.

Not just the substance of this picture and the overwhelming impact it had upon a world still suffering from the pounding of World War II account for the grandeur of its legend. Those are things one naturally assumes to be essential to any classic that we recognize today. The mere fact that *Open City* was made

The body of Pina (Anna Magnani), shot by Nazi soldiers as she ran after the van carrying away her captured Resistance lover, is tearfully embraced by her son, Marcello (Vito Annicchiarico).

under circumstances so difficult and even dangerous, and the fact that it marked the beginning of the Italian postwar neorealist surge—a movement so strong and antiformal it fairly shook the old foundations of fiction films—render this movie historically unique. Indeed, I would say this is the clearest watershed movie ever made.

Much has already been written about how *Open City* came to be, but I cannot forgo recollecting the circumstances. With Rome in a state of virtual chaos after the collapse of the Fascist regime but before the Nazis had abandoned it, it was officially declared an open city. Rossellini, who was thirty-eight and had been moderately conspicuous as a maker of documentary films, conceived the ambitious notion, along with a group of his Resistance-movement friends, to make a film that would give an honest picture of what life under Nazi rule had been. At daring clandestine meetings in the flat of an ardent patriot (actually it was Maria Michi, who played the role of the drug-addicted informer in the film), they worked out the idea for a screenplay, which was written tentatively by Rossellini, Sergio Amidei, and Federico Fellini, who was then virtually unknown in Rome.

True to his documentary training, Rossellini chose to make the film without professional actors, except for a well-selected few—Anna Magnani, Aldo Fabrizi, Marcello Pagliero, Harry Feist—people who had known all too clearly what Rome in those dark days was like. And when the time came for shooting, he took his meager little company into the streets for legitimate locations—into workers' apartments, a parish church, to wherever and whatever would afford them a feeling of authenticity. Financing for the production was scraped together from various ''silent'' friends, including an Italian countess and a Florentine merchant, and photography by Ubaldo Arata, one of the prewar Italian greats, was on bits and pieces of raw stock scrounged from the few operating studios and, after the city's liberation, from Allied military photographers.

Ironically, when the film was first shown to audiences in Italy, the reception ranged from moderate to indifferent—a phenomenon that was later ascribed to the painful familiarity of the people with the kind of dangers and hardships that were shown. It was only after *Open City* was virtually smuggled out of Italy and released in New York and London that its greatness as a drama of human suffering and heroism was

Pina (Anna Magnani), the strong and valorous Roman slum woman and Resistance sympathizer in *Open City*, makes her daily obeisance in the parish church.

Don Pietro (Aldo Fabrizi), the Roman priest who is condemned for aiding the Resistance fighters, prepares for his execution by a firing squad.

Don Pietro (Aldo Fabrizi), the Roman priest who aids the Resistance fighters, in *Open City*.

Marina (Maria Michi), who has betrayed her Resistance lover to the Nazi secret police in exchange for drugs, likewise betrays her own horror when she realizes what she has done. Ingrid (Giovanna Galletti), her Nazi seducer, is at right.

recognized and its impact as a truly new departure in film creation and artistry took hold. Thereafter it won several prizes at international festivals.

Not surprisingly, the story of *Open City,* when seen by young people today, far removed from the history and hysteria of World War II, may appear a rather ordinary recount of a grimly determined hunt by Nazi Gestapo and Fascisti for a tough Resistance leader in Rome and his eventual capture and killing under torture by command of the Gestapo chief. It is the sort of melodramatic story that has been done so many times since, and in locations and under circumstances conducive to a stronger sense of now, that a young person may be forgiven for regarding it today as an antique, deserving respect and admiration for its historical significance but rather commonplace and ho-hum as entertainment fare.

That wasn't the case when it opened in New York. It hit like a bolt of lightning with the electrifying first scene of a small detail of Gestapo jamming into a working-class apartment house and demanding to know the whereabouts of Manfredi, whom we soon were to learn was the head of the Committee for National Liberation, a potent Resistance group, and whom we saw, on the Gestapo's arrival, fleeing across the roof of the house. Everything about this beginning—the look of Germans arriving in the street, the interiors of the house, the fright and confusion of the two old ladies who met the pounding Gestapo at the door—had the convincing appearance of actuality. It seemed as though we were seeing a still-steaming documentary film.

As the story unfolded, as the audience was introduced to a tough, robust working-class woman, to a modest partisan priest, to an unprepossessing printer who was the woman's fiancé, all of whom were drawn into the action as accomplices to the fugitive—we quickly came to regard them as real. And an actress girlfriend of the fugitive, a surreptitious drug addict receiving her fixes from a woman Gestapo agent, loomed darkly as a person of whom to beware.

Along with the sense of tension and danger that prevailed from the start and grew as the net was drawn tighter on the fugitive and his friends, there was a goodly measure of humor and humane kindliness interposed to give full dimension to the people and lighten momentarily the suspense. But a crisis of shock came midway when the working-class woman was killed in cold blood by the Germans while running hysterically after a van in which her fiancé was being carried off following a flash raid on their apartment block. And from there on the route to the climax was stark and precipitate. The Resistance leader was captured after he had been betrayed by his jilted girlfriend in a fit of rancor toward him and also in her hunger for drugs. Taken with him on the threshold of escape to an intended hideout in a monastery was the priest, and the two were hideously tortured by the Gestapo until the leader finally dropped dead and the priest, refusing to talk even after being tortured and forced to witness the inquisition of his companion, was condemned and executed before a German firing squad.

This grisly climax to the picture was, of course, its most overpowering phase, and it capped with horror and outrage the heroic Resistance theme. It completed the paramount concept of defiance and loyalty to which all the Resistance people, even small boys, devoted themselves. That was their dominant purpose—resist! resist! resist!—and the loves and lives of the individuals were subordinated to clash and sacrifice. It was a drama of communal action, with no tinge of politics, although some at the time perceived it as Communist propaganda.

Under these circumstances, no attempt was made either by Rossellini or his writers to delve the depths of the characters. They were simply motivated persons, acting within the two-dimensional range of their intents. But strong personality and spirit were displayed by a few of them, most notably Anna Magnani as the volatile fiancée of the gentle, valiant printer (Vito Annicchiarico), already pregnant by him, yet ardent to assume the risks and burdens of being involved in a common cause. Her spirited aggression in the center of an angry, determined crowd of women raiding a bakery—a "celebration," the action was called—and her rough, ready wit and sarcasm with her family and friends established at once her charisma. Magnani was henceforth to be the paramount image of the strong woman in Italian films, a combination of peasant stolidness and matriarchal loyalty and wisdom, the very backbone of Italy, until superseded by the somewhat different images of Sophia Loren, Gina Lollobrigida, and so on.

Fabrizi was excellent as the partisan priest who regarded his assistance to his countrymen to be as normal and confidential as the vow of the confessional. He was a religious person in the truest sense of the word. And, indeed, the sober practice of Catholicism was evident and emphasized throughout the film. It was a duty in the lives of the people quite as dominant as their will to resist. A sense that they especially required it in the dark days of the Occupation was implied.

As the Resistance leader, Marcello Pagliero was intense to the point of seeming almost automatic, without evident passion or sentiment, long past anger or outrage, except in one rather banal scene in which he berated his girlfriend for being self-indulgent and without moral strength at a time when character was needed—thus offending her to the point of betraying him. And Maria Michi was believably unstable and pathetic as the girl.

Obviously Rossellini found it difficult to resist letting Harry Feist and Giovanna Galletti ham it up considerably as the brutal Gestapo captain and his velvety lesbian associate, but all other lesser characters were superlatively credible—particularly the youngsters who played a minor drama through the film as independent terrorists quite familiar with explosives and guns. And the final scene with these boys standing silently outside a prison fence watching the shattering execution of the priest by a firing squad, then turning away and walking bravely off down a hill toward distant Rome whistling "The Florentine Serenade," the familiar Resistance signal tune, was one of the most meaningful and moving scenes in postwar films.

Open City, a grimly ironic and sardonic title, we might note, marked a momentous beginning of a movement that still rumbles on the screen—so-called neorealism, which was given that loosely embracing name in recollection of a brief but robust outcrop of strong themes and naturalistic staging in Italian silent films.

THE LOST WEEKEND

1945

It is hard to believe now in these days of total candor on the screen that critics and the public expressed amazement at the release of Charles Brackett's and Billy Wilder's film version of Charles R. Jackson's novel *The Lost Weekend.* "Daring!" "Sensational!" "Horrifying!" were a few of the adjectives used to describe this now classic drama of four days in the life of a chronic drunkard. Audiences were stunned that the torments of a standard alcoholic were exposed with such honesty and realism as were exercised in this film. Customers came away from it staggering as though they had been slugged. And, most of all, there was disbelief and wonder that such a film should have come from Hollywood.

The reason was simple and also shameful. In all the years since the beginning of films, the subject of alcoholism, as well as that of narcotics addiction, was virtually taboo on the screen. Sure, the consumption of liquor and displays of drunkenness were familiar enough. They were not only common, but essential to the advancement of many popular themes. Comics, of course, used the bottle and its inebriating felicities with as much delight and extravagance as they used banana peels and custard pies. Moralists and temperance promoters brandished alcoholism as perhaps the most reprehensible reason for the ruin of careers and the breakup of homes. Occasionally a serious filmmaker such as D. W. Griffith, whose last film, *The Struggle,* was about the tearful decline of a problem drunk, would attempt to say something revealing about this modern social disease. But what they most inevitably produced were tiresome lectures on the shameful curse of drink.

Not until Mr. Jackson courageously opened up the topic of alcoholism in his intimately researched book and presented the problems of addiction with sophistication and sympathy, was the American reading public given a close, subjective look at the real psychological entanglement of a victim in this modern disease. The experience was so engrossing that the novel was a best seller for months. But it took the Messrs. Brackett and Wilder (and, I might add, Paramount) to have the courage to put it on the screen.

Confronted by his deeply anxious brother (Philip Terry) and his helpless girlfriend (Jane Wyman) with a hidden bottle of booze, Don Birnam (Ray Milland), is speechless with confusion and shame.

In one of the few black-comedy moments of *The Lost Weekend*, a bewildered Don (Ray Milland) is told that he won't be able to pawn his typewriter because it is the Jewish Sabbath.

The battered and exhausted alcoholic grovels along through a hideous bout of delirium tremens.

With a sharply observant camera tuned to a reportorial style that endowed this extremely personal drama with the appearance of a documentary film, Mr. Wilder as the director (his associate was billed as the producer and collaborated with him on the script) bore in directly and unrelentingly on the realistic flow of incidents that occurred in the crackup of their central character on a fearful four-day binge. It opened with an ominous refusal by the fellow to let the cleaning woman into the apartment he shared with his brother because he wanted to steal the wage money his brother had left for her. The theme of his mounting compulsion toward the bottle was taken up, and the dismal process of his debasement was started and followed through to the end.

The episodes were tepid at the outset—his hasty rush to a liquor store to buy two bottles of whiskey ("the cheapest") with the money he had filched from the maid; his stop-off for a couple of quick ones at his favorite bar on the way back home, and his attempt to keep the suspicious bartender from knowing what he had in the bag; and then his clear determination to make a weekend of it when he got home by carefully hiding one of the bottles in a lighting fixture overhead.

All of this behavior was laced with warning indications of his efforts at secrecy to keep his girlfriend and his successful brother from discovering what they already knew—although the girlfriend refused to admit it—that he was a hopeless alcoholic and there was nothing they could do.

It was these desperate endeavors on the drunk's part to try to conceal his weakness—let's call it sickness—from others and even from himself that were the most bleakly symptomatic and pathetic betrayals of his state, and it was these that inspired the viewer's sympathies in the splendid performance by Ray Milland. His cheap stratagems to fool his brother, to avoid facing up to his girl (whom he had failed before because of his insecurity), and especially his tale to the bartender that he was just about to write a novel that would tell the whole story of a man who was cursed by drink—these were the saddest indicators. His efforts to keep his self-esteem and his pitiful clinging to the fantasy of being a writer betrayed his deep-down lack of confidence and strength.

Actually, in Mr. Jackson's novel, the core trouble with this man—the thing that was gnawing his subconscious—was that he was a closet queen, an incipient homosexual, and he used the respectable excuse that he was revving up to write a novel to justify drinking and conceal his shame. But, alas, the fact of homosexuality as a matter for discussion on the screen was even more taboo than the subject of alcoholism in 1945. It was enough that the Messrs. Brackett and Wilder used the poor fellow's case of writer's block to explain his recourse to the bottle. They simply couldn't imply he was a secret homosexual.

Homosexuality was not essential to convince the audience of his frenzied need for booze—his endurance of the bartender's insults when he begged for another shot or two, his shame at being thrown out of a nightclub when he was caught taking a $10 bill from a woman's purse, his beseeching a prostitute for money, his trying to pawn his typewriter, and finally his being flung into the Bellevue Hospital alcoholic ward were evidence enough.

It was in the Bellevue snakepit that his real nightmare tortures began and the sensitivities of the audience became most subjectively involved. For it was here that his last sodden tatters of respectability were stripped away in revolting bed-to-bed encounters with drizzling sidewalk drunks, in helpless exposure to the taunting of a leering, sadistic male nurse, and in a hideous midnight awakening to the shrieks and screams of trussed-up inmates with delirium tremens. And when, in pajamas and a doctor's overcoat, he escaped from this horror to make his way home, he had yet to endure his final torment—a bout with DTs on his own!

The staging of this last experience, with the poor fellow cringing in a chair while phantasmagoric ro-

His craving for alcohol drives the penniless Don Birnam (Ray Milland) to beg for a drink from his not always friendly barman, Nat (Howard da Silva).

dents crawled out of cracks in the walls, bats flew screeching around the room, and horrifying noises filled the air, was the ultimate audience-grabbing triumph of Mr. Wilder's graphic style. And Mr. Milland's intense performance topped the horror. I don't believe that anyone who ever saw that extraordinary scene can possibly forget it or dismiss its shocking significance from his mind.

In the premiere version of the picture, a reasonably hopeful ending was contrived. The still loyal, loving girlfriend coaxed him back from the verge of suicide and aroused his resolution to write. That was a practical ending in 1945, when anything less heartening and reassuring might have meant commercial disaster for the film. But in later revival versions and nowadays on TV, the ending has been made more ambiguous and consistent with likelihood.

In a recent version of the final scene, the girlfriend, played by Jane Wyman, broke into the apartment and found the poor fellow crumpled on the floor, mumbling about the bats and rodents coming at him out of the wall. She tried to suggest he had had a nightmare, but he just fumbled pathetically with his hands and repeated a warning made by the bartender that the "ending" would be "like this" (he snapped his fingers weakly and forlornly) "or like that" (he snapped his fingers again). And he went on repeating the gesture until the scene faded. That's how this classic appropriately ends.

There have been several memorable pictures about alcoholism since *The Lost Weekend—Come Back, Little Sheba,* with Burt Lancaster and Shirley Booth in 1952, which was Hollywood's first intelligent tribute to Alcoholics Anonymous; *The Country Girl,* with Bing Crosby and Grace Kelly in 1954; and *Days of Wine and Roses,* with Jack Lemmon and Lee Remick in 1960, to name a few. And I daresay there will be others as this dramatic illness is more intensively pursued. But nothing, I predict, will hit the public harder than did *The Lost Weekend.*

Giuseppe (Rinaldo Smordoni), cruelly alienated from his little pal in the Roman prison, awaits his fate in a solitary cell.

SHOE SHINE

1946

Even as Roberto Rossellini was putting the final touches on his great trend-setting *Open City*, a second film that was soon to provide a surprise of equal distinction in the flow of Italian postwar films was being undertaken by Vittorio de Sica, a filmmaker who was clearly more experienced and, indeed, more interested and skillful in penetrating the depths of individual psychological reactions than was Rossellini. The film he was starting was *Shoe Shine* (*Sciuscia*) which, though it fell definitely within the genre of characteristic neorealism so far as setting, cast, and style were concerned, used the environment and the nature of postwar deterioration in Rome to surround an individual drama on a timeless tragic theme.

It was a story of the fatal corruption of two Roman shoeshine boys, one a smart, sturdy twelve-year-old street kid and the other his cheerful younger pal, who became innocently entangled in a petty black-market deal involving the sale of stolen blankets simply because this seemed an easy way to get enough money to buy a boyishly longed-for horse. Abandoned by the men who involved them when the woman they swindled turned them in, they were hauled off to city prison and there by slow degrees succumbed to the gross dehumanization of a brutish and degrading life in jail and a slow, senseless system of justice. In the end they were hopelessly divided and drawn into separate vengeful cliques until the death of one was caused accidentally by the other in an abortive attempt at escape.

So interesting was this haunting picture in the pattern of de Sica's career that comment upon it should be prefaced by a bit of explanation of his past. He had got into films as an actor in the early days of sound after making a conventional reputation as a matinee idol on the stage. Handsome, ebullient, and romantic, he seemed destined for a routine actor's life in a succession of shallow bedroom comedies (they used to call them "white telephones") in the years before the war. Indeed, he continued acting while Italy was deep in the war, and even after he became a top director, he frequently alternated as an actor until his death in 1974.

His introduction to directing was in 1939 with a little romance called *Rose Scarlatte* (in English *The Scarlet Rose*), which was of no distinction whatsoever, and was followed by several others during the war, the most significant of which was *I bambini ci guardano* ("The Children Are Watching Us") in 1944. This was an oddly bitter drama of the shock and disillusion of a boy upon discovering that his mother was an adulteress; a black, depressing theme which could have been taken as a guarded allegory on the disillusionment of a trusting people with Fascism.

Intended or not, de Sica therewith revealed himself to be more profound and concerned with human anguish than his earlier ventures foretold. So it was not altogether surprising that his first film after the war (excepting a minor item which he allegedly did "for the Vatican") was his immortal *Shoe Shine*, a film which proclaimed him to be what he often in later years asserted—"an artist of the poor."

This uncommon burst of deep compassion and concern for those whose lives were cruelly constricted and corroded by circumstances over which they had no control came from de Sica at a juncture when the ironies and cruelties in the lives of the Roman poor were too obvious and painful to be ignored. Already the spirit of solidarity and communal sacrifice within the working class that were exalted in *Open City* were cracking—or had cracked—beneath the strains of disorganization in government and the collapse of the Italian economy. Helplessness and cynicism were racking the people's minds. No wonder de Sica and others were moved to cry out in pain!

Such was the nature of *Shoe Shine*—a cry of outrage and anguish from de Sica and four other writers, including Sergio Amidei of *Open City* fame and the great Cesare Zavatini. But it wasn't simply outrage and anguish that this deeply devastating film conveyed. It was laced through with sympathy and pity not only for the two unfortunate boys but for the helpless parents and the burdened bureaucrats who had neither the means nor the capacities to save these inundated boys. The cry was against the terrible outrage committed upon all humanity by forces too powerful and impersonal to comprehend.

How strong were de Sica's feelings and his ability to convey them on the screen was illustrated at the outset in a lyrical introductory phase describing the delight and yearning that the two boys had for the horse, a plain old plug they went to visit every morning at a riding stable in the Borghese Gardens before going on to their shoeshining jobs. The morning mists, the sense of freedom in the open, the camaraderie of the youngsters and their pals swirled into an image of purity and innocence that was soon to be shattered and lost.

I will never forget the picture of the two youngsters, after they had made the modest sale of the blankets and had plunked down the money for the horse, sitting astride the animal and riding proudly down the Via Veneto as though they were young Augustus Caesars while their pals along the sidewalk cheered. Or the shot of the two proud possessors sleeping side by side in a manger of hay (could this have been symbolic?) in the stable with their prize.

But their euphoric state was exploded when they were picked up and hauled off to jail in a police van, with one of their playmates, a little girl, watching forlornly as they were driven away. And in jail, fingerprinted and locked together for a brief time in a cell,

Separated in prison from his pal, Pasquale (Franco Interlenghi), back to wall, broods helplessly and despairingly in a cheerless cell.

The inseparable buddies, Pasquale (Franco Interlenghi) and Giuseppe (Rinaldo Smordoni), count out their hard-earned liras to pay for the coveted horse.

they could only support their fading spirits by talking and dreaming of the horse.

Prison life, as the youngsters waited long and tediously to be put on trial, was strongly envisioned by de Sica as a round of dull and irritating constraints. There were bedbugs, hungry guards who stole from the food packages that were occasionally brought to the boys, beatings—or, rather, simulated beatings under the supervision of a harassed warden—to try to force them separately to break down and confess, clashes with characteristic bullies, lonely nights, and tears.

When the younger one, Pasquale, was put in solitary for participating in a fight, his alienation of the older, Giuseppe, was subtly begun. The latter's parents brought in a cheap lawyer to try to spring their now sullen son by getting him to put the blame for the swindle entirely upon the younger one. Thus, when the slowly crumbling youngsters were finally brought to trial before a weary judge, a hardening wall of bitterness and suspicion had perceptibly risen between them. Together they were sentenced to prison terms.

The rest of the film from this point was anticlimactic in a way because it shoved the now criminalized children into a prospect without joy or hope. Divided by fear and apprehension, each went his separate way, until Giuseppe, during a riot that broke out in the mid-

The two Roman shoeshine boys, Giuseppe (Rinaldo Smordoni) and Pasquale (Franco Interlenghi), make the mistake of selling black-market blankets to an incriminating customer in order to raise money.

dle of a pathetically mismanaged picture-show, followed through on an escape plan with some new pals and got away. Pasquale, the younger, suspecting they would go to get the horse, offered to lead the warden to the stable where he felt they would be found. And, sure enough, they were discovered as Giuseppe and another were riding away on the horse. A fight ensued between the two old buddies, Giuseppe was knocked off a bridge and killed, little Pasquale jumped down to weep beside him—and the riderless horse wandered aimlessly off.

Obviously this conclusion was a hasty summarization of an inevitable fate, and it wasn't made any more impressive by a bad studio-setting for the last scene. But by that time the viewer was usually convinced that the lives of the innocent youngsters had been shattered beyond repair.

Someone has said that de Sica had a skill for making the camera's eye so intrusively perceptive and searching that it was no longer an instrument of photography. It became the eye of the beholder. And that was certainly true. But he also had an infinite capacity for setting precisely the cogent scene and catching his actors in precisely the right expressions and attitudes to convey the essence of euphoria or pathos or whatever he wanted to reveal.

How he did this with his cast of nonprofessionals was a secret of his own sensitivities, but the evidence spoke for itself. The two youngsters—Franco Interlenghi as Pasquale and Rinaldo Smordoni as Giuseppe—were so true, so free of histrionic postures, so imbued with innate youthful dignity that one was caught up by their authenticity as much as by that of the Roman streets and the prison cells. Among the host of others in the film, Leo Garavagilia, who played the prison warden with an air of grim and despairing exhaustion, was the most impressive of the lot.

Perhaps it was because *Shoe Shine* came to us immediately after the war, when the feelings of frustration and anticlimax were setting in, that it made such a vivid impression and gave such a feeling of hopeless tragedy, more so than *Open City* or Rossellini's second classic of neorealism, *Paisan.** But there it was, stark and sober, and there it still is today—a grim memorial of a cruel and painful period that many people have been too happy to forget—and a fitting, almost providential prelude to de Sica's masterpiece, *The Bicycle Thief** (*Ladri Biciclette*).

GREAT EXPECTATIONS

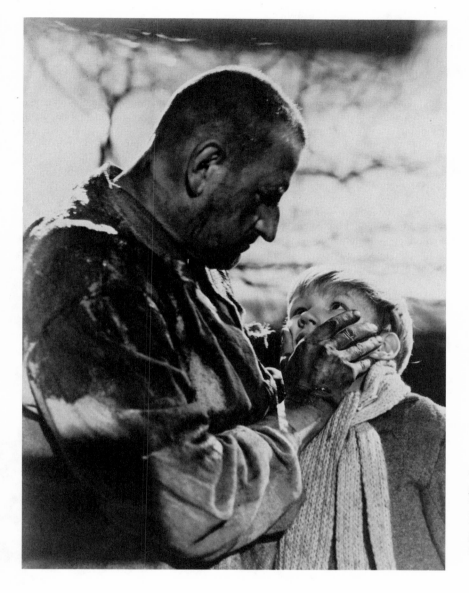

At the terrifying outset of *Great Expectations,* the escaped convict, Magwich (Finlay Currie), seizes the orphan Pip (Anthony Wager) in the lonely graveyard on the edge of the salt marshes.

1946

Critics and sometimes screenwriters have occasionally speculated that if Charles Dickens had lived in our day, this great nineteenth-century British novelist would have been a writer for the screen. The notion is based on the estimation of Dickens' genius for vivid imagery, for action-packed storytelling, and for his great gift in shaping characters. I don't want to make a speculation on that extraneous point just now, but it is certainly true that some fine movies have been made from Dickens' works.

There was the redolent *David Copperfield* that David O. Selznick produced back in the 1930s with W. C. Fields in the role of the flamboyant Mr. Micawber—a performance so magniloquent and droll that it almost overshone the rest of the picture and is the most memorable thing about it today. There were

An introduction to feminine beauty and haughtiness: Pip (Anthony Wager) joins the strange and wily Miss Havisham (Martita Hunt) as she presents her beautiful ward Estella (Jean Simmons) amid the clutter of her decaying home.

also the two superb adaptations that David Lean and Ronald Neame made from *Great Expectations* and *Oliver Twist* in 1946 and 1948, respectively. Of the two, I think *Great Expectations* was the more effective and enjoyable.

All of the charm and drama, all the full-bodied display of nineteenth-century characters and the rich atmosphere of Dickens' novel, were compressed—and compression was essential considering the scope of the book—in this two-hour-long telling of the story of little Pip, the poor country boy who was mysteriously provided with the means for becoming a fine gentleman, having thrilling adventures and learning some sober lessons along the way. And it was done with such understanding and taste, and such proper enunciation of the English dialogue, that it had an illusion of authenticity that no film made anywhere but in England could have had.

Who can forget the opening sequence with little Pip, the country blacksmith's humble ward, going out across the gray salt-marshes at fading sunset to visit his mother's grave in the empty churchyard, silent except for the creaking of wind-tossed trees, and suddenly, while kneeling beside the tombstone, having a

great hand clapped across his mouth and finding himself being held with suffocating pressure in an escaped convict's grasp? That beginning, I believe, was the most startling and electrifying I have ever seen in a film, and the image of the terrified child and the ferocious convict one of the most frightening and foreboding I can recall.

To be sure, the situation was not as dire as it first appeared. The convict was simply perishing for food and water, and he ordered Pip to go fetch them for him. Almost frozen with fear, Pip did so, without breathing a word to a soul, and watched with silent horror and compassion as the famished man ate greedily. But, shortly after, the convict was captured, and as he was taken away to the hulks, Pip watched him go in speechless bewilderment and with a child's uncomprehending sympathy.

This little scene, incidentally, of the convict being rowed away at night and looking back with a darkling expression at Pip standing alone on the quay imaged more of the nineteenth-century inhumanity to prisoners than might have been shown in a beating with whips.

A desperate plan to spirit the returned ex-convict Magwich (Finlay Currie), now a wealthy man, out of England is made by the adult Pip (John Mills), center, the beneficiary of the old man's largess, and his friend Herbert Pocket (Alec Guinness), in their elegant London digs.

Pocket (Alec Guinness) leads old Magwich (Finlay Currie), disguised as a river pilot, to a lonely inn on the lower Thames, whence an attempt will be made to smuggle him aboard a passing outbound packet boat.

The attempt to smuggle old Magwich (Finlay Currie) out of England has not succeeded, and now his grateful beneficiary, the adult Pip (John Mills), visits him as he lies dying in a prison hospital.

And, after that, who does not remember Pip being sent to the great, gray home of the eccentric and mysterious Miss Havisham, to gratify a whim of this strange lady, and being let in at the gate by the beautiful and haughty Estella, a girl of about his own age, and led to the dark and dusty chambers to meet poor, mad Miss Havisham? Those eerie encounters of the youngster with the lady and her snippy little ward in the gaunt rooms bedecked with cobwebs, where mice gnawed the ruins of a wedding feast, were so wonderfully expressive of horror, sadness, and mystery that they can well haunt the memory. Then Pip's burgeoning puppy love for Estella and his totally illogical fights with a whacky "young gentleman" named Pocket who kept insisting on being knocked down, filled out the atmosphere of strangeness in this phase of the film.

But, of course, since this was Dickens, the stringent anomalies of class had to come into the story, and they did as a consequence of Pip's exposure to Estella and his resultant ambition to become a gentleman. Though the idea completely astonished Pip's poor guardian, Joe Gargery, and provoked his humble wife, little Bridie, to exclaim, "Oh, I *wouldn't*, Pip!" he continued

to cherish the notion as he was apprenticed to the blacksmith's trade and accepted the fact that his boyhood and his visits to the great house had come to an end.

Then, lo, a few years later, what did we see occur but a visit from a ponderous London lawyer to Joe Gargery's humble home to convey the astonishing information that Pip, now grown into a fine young man, was in the way of having "great expectations." "He will come into a great property," the lawyer portentously said, but from a source that he was forbidden by the charge of the benefactor to disclose.

So off to London went Pip, with the prospect of becoming a "gentleman," saying good-bye with no great sadness to the gentle Bridie and Joe. And in London, under the guardian eye of Jaggers, the lawyer, and Wemmick, his sparrowlike clerk, he bought for himself a splendid wardrobe and was set up in a handsome apartment with—of all people—the "pale young gentleman," Herbert Pocket, with whom he had fought that long-ago day at Miss Havisham's. This coincidence naturally led to a suspicion that possibly Miss Havisham might be the mysterious benefactor, but Jaggers would not reveal a thing. All he did was continue to dole out the monthly allowance on which Pip so grandly lived.

And that he did to rare perfection, going to parties and balls, at one of which he met again the cruel Estella, now a beautiful and fashionable young woman. His ardor for her surged back more strongly, but she was evidently in love with a fop by the name of Bentley Drummil, who seemed a rascal at heart. This hindrance to Pip's social climbing was magnified when a visit from Joe, full of loving solicitude for him, reminded him of his meek and lowly past. When Joe left to go home, Pip reflected, "I realized that in becoming a gentleman, I had only succeeded in becoming a snob."

But he was snapped out of that mood shortly when, one night, returning to his digs, he found standing before his fireplace, wearing a black eyepatch and sinister-looking clothes, the convict whom he had befriended that night on the empty moors. The shock to Pip—and to the viewer—was almost as great as was that earlier scene, but this time the old man's emergence was for a purpose more amiable than the last. He had come, he told Pip, from far places (one thought of Australia) to have the satisfaction of seeing him, to see what a "gay one my boy has become!," and to pass the dumbfounding information that it was he, grown rich, who had set Pip up in such style. The implications were ironic: this patent criminal, still certain to be hanged if captured in England, having the wish to endow a poor boy who had befriended him to become a gentleman, and having the daring to risk his neck just to see how his dream had been fulfilled.

There was no time for amenities, however. Pip knew that he must arrange to get the old man out of England as soon as possible. So with Pocket lending assistance, in his eager mad-hatter way, they took the old man to a small inn on the lower reaches of the Thames—a gray, lonely area reminiscent of the salt marshes where Pip and the old man had met—and there awaited the opportunity to put him aboard an outgoing ship. This taut, precarious maneuvering was the most exciting business in the film, with the two young men rowing the old man (in a pilot's uniform) out upon the windswept river, deathly silent except for the splash of waves and the screams of gulls, to try to intercept the packet before a suddenly appearing boat with pursuing policemen in it rushed to cut them off. The race was hot and suspenseful, but sadly the policemen won and took the old man, badly injured, into

custody and thence to prison where he died before he could be hanged, but peacefully and gratefully because his beloved Pip visited and comforted him in the end.

Well, that was the sobering climax. Pip had been solemnly shown that it took more than money and social status to define a true gentleman. And he had further verification of it when he himself took desperately ill and after weeks of being in a coma discovered that he had been attended by his tireless, loving Joe. A return for recuperation back to the old blacksmith's home and the chances this gave him to again wander around Miss Havisham's great deserted house and to hear in his memory the echoing voices of those who talked to him there in his youth, completed his realization of the delusions of class. It was a truly Dickensian conclusion, and a reunion with Estella was an apt romantic dividend.

In the large cast of excellent performers, John Mills, of course, stood out in the role of Pip as the gracious and appropriately impressionable young man. Alec Guinness, still very young and agile, played Pocket, and Francis L. Sullivan as the bulbous Jaggers thundered with deep authority. Finlay Currie made Magwich , the convict, a beetling cross between a rascal and a saint, and Martita Hunt was elusive as mad Miss Havisham. Valerie Hobson as the grown-up Estella, Bernard Miles as kindly old Joe, Ivor Bernard as Wemmick, Anthony Wager as Pip as a boy, and Jean Simmons as the youthful Estella could not have been surpassed.

The script that was written in perfect tandem by Mr. Lean and Mr. Neame was a model of selection, and the direction of Mr. Lean, who only the year before had done the tightly constructed *Brief Encounter*, was notable for its tensions in close scenes, its exhilarating tempo, and its skillful synthesis of the many elements. The production designs by John Bryan and the musical score by Walter Goehr also deserve mention. Everything was memorable about this film!

But what I remember with most affection, outside of that shocking scene of Pip and Magwich in the graveyard and the first visit to Miss Havisham's, is the sweetness in the loving voice of Joe as he often addressed his deathless hero, "Dear old Pip, old chap!"

Here is a film which, like Dickens, will never grow old or dull, until man himself so thoroughly changes that there will be no more compassion in his heart.

In one of the more exciting and momentous scenes, the herd is started across the crucial Red River, boundary between Texas and Oklahoma.

RED RIVER

1948

Up to a point, Howard Hawks' *Red River* appeared to be well on its way to rivaling *Stagecoach* and *The Ox-Bow Incident* as one of the finest Westerns made. It had atmosphere, character, action, and an area of contemplation that had not been previously explored in movies except on a very modest scale. That was the

area of marshaling and moving a great cattle herd on the long trek from Texas to Kansas on the historic Chisholm Trail. And then, when the hardships and conflicts of the journey were almost at an end, the cattle, the cowboys, and the picture ran smack into "Hollywood" in the shape of a beautiful seductress played by Joanne Dru.

For two-thirds of its passage—perhaps even a little

more—this robust account of the contentions of two rugged, hard-bitten cattlemen, an older one, given to despotism and played in that vein by John Wayne, and a younger one, no less commanding but more considerate, played by Montgomery Clift, fairly reeked of sweat and cattle and strained with the brawn of men and beef.

From the moment this big, brawling picture faded in on the open Western plains and picked up a wagon train of settlers heading out toward the perilous frontier, it was obvious that this was not a cheap production, shot on a studio ranch, but a genuine excursion into the outdoors, full of sky and space. And from the point where Mr. Wayne and Walter Brennan as his devoted sidekick cut away from the train and took off to the southward to find a fertile cattle range of their own, you had the comfortable feeling you were riding with capable men toward a bold adventure.

That very night, the loners, who were trailing a bull and two cows, were attacked by Indians, whom they successfully beat off, and then the next day came upon a tough, sassy kid who was the lone survivor of a parallel attack on the wagon train. This kid had escaped with one vagrant cow—which was fortunate because Mr. Wayne's two breeders had been killed in the Indian attack. So, after a bit of rough debate in which Mr.

Tension mounts in the group of cowboys as the tyrannical Dunson (John Wayne) prepares to horsewhip a penitent malefactor, while Matt (Montgomery Clift), center, watches ruefully.

94

The great cattle drive from Texas to a thousand-mile-distant railhead is begun in *Red River*, with young Matt (Montgomery Clift) in the center of the three cowboys in the foreground.

The massive and grueling aspects of a legendary western cattle drive, as faithfully and thrillingly depicted in Howard Hawks' *Red River*.

The essential chuckwagon rumbles along with the herd, as young Matt (Montgomery Clift) trail-rides ahead.

A scene of visual excitement and dramatic triumph is enacted in *Red River* when the herd is finally brought to the railhead in Abilene, Kansas.

Wayne naturally took the upper hand, the two men, the boy, and the cattle set off again to the south to start a herd.

Fifteen years later, a spread of thousands of acres had been acquired somewhere in the panhandle of Texas by the simple expedient of eminent domain (and by killing the agent of the previous claimant, who was sent to order them off), a great herd of thousands of cattle had been raised from that one cow and one bull, the boy had grown into rangy manhood, and the time had come to move that herd to where it could be sold. But the boss, Mr. Wayne, whose name was Dunson, had grown no softer or more compassionate with the years. He was the same stubborn, unrelenting despot he was when he browbeat the boy.

And this was the issue that was dramatically posed in the film, and likewise the essence of the interest and the distinctive style of Mr. Hawks. Tough-grained, contentious masculine nature was what the director thrived upon, and he had plenty of it in *Red River*—and an actor who could play it in Mr. Wayne!

No sooner was that great herd gathered and started from the Dunson D-bar ranch (with a few hundred extra head of stragglers from other ranches whose brands had been "jumped"), off to a railhead in Missouri a thousand miles away, than the problem—aside from herding cattle and evading Indians and other natural perils—was how long the despotism of a hardheaded man could be endured. How long could Dunson's unilateral judgments in ruthlessly punishing men—horsewhipping one for accidentally starting a stampede, shooting another who threatened to pull out—be accepted, especially by Mr. Clift's young Matt, who had respect and a certain affection for Dunson, but knew that men could not be treated like steers.

The big showdown loomed when a crucial decision had to be made as to whether they should keep on to Missouri over the familiar route or take a new trail that was shorter to Abilene, Kansas, to which it was said—though not confirmed by more than rumors—that the railroad had reached. Dunson was for the old route. Matt and most of the cowboys were for the new.

The crisis came when Dunson was preparing to hang a man who had deserted along with two others. "You're not going to hang him," Matt said firmly when the judgment was pronounced to a campfire group. "Who's going to stop me?" snapped back Dunson. "I am," Matt replied and, in the usual fast recourse to firearms, beat Dunson to the draw and shot his pistol out of his hand.

That was the time for parting. Matt and the herd went off toward Abilene. Dunson and a couple of loyal followers, including the old cook, Brennan, who had been with him since the beginning, were com-

pelled to stay behind. But a parting crack from Dunson warned Matt that sooner or later he (Dunson) would catch up and kill him.

This was also the point of parting from the tough, honest fiber of the film—from the strong and believable fabric of conflict between the two men and particularly from the thrilling details of the herd. The sheer particulars of the cattle drive, moving on the trail like some great nomadic migration, of trying to control the wild stampede that was caused by nothing more than a sugar-stealing cowboy rattling a few chuck wagon pans, the momentous crossing of the Red River, with the cowboys carefully guiding the swimming herd—all of this was photographed and made exciting as though it were happening in a documentary film. Indeed, a documentarian might have been less bold than Mr. Hawks.

Only one further sequence had the gusto and the rugged poetry of this part of the film. That was when the weary, anxious cowboys brought the herd into Abilene, moving it boldly and majestically across the railway tracks and through the town's crude streets.

The rest was just a commonplace account of the meeting of the herdsmen with a standard studio wagon train, a conventional fight with attacking Indians, in the midst of which a cheeky girl (Miss Dru) alternated shooting at Indians and tossing wisecracks at Matt, and finally a standard confrontation between Dunson and Matt in the streets of Abilene, ready to slug it out until prevented by the sassily taunting Miss Dru.

Fortunately, this part of the picture, though obviously unoriginal, still had enough Hawksian flavor to make it endurable. In its way, it rather fitted in with the Western fictional elements in the script of Borden Chase and Charles Schnee, such as a running gag about false teeth between Mr. Brennan and an Indian and a totally superfluous scene in which Dunson advanced the proposition to Miss Dru that she have a son by him.

But despite its flaws and despite the possibility that *Red River* may seem too long and drawn-out today, I do not hesitate to recommend it as one of the classic Western films.

THE RED SHOES

1948

Out of the handful of movies that have boldly attempted to intrude into the rarefied precincts of the ballet world—films such as Jean Benoit-Levy's *Ballerina* and Ben Hecht's *Spectre of the Rose*—the most successful in capturing the arcane romance of that world has been Michael Powell's and Emeric Pressburger's magnificent *The Red Shoes*. Written, produced, and directed by those two artful Britishers whose imaginative creations ranged from their supernatural *Stairway to Heaven* to their operatic *Tales of Hoffman*, this picture was released a few years after World War II and despite little initial fanfare became an immediate success. Audiences drawn in vast numbers from the ranks of more than pure balletomanes eagerly flocked to see it; it ran in New York for two years, and today is a perennial favorite for revival and showing on TV.

Where there have been many pictures in which ballets have been performed, most often musical pictures in which the ballet has usually been the artistic pièce de résistance, *The Red Shoes in toto* had the structure, the flow, and the spirit of an operatic dance. Not only was its story a frankly theatrical affair, true to the traditional expositions of romance, but it was played by a splendid cast of actors who had the natural grace of ballet performers—which, of course, the majority of them were.

Clearly it was created out of a basic and valid idea—that ballet is enchanting and that it feeds upon dedicated souls. And it was made for no other purpose than to avow that concept with the proof of beauty such as the ballet choreographer and the artful filmmaker command.

I am not suggesting that the working world of ballet is as glamorous and exalted as it was made to appear in this lovely film. It is probably somewhat closer to the untidy, frustrating world that Ben Hecht rather cynically suggested in *Spectre of the Rose*. And, as a matter of fact, in a comment upon *The Red Shoes* Agnes De Mille, who herself knew something about it, being a distinguished creator of ballets, spoke of the "happy, healthy youngsters" in it, who were like "a traveling university." "Nothing," she exploded,

The young ballerina (Moira Shearer) is elevated, literally and symbolically, to new heights in this fluid tableau in the *Red Shoes* ballet.

"could be farther from the truth!" But granting the justice of the purpose of the Messrs. Powell and Pressburger, they achieved the illusion as finely and tastefully as one could wish.

Their drama of an English ballet dancer who got herself into a famous troupe—the name was never mentioned, but it was presumably the Monte Carlo Ballet—became its prima ballerina, and then defied the domineering impresario by being in love with a young composer, was right in the rich, romantic groove. Nothing could be more touching than the torments of one deciding between the demands of art and love. And when this poignant dilemma was finally symbolized in a ballet about a beautiful fairy-story

One of the top male dancers of the ballet company, Ljubov (Leonide Massine), introduces himself to the charming but unknown member of the chorus, Victoria Page (Moira Shearer), early on in *The Red Shoes*.

Vicki is congratulated on her selection to dance the prima role in the Red Shoes ballet by the aged ballet master Ratov (Albret Basserman). Concurring are (from left to right) Boles Lawsky (Robert Helpmann), Livy (Esmond Knight), and Ljubov (Léonide Massine).

youngster who became bewitched by a pair of dancing shoes, the elements formed an amalgam that was almost impossible to resist.

Impossible, that is, in view of the imagination and taste with which both the romance and the ballet were put together in the film. The pictorial details of the story were merged so smoothly with those of the dance that the story itself became the medium of a rapturous experience. And so deftly did Moira Shearer as the heroine drift between the joys of her budding romance and the transports of her *Red Shoes* ballet that it seemed she was constantly performing an impassioned pas de deux. Scenic arrangements, especially in the

actual ambience of Monte Carlo, and a harmonious use of color such as few films up to that time could boast, assisted in creating illusions of both the glamorous ballet world and the fanciful imagistic regions in which the performing dancer dwelled.

Building out of the details of the intimacies and activities of a highly disciplined ballet company—the patient planning, preparation, and drills not only by the members of the chorus but by the principal dancers themselves; the badgerings, the conflicts, and the agonies of the ballet master, with the impresario standing coolly and imperiously behind him; the sleek performances of bits of known ballets—the steady flow of

The little dancing girl (Moira Shearer) is drawn from the security of her home by the master of the magical dancing shoes (Léonide Massine) in *The Red Shoes* ballet.

The two principals, portrayed by Robert Helpmann and Moira Shearer, perform a duet in the allegorical *Red Shoes* ballet.

Moira Shearer as the ballerina in a fanciful episode from *The Red Shoes* ballet.

the drama was toward that premiere presentation of *The Red Shoes*. Crucial in this buildup were the eye-to-eye clashes between the beautiful young ballerina and the impresario wherein he tried to command her to give up her affair and she as stubbornly insisted on her right to love. And perhaps the most breathtaking sequence—outside of the ballet itself—was that in which the chastised ballerina was unexpectedly summoned from her hotel at twilight to be told by the brooding impresario that she had been selected to dance the leading role.

I will not attempt to give you more than a brief description of that ballet, which was arranged by Robert Helpmann, who also performed in the film, from the

A group of hypercritical professionals—Moira Shearer, Robert Helpmann, Anton Walbrook, Esmond Knight, and Léonide Massine—study an off-camera performer during auditions for the prima role for *The Red Shoes* ballet.

A glowing and dramatic moment in the dancing of the tabloid ballet of *The Red Shoes*, when the Clown (Leonide Massine) tempts the young ballerina (Moira Shearer) with the pair of magical ballet slippers, while she is held by the arm of the Lover (Robert Helpmann). *McGraw-Hill Films*

Hans Christian Andersen fable of the little girl whose dancing shoes carried her to destruction. It was set to a stunning musical score by Brian Easdale and ran a full twenty minutes, making a complete ballet.

The structure and staging, while drawing from the crafts of the stage, were intrinsically cinematic, comprising a blend of music, movement, color, and frequent abstract imagery. From the usual inescapable confines of the scenic limitations of the stage, it flowed into regions conceived in the dancer's mind. Dissolves from the figures of Miss Shearer and Mr. Helpmann in conventional ballet scenes carried into compositions of undulating flowers and birds and on into darker phantasms of arms and bodies writhing painfully in caves. The variety of images was myriad, but the camera always returned to the poignant theme of the story and the substantial artifice of the whole.

Perhaps in the film's totality a bit too much stress was placed on the vehemence of the impresario, whom Anton Walbrook played with an air of cool detachment and ascetic sovereignty. Perhaps Marius Goring was too softly effeminate to be entirely satisfactory as the object of the ballerina's love. Léonide Massine was waggish and impulsive as the ballet master and dancer of the role of the village buffoon in the focal ballet, and Mr. Helpmann and Ludmilla Tcherina were superior premiere dancers. And Miss Shearer, with her green eyes and red hair, her freshness and her youthful, pliant grace, was a winning figure on the cinema scene.

The climax, when the ballerina, in fear of losing her lover, was impelled to chase after him into the nighttime and plunged over a parapet, was too contrived and melodramatic. And the final fadeout in which the impresario came before the curtain to announce the young ballerina's death and the village buffoon sadly held up the symbolically fateful red shoes was sentimental cliché, but nevertheless by that time the film had captivated audiences with its romantic charms.

Shortly after the opening of the picture, Miss Shearer arrived in New York as the second ballerina with London's Sadler's Wells Ballet, in which Margot Fonteyn was the prima and, of course, drew the rave reviews. But so insistent were the calls and letters to the management that program schedules had to be rearranged. The public—the new aficionados—were demanding to see more of the girl who had danced the unforgettable *Red Shoes*.

THE SEARCH

1948

A viewer's emotional responses to a particular picture at a particular time are usually to a large extent affected by the immediacy of the substance of the film—by the viewer's own closeness and sensitivity to the content of the drama. Cause and effect are correlative to the degree with which one identifies. I make this observation by way of introducing the remarkable little Swiss film *The Search*, which was directed by an American, Fred Zinnemann, and was sent to this country by producer Lazar Wechsler in 1948.

At the time it came out, I and others were profoundly moved by it and were loud in our praises, citing it as a rare artistic film. It had to do with the lost children of Europe—one in particular—whose homes had been wrecked, whose families had been wiped out or scattered, and whose lives had been scarred by the devastations of the recent war. A more tragic and heartbreaking subject could not have been imagined at the time. So no wonder we critics and our readers responded with deep sympathy.

In the years that passed, I carried that poignant picture in my memory along with those other splendid pictures about children devastated by war, Vittorio de Sica's *Shoe Shine* and René Clement's *Forbidden Games.** I thought of it with such affection that, when I came to prepare this book, I felt it was one that I would surely be eager to include. But then came that fearful moment when I had to see it again to make sure it hadn't diminished, that it was as fine as I first thought it was.

Well, the fact that you now find it included in this book is the evidence that I wasn't disappointed—that

Resisting with the child's hysterical terror of anyone in a uniform, little Karel (Ivan Jandl) is brought by his beneficent captor, the American Military Government officer (Montgomery Clift), into the latter's apartment in a devastated German city.

The small hero, in knitted cap, arrives with a group of lost children at a reception center at the beginning of *The Search*.

An officer (Montgomery Clift) of the American Military Government in postwar Germany spots and stops to pick up a lost child (Ivan Jandl) amid the ruins of a bombed-out city.

Homeless and lost children picked up across war-torn Germany after World War II are registered at the United Nations Relief and Rehabilitation camp in southern Germany in this scene from *The Search*.

despite certain minor weaknesses such as excess of sentimentality in some spots and a few stretches that are tediously verbose it still stands up as a graphic depiction of cruelty done to innocent children. It is an honest and lasting summation of one of the residual agonies of the war.

At first it may seem to one who views it now without that original emotional conditioning as though it might have placed too much emphasis on the crisis of one small boy. But then it should be apparent that this lad did emerge from a group of displaced children, and that the tragedy of all these children was personified by him. And to the possible protest that the predicament of our little fellow was too happily resolved, I can only say that I do hope such endings might have been frequent. At least it did represent hope.

The Search was the story of a small boy who arrived with a gaggle of other forlorn little waifs in a United Nations Relief and Rehabilitation camp in southern Germany shortly after the war. Silent, solemn, bewildered, these children were like frightened animals, as wary of those who wanted to help them as they undoubtedly had been of the Nazis who had brought them to this state. Often powerless to tell even their names and backgrounds—this boy was totally mute—they huddled together in a bond of common terror and comforted themselves with pitiful relics of their past. One little girl cuddled closely to the broken head of a doll. Our little boy clung desperately to a knitted cap.

So intense were their suspicions and confusions that when a small group was later being moved in an ambulance marked with a red cross to a more permanent camp they were suddenly struck with the notion that they were being taken off to be gassed, and a couple of them, including the boy, broke open the door and escaped.

Trying to cross a river with a companion, the two were caught by the current. The companion was washed away, but little Karel, our youngster, managed to reach the other side, minus his cap.

Wandering alone among the ruins of a bombed-out city—it might have been Munich or Cologne—he was spotted by a young officer of the American Military Government, who caught him and took him to his home. There this young man, with the compassion—and sometimes the irritability—of an older American brother, and with the counsel of another officer who shared the apartment with him and was the father of children back home, struggled patiently to gain the confidence of the youngster, to teach him to speak English, and finally to reconcile him to the thought that his mother was dead.

Meanwhile, the mother, a survivor of a Nazi concentration camp, had been hopefully looking for the youngster in a number of children's camps, with successive choking disappointments and heartbreaking experiences. Finally she reached the center where we had seen the group of children initially screened and was shown the cap which she recognized as one that she had knitted. It had been picked up farther down the river, along with the body of the other child, so it was assumed that Karel, too, was dead. Desolated, the mother was persuaded to give up the search and prepared to leave.

She had gone to the railway station and was on the point of boarding a train, when the young officer who had befriended Karel drove into the center with him and turned him over to the director. He had suddenly been ordered home and was not able to take the lad with him, as he might have taken a pet—which, indeed, seemed almost to be the nature of the attachment of the young man to the boy. (This is the best explanation I can give you of why he hadn't turned him over before.)

From bits of information she was now able to draw from the boy, the director suddenly suspected that he was the one the mother sought. A rush to the railway

Karel (Ivan Jandl), the lost child now restored to health and taught to speak English, is turned over to the director of the UNRRA camp, Mrs. Murray (Aline MacMahon), by his departing benefactor.

Joyous reunion at last. The mother (Jarmila Novotna) and her boy (Ivan Jandl) at the end of *The Search*.

station in the officer's jeep brought them there just in time to see the train departing, but fortunately the mother had held back at the last moment from getting aboard and was walking dazedly away from the station when the jeep drove up.

Some must have felt that her miraculous hesitation and the subsequent twist that was then arranged for the mother to discover the youngster—he was placed in a group of children passing her along a sidewalk and it was there that she suddenly saw him—was too contrived and emotionally overdone. I felt—and still feel—that it was valid as an essential catharsis for all the foregoing agony. I don't think that audiences could have stood it if the mother and her child had not been brought together in the end.

Further, and this is very important, a major stress in the film was on the innate hunger in the youngster—and in all youngsters—for a mother's sheltering love. While Karel was still with his benefactor, he was suddenly profoundly moved without knowing why when he saw a picture of a mother dog nursing a litter of pups. He was so upset and bewildered when the wife of the other officer in the apartment arrived for a visit that he hysterically fled the apartment and again went wandering through the ruins. At dawn he found himself standing outside the significant high-wire fence of a factory, scanning the faces of the women workers as they wearily came out. The essential need of the mother-child relationship was the real dramatic crux of the film. To have been denied at least an illusion of its fulfillment would have been to conclude in cynical despair.

Mr. Zinnemann and his writers, Richard Schweizer, David Wechsler, and Paul Jarrico, had included sufficient frustrations to carry the impact of harsh realities. One tormenting scene in which the mother confronted a little Jewish boy who had assumed the identity of Karel so he could shelter himself in the Catholic choir was pregnant with helpless emotions—the petrifying fear of the boy that he would be fatally segregated and the grief of the mother at finding he wasn't her son.

As the mother, Jarmila Novotna, a distinguished opera singer, was lovely and restrained, only appearing artificial in one family flashback sequence which was itself a bit absurd. Montgomery Clift was fine as the American officer, completely matter-of-fact and in tune with the clear, realistic environment of postwar Europe that Mr. Zinnemann faithfully reproduced and photographed. Aline MacMahon was impressively bureaucratic but compassionate as the UNRRA center director, and Wendell Corey gave low-key substantiality to the other officer.

But it was a little Czech boy named Ivan Jandl, whom Mr. Zinnemann had found in a group of Prague schoolchildren, who dominated the film. With a sad little face atop a slight frame, melting appeal in his thin voice, when he found it and spoke with an accent (others spoke in English or German), and with such birdlike responses and agility when he moved about that he gave the impression of an early Christian innocent marked for brutal sacrifice.

Today there is little recollection of those children who were lost after the war. Those that survived are now middle-aged, and their adjustments, whatever they were, have been made. The dilemma of their futures is forgotten. But *The Search* remains as a fine memorial of a tragedy that once deeply disturbed us and is a reminder of the ageless potential for cruelty in evil, misguided men.

Willie Stark (Broderick Crawford), now consumed with a passion for political power, is accompanied by his friend (John Ireland) as he reviews a detail of his personal "storm troopers."

ALL THE KING'S MEN

1949

Surely no one could have foreseen at the time of the release of Robert Rossen's movie from Robert Penn Warren's novel *All the King's Men* how darkly this thundering melodrama about an unscrupulous political leader in the South cast an ominous shadow of future happenings on the American political scene. Although it was patent that the novel—and the movie, of course—were prompted by the awesome and ambiguous aspects of the sordid career of Huey Long, a for-

mer governor of Louisiana and then a United States senator who was killed by an assassin in 1935, the presentiment given in the picture of the kind of violence and seeking after power that were to prevail on the national scene in the next two decades mark it today as prophetic.

When it came out, we generally hailed it as one of those blistering postwar American films that were more or less inspired by the example of the Italian neorealists to cast an unrelenting spotlight on some of the seamier sides of American life. Like a few of the prewar sound films—the gangster classics especially—it made a distinct contribution to public awareness and emotional concern. After all, this *was* a picture about a type we *had* observed. But the clanging alarm it sounded about the danger of unscrupulous men capturing and using high office to aggrandize themselves and the hideous preview it gave us of political assassination in this country were admonitions that only later struck home.

So this historical perceptivity is one of the reasons why *All the King's Men* still stands out as a great American film.

But beyond that—which was clearly not its virtue in 1949—it was a turbulent and engrossing contemplation of a few hectic years in the life of a self-made and self-styled backcountry, dirt-road, red-necked hick who clawed his way up from that environment to supreme political power in an unspecified Southern state and crudely indulged his towering ego until he was killed by an avenger's gun. With aggressiveness and vitality of an order seldom seen in fiction films, it ranged from raw-boned melodrama to dark psychological depths. Consistency of dramatic structure—or of character revelation—it did not have, but it throbbed

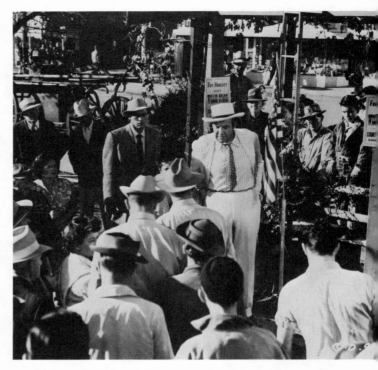

The back-country hick lawyer, Willie Stark (Broderick Crawford), angered by evident misappropriation of public funds, begins his first, honest try for public office, accompanied by a lone newspaper reporter (John Ireland), left.

Willie Stark (Broderick Crawford) attends with interest an attempt by his newspaper-reporter friend (John Ireland) to make a deal with a small-town political leader (Ralph Dumke).

106

The campaign headquarters of the increasingly ambitious and successful Willie Stark hums with activity. Briefing him are his dynamic and cynical associate, Sadie Burke (Mercedes McCambridge), and his reporter friend (John Ireland).

Willie Stark (Broderick Crawford), now a political power, unleashes his wrath upon his contemptuous son (John Derek), in the presence of Mrs. Stark (Anne Seymour) and his still loyal friend, Jack Burden (John Ireland).

A hypocritical show of family harmony is made for the benefit of photographers by Willie Stark (Broderick Crawford), surrounded by his father (H. C. Miller), his wife (Anne Seymour) and his son (John Derek), in wheelchair, on the porch of his old back-country home.

with superb pictorialism to match that of the finest documentary films, and it popped with the kind of realism that was evident in John Ford's earlier *The Grapes of Wrath.**

Because of this rich pictorialism, which embraced a wide and fluid scene, it gathered a frightening comprehension of the potential of demagoguery in this land. From narrow and ugly illustrations of back-room spittoon politics to wild illuminations of howling political mobs, it caught the dreadful aspects of mass ignorance and high-class greed when stirred by deceitful politicos. It visioned the public spellbinders and the back-room hypocrites for what they were, and it looked on extreme provincialism with a candid and cynical eye.

In short, Mr. Rossen assembled in this starkly unprettified film a piece of pictorial journalism that was remarkable for its brilliant parts. It fairly observed the beginnings of a Huey Long type of populist in an humble and honest night-school lawyer in a sleepy courthouse town, earnestly fighting the bosses to try to get something done for the benefit of the poor—the lanky, foot-shuffling dirt farmers, their overworked

The irate father of a girl who has been killed in an auto accident with young Stark assails an insensitive Willie (Broderick Crawford) and his anguished wife (Anne Seymour) in the foyer of the governor's mansion.

wives, and their underfed kids. It followed this disillusioned fellow as he absorbed politics and discovered the strange intoxication of his deliberate cracker-barrel charm. And it raced with him through crooked campaigns and finally landed him squarely in the governorship.

But in the course of this progression, our hero, Willie Stark, profoundly changed. From a decent and gullible decoy to trap the "hick vote" for the state machine he metamorphosed into a crafty lone-wolf professional pol, making deals with anybody who could help elevate him to power, always on the pretense he was doing it "to get the things people need." Thence he propelled into the posture of a ranting and snarling demagogue. He hobnobbed and played ball with the wealthy while striking his pose as the people's friend, and he used his accumulated leverage to command the radio and press. Altogether Willie became a vicious and menacing sort.

In his private life, too, he metamorphosed. From a loving and considerate family man, he turned into a scoundrel who neglected his wife, browbeat his son, and took as his mistress the fiancée of his press representative, who was also his best friend. And when the legislature threatened to impeach him, he tried to blackmail an old, respected judge who had been one of his early supporters, and drove him to suicide. It was this treachery that incited a liberal-minded nephew of the judge to go gunning for Willie and finally shoot him down on the steps of the state capitol from which Willie was roaring a blast of rhetoric to a wild, idolatrous mob while the state militia was gathered to help him seize absolute power.

All of these things Mr. Rossen pictured stunningly. The final episode of mob hysteria and personal violence fairly burst with savagery. But in his parallel endeavors to transfer from Mr. Warren's book some clear understanding of Willie, he met with less success. In fact, the midsection of the movie, which was almost entirely concerned with the nerve-racking impact of the fellow upon his wife, son, mistress, and friends was a baffling confusion of dramatics that was saved only by the abundant pictorial detail.

Contributing to the film's success was the raw performance that Broderick Crawford gave as the big, brawling, boisterous, hick lawyer who made himself a briefly reigning king. Mr. Crawford packed energy and color into every delineation he gave, whether it was of the enthusiastic bumpkin or of the scowling and drunken demagogue. And although it was difficult to fathom why Willie really went the way he did, shifting so swiftly in his nature and his ideologies, it must be said that Mr. Crawford made the portrait of an egomaniac exciting and compelling.

Less could be said for other principal performers in the film, not so much because of their own shortcomings as because of the limited roles they had to play. Joanne Dru was a pretty, well-dressed cipher as the mistress who made the switch for reasons completely indecipherable, other than perhaps because the press man from whom she defected was so insufferably dull. As John Ireland played him, he was a gangling, deadpanned dolt whose only assistance to Willie seemed to be to introduce him to the country-club crowd.

Shepperd Strudwick likewise fumbled vaguely as the nephew who eventually pulled himself out of a mood of genteel benevolence into a state of vengeful savagery sufficient to arouse him to fire the fatal shot, and tight-mouthed Mercedes McCambridge was merely picturesque and acid-tart as a cynical mercenary for Willie. Raymond Greenleaf as the judge, Katherine Warren as a Southern society dame, and John Derek as Willie's sullen offspring were standard Hollywood types. However, Will Wright and Ralph Dumke were as solid as potbellied stoves in the roles of country politicians, and virtually everyone who came on the scene as tub-thumpers, shills, or just plain people enhanced the credibility of the tale.

I would not suggest for one moment that this film was by any means the last word on demagoguery and its dangers in our "democracy." But it put forth a powerful conjecture on the potentialities of peril, given the proper soil conditions, making it an exciting, engrossing show.

A salient encounter between Lucas Beauchamp (Juano Hernandez) and Vinson Gowrie (David Clarke) in a lonely woods.

A country store in Mississippi is the scene of this strained interlude, remembered by Chick Mallison (Claude Jarman, Jr.), the boy at far left, as the proud and independent black farmer, Lucas Beauchamp, makes his purchases amid a gathering of resentful whites, notably Crawford Gowrie (Charles Kemper), at right in the railroadman's cap.

INTRUDER IN THE DUST

1949

It is hard to believe now that the subject of race relations in the United States—one which has become in three decades perhaps the most obvious and urgent issue in our national life—was avoided by filmmakers prior to World War II, or else regarded from the indulgent white man's point of view. After D. W. Griffith's *The Birth of a Nation*, which was an out-and-out white supremacist film and caused great indignation among intellectuals, black and white, the subject was either avoided or touched on affably in Hollywood. Blacks were portrayed either as servants or as congenial entertainers, such as Sam in *Casablanca*, until after World War II.

Then long-felt resentments against racial discrimination and injustices, further aggravated and made apparent by gross inequities toward blacks during the war, finally brought on the explosion of the issue in violent protests in the South and the Supreme Court decision against segregation. Once the issue had become a matter of general concern, filmmakers began to deal with it—frankly but gingerly.

The first postwar film to broach the issue of black-white discrimination was made very much under wraps by Stanley Kramer, a young war veteran turned producer-director. It was *Home of the Brave*, and it told a brooding story of a black soldier who had to be returned from the South Pacific suffering from "shell shock" because of the harassment he had received from his bigoted white "buddies." It was followed within a year by a procession of race-conscious dramas—Louis de Rochemont's *Lost Boundaries*, Elia Kazan's *Pinky* and, most realistic and searching of all, Clarence Brown's magnificent rendering of William Faulkner's novel *Intruder in the Dust*.

Here at last was a Hollywood picture that slashed right to the core of racial antagonisms and social divisions in a typical rural area of the South—a picture which smashed the hollow pretense of white supremacy and did it in terms of visual drama and realistic action at its best. Even if its broader meanings and its

Chick (Claude Jarman, Jr.), saved from an icy river by the farmer, Lucas Beauchamp (Juano Hernandez), is revived by the latter in his humble home.

more accusative overtones were missed by some prejudiced viewers, those same viewers could experience its impact as a thriller. This was because the story, which Ben Maddow expertly derived from Mr. Faulkner's novel, and which Mr. Brown boldly put upon the screen, was a solemn and spooky mystery that eerily emerged from a succession of stark discoveries, reflections, and shocks. On the surface it was the story of a courageous and desperate attempt to save an innocent black from lynching at the hands of a Mississippi mob—a story of how three people, an old

white lady and two fearful boys, one of them black, on the word of a black man, who was being held in jail, slipped out of town at midnight and secretly opened a grave to discover the startling evidence that helped to prove the man innocent and save his life. It was further—simply on the surface—a story of shrewd detective work by an honorable white lawyer and a sheriff that exposed the real murderer. More than taut, chilling melodrama, however, this film gave a horrifying view of an irrational surge of racial hatred.

From the opening scene in the quiet streets one Sun-

A grave is opened surreptitiously by Chick (Claude Jarman, Jr.) and Aleck (Elzie Emanuel) in search of crucial information in *Intruder in the Dust,* as a brave accomplice, Miss Habersham (Elizabeth Patterson), holds a light.

A valiant Southern lady, Miss Habersham (Elizabeth Patterson) sits in the doorway of the courthouse and jail in a Mississippi town to prevent an intending lyncher, Crawford Gowrie (Charles Kemper) from entering.

"There he goes—proud, stubborn, insufferable, but the keeper of my conscience." The lawyer, John Gavin Stevens (David Brian), rings down the curtain on *Intruder in the Dust* with these words, addressed to his stalwart nephew, Chick (Claude Jarman, Jr.), as these two champions of the black man, Lucas Beauchamp, watch him walk among the Saturday-morning swarm in Jefferson, Mississippi.

The proud and defiant Lucas (Juano Hernandez), now cleared of suspicion of having murdered a white man, crosses the street of the Mississippi town to settle his account with the white lawyer who represented him.

day morning in this sleepy Southern town—it was actually Oxford, Mississippi, where Mr. Brown, with the help of Robert Surtees, photographed most of the film—it was plain that this wasn't the sort of picture that one usually saw in those days. The town was indelibly authentic, the drowsing idlers looked rawboned and real, as ominous news spread among them: a white man, "one of the Gowers," had been murdered out in the country and a black man was being "brought in" for the deed.

Then, thumping into the town square came the sheriff's dusty car, one tire flat and the siren moaning. Tension was immediately drawn. In the car was the manacled black, a proud and haughty man, and outside, watching, were the faces of a gathering crowd.

In the white church nervous worshipers listened gravely to that telling siren's moan. The respectable town of Jefferson was preparing to allow "justice" to be done.

But justice—or at least that sort of "justice" to which the South had been submissive in the past—was not done, as anticipated, in the next thirty-six hours, while the black waited quietly in his jail cell and the crowd swelled menacingly. And it wasn't done because a sixteen-year-old white boy, son of one of the "solid" families in town, whom the black man had once befriended and thereby put into his debt, could not smother the dictates of his conscience beneath the blanket of a traditional code.

It was this lad who heeded the black man's urging

that, if they opened the murdered man's grave, they would find that the bullet that killed him had not been fired from the black man's gun. This routine piece of crime detection had obviously not been done by the local law enforcers because it was a hated black man charged with killing a well-known white. But the boy, after trying unsuccessfully to get his lawyer-uncle to intercede, rallied the only other help he could think of, a gentle lady and her black houseboy, and went out to open the grave.

Imagine their astonishment and horror when they found, by a flickering hand-held light, that the freshly dug grave was empty. Filling it in again, they went home, and the next day the lad told his uncle, who was now willing to persuade the sheriff to look for himself. Sure enough, they found the body was missing, and this led to the weird discovery that it had been removed and buried in quicksand on the bank of a nearby creek—and that the bullet which killed him had not been fired from the black man's gun!

All of this gruesome detail—the whispered talk of the boy with the prisoner through the bars of his cell, the midnight discovery in the graveyard, the second opening of the grave, and the ensuing pursuit with bloodhounds to the quicksands from which the decomposing corpse was disinterred—was evolved with blood-chilling realism against the intercut details of the mob building up and being urged to take action by the snarling brother of the murdered man.

It was in this phase of the picture, when the sheriff came back to town with his grisly information to find the lynch-hungry mob in the town square, with a store gramophone blaring an ugly jazz tune and the whole pervaded by a carnival atmosphere, that the hideousness of racial hatred and the thirst for vengeance was most vividly revealed, and the threat of impending disaster was most tightly and painfully drawn.

The rest of the film was quite as gripping and disturbing as it went on to tell how the sheriff, now perceiving that the black man had been framed, released him and sent him home to be a decoy while the sheriff and his men hid near the house to apprehend whoever might come to get him—which, sure enough, turned out to be the brutish, mob-leading Gower brother who had committed fratricide.

But the epilogue was particularly admirable. On the following Saturday, the now exonerated black man came into town, still wearing the frock coat and sombrero which he was wearing when he was first brought in, strode disdainfully through the clusters of staring people in the streets, went up to the lawyer's office, and insisted on paying what he could for the lawyer's services, which was two silver dollars.

This confrontation between the two proud and honorable men, each knowing the gulf between them and neither ready yet to give an inch, but well aware that they had been drawn closer by a tie of mutual ordeal and respect, was the ironic capstone to the substance of this film. It did not pretend to a happy ending, a pat solution for the problems that had set the white man against his black neighbor for generations past. But it viewed the situation succinctly in terms of forthright individuals. And the last words of the lawyer, as he watched the black man go down to the street and walk away with his head high, "There he goes—proud, stubborn, insufferable—but the keeper of my conscience," were the words of a white Southerner who thus acknowledged that he had a burden of age-old guilt with which to struggle toward some sort of resolution in his own mind and heart.

Much of the power of the picture was in the honesty with which it was played, especially by Juano Hernandez as the black victim. He was nobody's humble Uncle Tom, but a strong and apparently prosperous farmer with such knowledge of and pride in himself that he would rather be lynched than surrender his dignity. One scene in a complementary flashback, when he came into a country store amid a gaggle of contemptuous bumpkins, made his purchases, and silently walked out, was a fulgurant illumination of why he was so resented by the Gowers.

Young Claude Jarman, Jr., as the schoolboy who had the pride and the audacity to do something wholly unconventional to repay the man who had saved his life, gave an engrossing indication of a youngster growing up, having his eyes amazingly opened, and being changed by what he had seen. David Brian as the small-town lawyer, Charles Kemper as the porcine murderer, and Elizabeth Patterson as the gentle Southern lady who had the courage to help open a grave and later sit in the door of the courthouse and defy the lynchers as they came with gasoline to set fire to the building and burn out their man, were excellent, along with Will Geer, who made the sheriff a credible Southern type.

Intruder in the Dust is not often shown in revival these days. That's a shame, because it bears repeated seeing as a continually valid antiracist film.

ALL ABOUT EVE

1950

Back in the early 1930s, when it was considered quite clever and chic among the New York literati and especially the people of the Broadway stage to sneer at the "vulgarity" of the movies, George S. Kaufman and Moss Hart wrote a satire called *Once in a Lifetime*, which was a classic putdown of Hollywood. Nothing before or since quite managed to make the people of the studios and the stars look quite as foolish and self-centered as this skin-peeling satire did, with the possible exception of Preston Sturges' *Sullivan's Travels* or Billy Wilder's *Sunset Boulevard.**

Oddly enough, the movies never got even until Joseph L. Mankiewicz's brilliant *All About Eve* was released in 1950. Then, with this devastating comment upon the egos of stage people—those supposedly selfless custodians of the Temple of Thespis and the arts—Mr. Mankiewicz debunked the theater myth—the theater, as distinct from Hollywood—in a manner so skillful and absorbing I don't see how it can ever be surpassed.

Focusing on a personality clash between two formidable ladies of the footlights, one a brilliant and long-established star and the other a ferocious newcomer determined to claw her way to the top, Mr. Mankiewicz synthesized some of the more lurid legends of idolized theater stars, old tales of production-level battles, ugly stories of certain bitchy journalists, and a flash or two of the stylish ambience of Broadway. It was obviously a very special milieu about which Mr. Mankiewicz was very knowledgeable. Like a onetime rumored lover who had had a secret affair with the lady and found her wanting, he plainly felt free to kiss and tell.

The consequence might have been routine and parochial if Mr. Mankiewicz, as his own screenplay writer, had not directed with extraordinary wit and if he had not had his clutch of theater people played by an excellent cast—a cast which might have rivaled any Broadway cast available at that time. This was an incidental triumph: *All About Eve* was better than most vaunted Broadway plays.

Credit for this particular success had to go, by and large, to Bette Davis, who played the leading (though

not the title) role. As a top-ranking star of the American theater—someone comparable in those days to Helen Hayes, Katharine Cornell or Tallulah Bankhead—she found herself pursued and craftily used by an aspiring actress with murder in her eyes. Miss Davis was indubitably the image of a reigning aristocrat. Her cool self-assurance and condescension when chatting with friends and fans, her glibness and prickly sarcasm when sparring in professional repartee, marked her as one who had clearly acquired her au-

En route for a stint in Hollywood, Bill (Gary Merrill), the Broadway director and lover of Margo (Bette Davis), tries to reassure her as he bids good-bye.

114

A resentful and angry Margo (Bette Davis) shoots some poisonous remarks at the viciously conniving Eve (Anne Baxter) at a theatrical party, to the amazement and delight of a group of important onlookers.

Barbed words and polite insults fly between the star, Margo (Bette Davis), and the powerful drama critic, Addison De Witt (George Sanders), as his current adornment (the newcomer Marilyn Monroe) takes it all in.

One of those fateful moments in *All About Eve*, when Margo fails to show up in time for a rehearsal of her new play and the director, Bill (Gary Merrill) agrees to let Eve (Anne Baxter) read the part. Handing him the script is the producer, Max Fabian (Gregory Ratoff), while the playwright (Hugh Marlowe) and his wife (Celeste Holm) watch anxiously.

Meeting backstage to discuss the potential nuisance of a stage-struck girl are Margo, her maid Birdie (Thelma Ritter), and her best friend, Karen (Celeste Holm).

thority and skill by waging her own battles to play the great heroines.

But under her queenly exterior—the one that was visible and adored by the idolatrous public—there lurked a vain and vulnerable woman, strangely unsure of her charms, racked with doubts and misgivings about her ability to hold her man, and haunted, above all, with the specter—the obsession—of growing old. When she perceived that she was being exploited and menaced by this deceptively worshipful young actress who used the bodeful stage name of Eve, she slipped (temporarily) into betraying her own murderous guile and bitchery.

Hers was a splendid performance—the best, I think, Miss Davis ever gave—and the irony was it didn't win an Oscar, though the film and Mr. Mankiewicz did.

So, too, did veteran George Sanders, whose brittle performance in the role of a powerful and caustic drama critic was close on Miss Davis' heels. Dressed to sartorial perfection—far beyond the taste and the means of any drama critic of my acquaintance, excepting the late George Jean Nathan, who *was* a careful dresser and a brutal critic like this Addison De Witt—Mr. Sanders fairly oozed sangfroid and savoir faire while going about his favorite pastimes of juggling careers and chasing girls. He was the deus ex machina, the chief manipulator in the piece, whose insights into

The coveted Sarah Siddons Award for Distinguished Achievement in the theater goes to the parvenue, Eve (Anne Baxter), center, rather than to her more deserving patroness, Margo (Bette Davis), in *All About Eve*.

the natures and weaknesses of the dames allowed him to manipulate them in print. The invention and use of this character by Mr. Mankiewicz was one of his keener creations because it subtly exposed the power of criticism and publicity in making or killing reputations in the theater. I also suspect it gave him a bit of vengeful satisfaction, too.

All About Eve opened sweetly upon a gathering of theatrical elite attending the annual presentation of the envied Sarah Siddons Award for Distinguished Achievement. The award went to Eve, who was played by Anne Baxter with balanced measures of unction and stealth. And while the presentation speech was flowing, the muted voice of Addison came in to explain confidentially to the audience that this award was originally meant for the star, Margo Channing, who was also in the gathering, but. . . . Thus the film led into a flashback of the story of Margo and Eve.

It was a constantly captivating story of how a conniving, stage-struck girl worked her way into the friendship of Margo (by playing on her vanity and sentiments, of course), became her secretary and confidential servant, engaged herself with Margo's lover and friends, and eventually tried to steal not only the lover but Margo's current sensational role (which she finally did, with the help, however, of wily Addison and a stupid blunder by Margo's best friend). It was an absorbing continuity, first, of delicate thrusts and counterthrusts, which became more vicious and slashing until that ultimate humiliation of the bestowal of the award upon Eve, who thereby seemed to have her triumph. But Margo got the last word!

I cannot recount in detail the successive witty scenes and sequences, such as one of a party at Margo's to welcome her lover home from Hollywood, which degenerated into a jangle of testy insults and bitcheries. There was so much headlong movement in the picture it was hard to realize it was mostly conveyed in dialogue. Superfluous, however, was a postscript in which Eve, having won, but all alone, was conned in much the same fashion as was Margo by another aspiring, conniving girl. The scene was just a bit too pat and obvious, since the irony had already been conveyed.

But that passed for anticlimax. The moral—if moral is the word—was drenched in the implications of continuing irony. For the idea that Mr. Mankiewicz presented in this film, with so much more scope and penetration than anything in *Once in a Lifetime*, was that people who are lured into the luxury of the exhibitionist's trade are trapped in a cannibalistic business that feeds upon their own vain weaknesses.

I must not leave it without mention of some others in the cast—Gary Merrill as Margo's shrewd director, patient lover, and understanding pal; Celeste Holm as the wife of her boyish playwright (Hugh Marlowe) and her closest, most gullible friend; Thelma Ritter, a superb character actress who slyly stole a few scenes as her maid and; oh, yes, in the role of a protégée of Addison, a burgeoning star in Hollywood, Marilyn Monroe.

THE THIRD MAN

1950

If ever there was a movie in which a musical instrument played a leading role—indeed, a role so expressive and pervasive that it all but dominated the whole—that movie was Carol Reed's and Graham Greene's superior mystery-thriller *The Third Man,* which David O. Selznick brought from Europe just five years after World War II. And the instrument was a zither, one of those strange combinations of strings that was and still is the special spokesman for the vagrant moods of the Viennese cafés.

Soft and sad at some moments, strident at other ones, commanding those occasions when it was allowed to intrude its voice, this zither became the keen observer of and commentator upon all that occurred in this mystifying romance set in the Vienna of the immediate postwar. It sang when the mood was hopeful, it cried when the mood was sad, it growled when the action became menacing, it whispered when mischief was afoot. And always it forced its rhythms, weird and insistent, upon the mind as events of a strange and violent nature were excitingly played upon the screen.

It was, indeed, as though this zither were the harp of one of the ancient jongleurs who recounted stirring legends in the castle banquet halls. It had its own personality, its own melodic point of view, and it was always two beats ahead of the audience in grasping a shock or a change of mood. And, properly, this participant was never seen. Only at the start of the picture did its vibrating strings traverse the screen as the credits were duly displayed. Sadly, its insinuating music twanged and pinged out the melody that has since become famous and universal as "The Third Man Theme." As soon as the credits were finished, the strings disappeared, to be seen no more.

The incredible thing is that this factor, this importance of the zither in the film, was not designed or intended until the film was finished and ready to be scored. It was only then that Sir Alex Korda, who was the actual producer, was struck with the brilliant idea of allowing the distinguished Viennese zither maestro, Anton Karas, to write and play the singular score. This was viewed with some misgiving by his associates—until the finished picture was shown to them.

The first and startling appearance of Harry Lime (Orson Welles) out of a night-shrouded doorway in the silent streets of Vienna.

119

In the dark and rubble-strewn streets of postwar Vienna, Holly Martins (Joseph Cotten), accompanied only by the muted and haunting music of a zither, seeks his boyhood friend, Harry Lime.

The two American boyhood friends, Holly Martins and Harry Lime, turned international black-marketeer, have a decisive rendezvous in a gondola of a giant Viennese ferris wheel.

Then they reacted with amazement and delight. History had been made.

Let it be noted, at the same time, that this stroke of superior artifice was entirely consistent with the nature and the spirit of the film. For *The Third Man* was itself a brilliant fabrication of such materials as were most congenial with Mr. Greene and Mr. Reed. It was a slick and polished package of melodramatic surprises and twists.

Right after the credits were run off and the zither had been introduced, a voice intruded on the sound track as shots of postwar Vienna were shown. It was the voice of the principal character, Holly Martins, an American Western fiction writer, played by Joseph Cotten, who introduced himself. Glibly, sardonically, he briefed us on Vienna in those grim, black-market days and explained that he had come to this strange city to look up a boyhood friend. But no sooner had he got his bearings and gone to the apartment of his friend, Harry Lime, than he was shocked to be told that his friend was dead—run down by an auto in the streets. He learned that the burial was taking place that very afternoon, so he went to the cemetery and found an odd group at the grave. It included a quietly grieving woman and a scattering of silent and stoical Viennese. So cryptic was the service that Holly was plainly mystified, and went back to Harry's apartment to try to find out what more he could. Everyone asked seemed evasive, until one fellow guardedly said, "I wondered whether it was really an accident." And that set Holly off. Had Harry possibly been murdered? And, if so, why and by whom? Holly assigned himself to find out. Thus the search began.

It would be difficult and tedious for me to detail the many incidents and surprises in this search—how Holly found himself obstructed by a curious wall of silence at first, as everyone seemed to fall mute at the mention of Harry Lime's name; how neither the grieving woman who was at the graveside (and who we soon learned was Harry's Russian-exile sweetheart) nor Major Calloway of the International Police was greatly disposed to talk about it; how Holly eventually found that there were more than the reported two witnesses of the accident—there was a third witness, the mysterious "third man"—and how this piece of information led on to the staggering surprise of being told by a now annoyed Calloway that Harry was actually up to his neck in crime. He was engaged in the black-market traffic in penicillin, a most rare commodity, and for his participation in this racket, anything could have happened to him.

Well, the anything was that Harry, as Holly suspected, was still alive—a fact which was soon corroborated by Calloway's opening the grave and discovering that the body was not Harry's but that of another racketeer. And this new twist started Holly on a wild hunt for Harry himself.

Again the onrush of details was too swift and labyrinthine to now recount, except to cite the startling moment when Holly, chasing a frightened cat through a night-dimmed street (and let's not go into how *that* happened), suddenly saw Harry standing in a door, looking as sinister and mystic as only Orson Welles, who played the character, could; and later had a rendezvous with him in a gondola of a giant Ferris wheel where his old friend rather sadly confessed his guilt, "Old man, you should never have gone to the police; you should have stayed out of this."

Indubitably, a powerful element in the attraction and appeal of this film was the strain of wistfulness and pathos toward the end. For, after the crowded crises of the early phases had been passed and Harry had been isolated as the singular quarry of the chase, the irony of Holly pitted against his boyhood friend

Holly Martins (Joseph Cotten) waits as Harry Lime's Russian-émigrée girlfriend (Alida Valli) makes a fruitless effort to get some information about Harry.

Searching for Harry Lime in the Viennese sewers are British Intelligence Major Calloway (Trevor Howard), the American Holly Martins (Joseph Cotten), and Sergeant Paine (Bernard Lee) of BI.

and leading the chase to destroy him in the bowels of the Viennese sewers was such as to fill one with sadness and nostalgia—a mood which the zither music much enhanced.

The last scene in the picture, when poor Harry had been finally laid to rest in the same graveyard where his surrogate scoundrel had been buried at the start, and his sweetheart, still loyal and defiant, was walking away from the burial all by herself, down a long, empty avenue of bare trees, with only Holly, who had decoyed and betrayed his friend, silently, discreetly standing to one side, watching her, became—thanks to that zither—one of the most touching endings I have seen. All the sadness and social desolation of postwar Vienna were in that scene.

Mr. Greene has subsequently given credit to Mr. Karas and his zither for making it a fadeout of haunting retrospection instead of the anticlimax he feared it might be. I thoroughly agree with his reflection. The lament of the zither still echoes in my mind.

The images of all the actors dwell there hauntingly, too—Mr. Cotten, intense and sweetly naïve, bum-bling clumsily through dark and sinister realms; Mr. Welles, treacherous, headed straight for a violent fate; Alida Valli, remote and defiant as Harry's loyal girl; Trevor Howard, efficient in his duffel coat and beret as Calloway. And others, too, come to mind in vivid profile—Bernard Lee as Calloway's Cockney adjutant, Ernst Deutsch as the one helpful "witness," and Eric W. Ponto and Siegfried Breuer as Viennese types.

Although Mr. Greene has flatly stated (in the preface to the novel he derived from his original screenplay) that he had no wish whatsoever to arouse anyone's political emotions by the cross ruff of international tensions in his plot, and especially the actions of the Russians in trying to capture Harry's girl, there was definitely a sense of smoldering conflict between the Russian and Allied zones. One can still sense the air of Machiavellian intrigue that hung over postwar Vienna from this great film. Not that it was political in any positive sense of the word, but that element certainly was a factor, along with its mystery and romance—and with the character of the zither—that made *The Third Man* the chef d'oeuvre that it was.

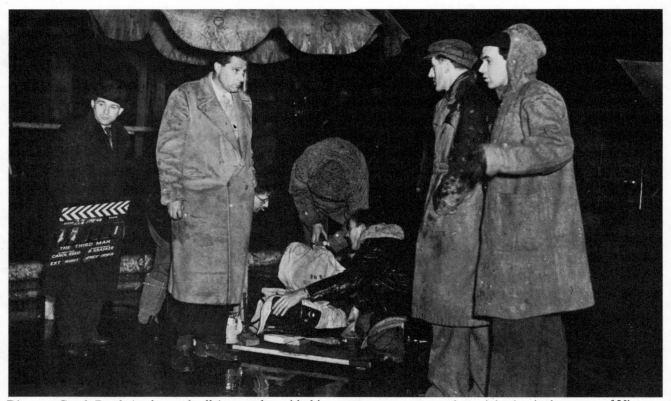

Director Carol Reed (under umbrella) consults with his camera crew on an outdoor night shot in the streets of Vienna for *The Third Man*.

THE LAVENDER HILL MOB

1951

For a period of roughly twelve years, beginning in 1946, there flowed from Britain's small but prolific Ealing Studios a run of such charmingly nimble and witty screen pleasantries that the most flattering thing a critic could say of a picture was that it had the wit of "an Ealing comedy." They were lively, ingenious little pictures on unusual, surprising themes having intimate connection with British locales and personalities, and they were invariably beautifully acted by a loosely knit group of "Ealing types," of which the rising Alec Guinness was a particular boast.

His early appearance in the impish *Kind Hearts and Coronets*, wherein he first showed his versatility by playing a total of eight roles—assorted members of an aristocratic family who had to be eliminated by an ambitious kinsman before he could inherit the family coronet—revealed the particular genius of Mr. Guinness for subtle comedy and started him off on a passage of no less than six Ealing films. Of these, I have chosen *The Lavender Hill Mob* as the most representative of *his* dexterity and of the kind of film made by the studio.

Like so many others of that genre, its cachet was a blithe irreverence toward middle-class morality. Its hero was a mousy bank clerk, peering out from behind his steel-rimmed glasses and from under his squarely set bowler hat, who quietly concocted a maneuver for stealing a fortune in bars of gold, which it was his job to keep an eye on, and smuggling it to France in the form of small souvenir replicas of the Eiffel Tower.

In the first place, the thought of such a caper being conceived and engineered by one of those modest little servants on whom the British banking system relied was itself a delightful impertinence, a jab in John Bull's complacent hide. And the types he got to help him were members of the scrupulous working class. There were a couple of Cockney individuals, faithful family men, but slightly given to pursuing a vagrant quid or two. And the first assistant henchman to the bank clerk, whom of course, Mr. Guinness played, was a genteel but windy high binder played by Stanley Holloway.

This latter individual was as seemingly guileless in his robust way as was the little bank clerk, as much a bastion of the British bourgeoisie. He seemed a hearty fellow, a modest keeper of a souvenir shop by trade and an amateur artist by avocation. As honest as such fellows come. But the moment he heard of the bank clerk's tentative plan in the parlor of the Balmoral Private Hotel on Lavender Hill where both of them lived, and remarked with obvious admiration, "By Jove, it's good we're both honest men!" you knew, first, they weren't and, second, that it would be no time before the scheme was set afoot.

But they had to have what the bank clerk professionally called a "mob" (he was an ardent reader of crime fiction) and, since they didn't know to whom they might turn, they simply stood in a crowded London bus and talked loudly about a large sum of money being in the safe of Mr. Holloway's shop. Sure enough, that night two burglars broke into the shop and were met with cordial invitations to join the mob, which they happily did.

The action from there on was rapid and full of slip-ups, as arranged in the script of Ealing's favorite and most prolific writer, T. E. B. Clarke. The bank clerk was to ride, as was his custom, in the armored van in

Still whirling around in circles after a rapid descent down the stairway of the Eiffel Tower, Holland (Alec Guinness) and Pendlebury (Stanley Holloway) can't quite organize themselves in time to waylay the group of English schoolgirls departing with the last of the precious souvenirs at right.

Pendlebury (Stanley Holloway) and Holland (Alec Guinness) are stopped for lack of tickets as they attempt to board a Channel steamer in pursuit of the schoolgirls, who are unsuspectingly returning to England with their precious gold souvenir miniatures of the Eiffel Tower.

which the bullion was transported from the refinery to the vaults, and his henchmen were to be in various places from which they could converge and hijack the van. But, of course, certain accidents befell them, such as Mr. Holloway being nabbed for unconsciously trying to shoplift a painting in the gallery in which he was supposed to be browsing, and Mr. Guinness had a bit of a problem with the driver of the truck. But eventually, after being detected and chased by the police,

The last of the precious souvenir miniatures is given as a present by one of the innocent schoolgirls (Alanna Boyce) to—of all people!—a London policeman (Meredith Edwards).

they got the gold stashed in a safe place and Mr. Holloway out of the clutches of the law.

Then began the second phase of the maneuver—getting the gold molded into souvenirs and shipped off in innocent packing cases to a helpful merchant in Paris. When all was completed, the four ''mobsters'' celebrated in the Tower Room of a London hotel and, in anticipation of their fortune, got deliriously drunk. Mr. Guinness simulating inebriation was always something to see!

But when Mr. Guinness and Mr. Holloway got to Paris and made a courtesy trip to the top of the Eiffel Tower, what was their horror to discover that their little replicas had not only arrived but, owing to someone's misunderstanding, were already being sold for modest sums. As a matter of fact, the last of them had just been vended as souvenirs to a departing group of English schoolgirl sightseers.

So now began the third round of frenzy, with the fellows tumbling down the steps of the tower (because they couldn't crowd into the elevator), continuing to spin around dizzily when they reached the ground (an old Keystone comedy bit), and chasing off in a taxi after the schoolgirls, who had already boarded the Calais train. Wild confusions with the guards at the train station and with the ticket takers at Calais impeded their pursuit, and they only caught up with their quarry after a convenient dissolve and a cautious and gentlemanly visit to their starchy school.

In ways to which we weren't made privy (such details being blandly overlooked in a farce as fast and furious as this one), they got all the replicas back except one which was stubbornly held onto by a little demon who might have been a harbinger of the swarm of schoolgirl monsters in a later gem, *The Belles of St. Trinian's*. She resisted all their importunities because she wanted to give her souvenir to a friend, who turned out to be a crossing policeman to whom she took it at the Metropolitan Police Training School. There, without further taxation of their frazzled nerves or ours, the two snatched the prize off the table of the policeman and raced out into the street, where they shanghaied an empty police car and beat it away, with other cars after them.

This final chase through the streets of London, with Mr. Guinness confusing the pursuers by giving false information about their whereabouts to the central dispatcher over their two-way radio, was neo-Keystone burlesque, with the whole thing coming to an end

In their hideaway foundry in London, the two ingenious but unlikely smugglers, Pendlebury (Stanley Holloway) and Holland (Alec Guinness), transmute stolen gold bullion into innocent-looking souvenir miniatures of the Eiffel Tower for illegal shipment to France.

when the car of the culprits smashed into that of an innocent motorist, and somehow wires got tangled so that the radio suddenly began blaring "Old MacDonald Had a Farm."

A genial and characteristic epilogue saw the smiling bank clerk walking away with a companion from a sumptuously spread dining-room table in a South American hotel. We had seen him there in the beginning of the film, telling his story and squandering money lavishly. Then we saw he was wearing handcuffs, an Ealing way to let us know the jig was up.

Of course, it was not just the story that was so disarmingly droll. Stories of amateur criminals getting themselves all tangled up in comical situations had been done on the screen before. It was the aspect of seeming innocents so recklessly involved in a project that hardened professionals would avoid as too dangerous, which made this film unique. The acting of Mr. Guinness and Mr. Holloway was so perfectly timed and meshed that their gestures and facial expressions seemed to counterpoint rhythmically, as did Sidney James and Alfie Bass as their Cockney confederates. Charles Crichton, the director, so accurately maintained the pace of the mischief that a viewer could hardly draw a relaxed breath.

Two interesting things I've failed to mention: First, the London police were ridiculed roundly for *their* bumbles, especially when they failed to perceive the little bank clerk, whom they had in custody for a brief period after the hijack, as the proclaimed "mastermind" of the job; and, second, the pretty young thing in the prologue to whom Mr. Guinness grandly gave a princely sum presumably for services rendered was Audrey Hepburn, no less! That gives you an idea. She was then an extra at Ealing Studios!

Other films that Mr. Guinness made for Ealing were *A Run for Your Money, The Man in the White Suit, The Lady Killers* (in which Peter Sellers made his debut), and his only commercial failure, *Barnacle Bill.* Just a few of the other films made at Ealing were *Passport to Pimlico, Whisky Galore* (called in America *Tight Little Island*), and the whimsical *The Tittfield Thunderbolt.*

It was economics (British films seldom sold too well abroad except such immense successes as *Great Expectations* and *Henry V**) and the dethroning of the acknowledged genius loci, Sir Michael Balcon, as studio head that finally brought about the decline of this distinguished institution. The extinction of Ealing Studios was indeed a great loss for British movies and for cinema lovers all over the world.

UMBERTO D

1952

The lonely old Roman pensioner, Umberto D (Carlo Battisti), clasps his sole remaining companion, his dog Flick.

Old age has never been a topic of particular interest to makers of films for a very obvious reason: It is not one that particularly appeals to the vast majority of moviegoers, not even to those who *are* old. Age, at best, is a condition that merely symbolizes the ultimate stage of fulfillment of the work ethic and moral respectability. The place of old people in movies is generally that of genial contrasting characters to those who are young, aggressive, and usually sexual. At worst, old age is a plateau with no horizon except death. It is not a human condition that invites wishful fantasies and dreams.

That is why it was uncommon for Vittorio de Sica to choose to make a film that was totally concerned with the impoverishment of an old Roman pensioner while he was still in the first flush of triumph and success with *The Bicycle Thief.** No one obsessed with box office could possibly have approved his choice of the subject of old age at that particular stage of his career. But de Sica and his favorite scriptwriter, Cesare Zavattini, were bent on making such a film for personal reasons that were heedless of commercial advantage. Being humane individuals, as their previous successes together showed (*Shoe Shine, The Bicycle Thief,* and *Miracle in Milan*), they wanted to dramatize the pathos, and by implication, expose the larger social tragedy of those who had spent their lives working in small white-collar jobs and, when old, alone, and of no more commercial use, were cast aside. Further, de Sica was anxious to make a film that would suitably serve as a memorial to his father, who himself had been a modest pensioner. The consequence of their determination was the classic *Umberto D.*

I still find it vastly unsettling to my emotions and sensibilities to see again this lovely picture, which was a model of simplicity and concentrated neorealism within its limited cinematic frame. For it did nothing more than consider the plight and destiny of its gentle, aging hero who had only the companionship of his dog Flick and the casual friendship of a rooming-house slavey to comfort his loneliness. There was no oversentimentality in it, no playful old codger clichés, al-

Isolated as compassionate friends in a Roman rooming house are the old pensioner, Umberto D (Carlo Battisti), and the pregnant slavey, Maria (Maria Pia Casilio).

On his way to "a new place," the old Roman pensioner, Umberto D (Carlo Battisti), tries to leave his little companion, Flick, at a boarding kennel, but finds he hasn't the heart to do it.

though there were many touches of humor and amusing glints of stubborn character. The only thing that could possibly have rescued the old gentleman from his obvious destiny was a fictional contrivance of some sort, and that the authors would not provide.

Opening on a nondescript gathering of angry, shouting old men in front of a government building demanding payment of their pitifully small pensions—a scene which adequately defined the extent of the social problem before the men were dispersed by the police—the drama was then confined to the endeavors of the one old man to sustain himself and his dog. A stop at a government mess hall where he was surrounded by other old men, all of them neatly dressed in worn clothes and quietly dignified—and where he slipped his own plate of pasta under the counter to feed his dog—then on to his lodging house where he was briefly locked out of his room while a transient couple used it for a "matinee"; it was clear he was in peril of being thrown out by a pitiless proprietress who was demanding his back rent.

Such was the substance of the drama: the feeble but determined efforts of the old man to sell his few valuable possessions—a watch and some scientific books—to give him enough money to hold on to the tiny room he had called home for years. In a pitiable endeavor to stave off immediate eviction, he secretly called a charity hospital and had an ambulance come to fetch him. But, of course, it was a losing battle. When he returned to the rooming house, after an amusing interlude in the hospital, he found his room was being dismantled and that little Flick had been lost. Desperately he went to the dog pound to try to

Departing forever from his meager home of many years, the old pensioner, Umberto D (Carlo Battisti), and his dog, Flick, board a streetcar in the Roman dawn.

find it, and there he blankly observed the matter-of-fact facilities for destroying unclaimed dogs. But de Sica did not dwell on this experience to milk an agonized response or do more than suggest a gruesome metaphor.

The old fellow found his pup and, on the way home, he saw an old man successfully begging. So, in front of the Pantheon, he made a tentative, embarrassed try to stick his hand out for money. But when a

In the portico of the Roman Pantheon, the destitute old pensioner, Umberto D (Carlo Battisti), pauses with his dog, Flick, before making a humiliating endeavor to beg.

passerby stopped and was about to put a coin in his upturned palm, he quickly turned it downward. He could not endure the humiliation of accepting alms. Then he had Flick sit on his haunches and he put his neat black fedora in the dog's mouth, while he himself slid into the shadows of one of the pillars of the ancient building. But this time a friend who was passing recognized the dog and, discovering the old man lurking in the shadows, greeted him cheerily, laughing at the dog and assuming the old man was playing a trick.

This time, back at his lodgings, he found his room totally torn apart, furniture moved out, a hole broken through to another room. The landlady was having the house renovated so she could get married. The silences of the old gentleman, his tacit despair, and the evidences of surrender written on his face and in his eyes were clearly prefatory to the thought of suicide which was implied when he went to the window and looked out upon the glistening street four stories below. But he put the thought from his mind at that point when he turned back and saw Flick lying quietly on his bed.

At dawn the next morning, however, he packed his sole valise and left the house, with only a poignant good-bye to the awakened slavey, who was astonished and saddened by his departure. To her anxious inquiry as to where he was going, he simply said, "I am going

to a new place." And then, his last word to her from down the stairs, where he paused for a moment, was, "Give up the man from Florence," meaning one of the two young soldiers (she wasn't sure which) who had got her pregnant.

An attempt to lodge the dog at a boarding kennel with a payment to the scruffy proprietors of all the money he had was abandoned when the dog showed fear of other barking and snarling animals. So off to the outskirts of the city he went and there, with the dog in his arms, he stood on the tracks at a railway crossing and waited for a passing train to kill them both. But a sudden struggle by the dog to leap out of the old man's arms just as the train came upon them tumbled the old man off the tracks, while the dog itself disappeared. Dazed, the frightened old gentleman stumbled to his feet and looked blankly at the train roaring past, not knowing—and terrified to imagine— what he would see after it had gone by. But as it did, he saw the animal calmly sitting and looking at him on the other side of the track, the image of unshakable trust and undying loyalty.

Well, that was obviously the climax and conclusion of this poignant account. Nothing more could be said or imagined about its abject finality. The rest of Umberto's story was as classically undefined as was that of Charlie Chaplin's put-upon Little Tramp as he walked off into the sunset at the end of one of his films. So de Sica and Zavattini concluded this one similarly with the old man and his small companion frolicking wistfully in the beams of autumnal sunshine down a lengthening alley of trees. It was a fadeout that could be taken as a metaphor for death, for there surely was no other haven for this lonely, abandoned pair.

It was evident that de Sica did not intend or expect this drama to manifest the substance and the logic of a ''well-constructed'' film. At no place was the background of the old man described or explained. He was simply an individual, forsaken and alone—let us say, the personification of the irony of old age, a relic of the past, now possessed of nothing more than pride and dignity.

The fact that de Sica could convey this in the language of visual images, the old man against the setting of the cheap and sleazy rooming house and the hard, cold streets and ancient buildings of a remote, impersonal Rome, was again a token of his cinema artistry. He could animate the life of human beings against the imperviousness of stone. And he used a true Roman for his hero. In Carlo Battisti, a college professor who had never acted before, he had a splendid image of the persona he wished to show: quiet, dignified, impassive on the surface, yet clearly full of anguish underneath, smoldering with moral outrage, indignation, and grief. But he never appeared self-pitying, nor did the authors indulge such a state. He was the ultimate manifestation of the finality of age.

As the slavey, little Maria Pia Casilio was his counterpart in many ways, equally lonely, neglected (except by the young soldiers in the barracks across the way), facing the forlorn prospect of bearing a bastard child, yet brave and maintaining her composure with her measure of dignity. The little things she did for the old man and what he tried to do for her were the sole tokens of human compassion and generosity in the film. For Lina Gennari's landlady was a lump of selfishness and vanity, and all other passing individuals were merely beings that paused for a moment, then went their ways.

I don't imagine anybody, including de Sica, ever got much money from *Umberto D,* but I would think it was one of the most rewarding films the great director ever made.

SINGIN' IN THE RAIN

1952

In my original *New York Times* review of Stanley Donen's *Singin' in the Rain,* which is now generally acknowledged to have been one of the great musical movies of all time, I expressed my enthusiasm for it, as virtually every critic did, but I found the title mystifying. Said I, "It has no more to do with the story than it has to do with performing dogs."

As a matter of fact, I even offered, further along in my review, to give a new spring hat to anyone who could tell me what the point of it was, and I still don't understand why I wasn't inundated with replies. For didn't any of my readers remember that "Singin' in the Rain" was one of the great old song numbers in the first *Hollywood Revue,* a potpourri of random songs and dances, elocutions, and vaudeville skits, thrown together by the people at Metro-Goldwyn-Mayer at the time of the frenzied transition to sound in 1929? And didn't I see, since the topic of the delightful film under review was the turmoil of Hollywood in making the fateful change, that the title of the film was, indeed, as reasonable and likely a choice as could have been made, especially since the song was resurrected to provide the star, Gene Kelly, with the big hit number in the film?

Well, I soon was discreetly enlightened by the people at Metro-Goldwyn-Mayer, and I have long since expressed my apologies to everyone concerned. And I have also claimed charter-member status in the now multimillion-members club which holds that this grand old movie was one of the wittiest, liveliest, and best musicals ever made.

It was also—and this is something which I have continued to find a major joy—unblushingly cannibalistic. It gorged itself on its own medium. For it dared audaciously to spoof its antecedents, the primitive ear-

In one of the great solo dances in screen musical comedy, Don (Gene Kelly) performs the rhapsodic "Singin' in the Rain" piece.

ly sound films, their titanic fumbles with music, cameras, and microphones, and their endeavors to create illusions with machinery its operators knew little about. It was, indeed, unique.

Oh, yes, several films before it had tried to poke irreverent fun at the early moviemakers—the Keystone comics, the flapper stars, and the salad-days producers and directors who wore puttees and gave directions through megaphones. But nothing had yet played such havoc with the problems of the great silent stars in adapting their voices as did the remarkably candid *Singin' in the Rain.*

I maintain that a lot of the credit for it was deserved by Betty Comden and Adolph Green, who wrote the story and the screenplay, and also by Producer Arthur Freed, who, with Nacio Herb Brown, had written the title song for the *Hollywood Revue.* All three were loving votaries of the movies as they used to be and totally steeped in the knowledge and appreciation of the transitional years. The result was a masterpiece script which Mr. Donen, his designers and actors made come to brassy life on the screen.

A cardinal feature of the story was that it began in the silent years and established a hyperbolic concept of Hollywood in those times, with Mr. Kelly aping the behavior of a famous movie star attending the premiere for his latest swashbuckling film, all to set up an ambience of legendary extravagance and bad taste. It was also an occasion to acquaint us with his gaudy costar, a shapely blonde with a guttersnipe voice and a jealous nature, whom Jean Hagen magnificently burlesqued.

Miss Hagen inevitably became the nub of all the technical hang-ups and hassles when sound, the monster, suddenly arrived and made it vital that dialogue and music be hastily dubbed on their new film, *The Dashing Cavalier.* Haughtily resistant, she couldn't come through with a voice. Her lines sounded like back-alley shrieking and her protests were equally shrill. Poor Douglas Fowley as her director was plunged into apoplectic rage, and Mr. Kelly, trying to be fair about it as her costar, was totally nonplussed.

Likewise, the mortally stricken siren was paralyzed when it came to doing some big dance numbers for the

While vaudeville is in flower, the budding team of Cosmo Brown (Donald O'Connor) and Don Lockwood (Gene Kelly) do some lively cultivating on the road to Hollywood.

Though extraneous to the story, the dancing of Don (Gene Kelly) and Cyd Charisse to a medley of old tunes in the "Broadway Ballet" number proves one of the exciting delights of *Singin' in the Rain*.

Before everything went haywire with sound in Hollywood: the popular stars Don Lockwood (Gene Kelly) and Lina Lamont (Jean Hagen) serenely rehearse a scene for their ill-fated silent film, *The Dashing Cavalier*. Under the direction of Roscoe Dexter (Douglas Fowley), Cosmo (Donald O'Connor) provides a bit of music to put them in the mood.

reconstructed film, which would now be given a new title, *The Dancing Cavalier*. Not only was she unable to so much as move her two left feet, but she couldn't have begun to keep up with Mr. Kelly, who was, as everyone knew, a dancing fool. This fact had been carefully established with an early flashback of his boyhood years in vaudeville and in his constant association with Donald O'Connor, who was almost as deft a dancer as he.

Already Mr. O'Connor had demonstrated his nimble feet—and the choreographic ingenuity of Mr. Kelly, Mr. Donen, and himself—by romping through an acrobatic routine to the music of "Make 'em Laugh," and he and Mr. Kelly had teamed in "Moses," a deliciously comic pantomime. And already it had been arranged for Mr. Kelly to have a standby in the wings, ready to go on for the waning Miss Hagen.

This charming standby was Debbie Reynolds, a cute little extra girl, whom Mr. Kelly met at the premiere party (she was there to do an act with other girls

The four principals of *Singin' in the Rain*—Kathy (Debbie Reynolds), Don (Gene Kelly), Lina Lamont (Jean Hagen), and Cosmo (Donald O'Connor)—have a slight problem in communication.

From Don's (Gene Kelly) rhapsodic "Singin' in the Rain" number.

to the music of the pleasantly nostalgic "All I Do Is Dream of You"), and he had taken her off in his roadster, just as was done by the famous-star hero with the little hopeful in the oldie, *A Star Is Born.* As a matter of fact, this opening sequence virtually parodied that famous 1937 film.

So, when Miss Hagen couldn't manage her role, it was capable Debbie who was rung in to help Mr. Kelly and Mr. O'Connor salvage *The Dancing Cavalier* by fitting it with modern-dance numbers, one of which had the three stepping out to the lively air of "Good Morning" and the other—by far the best—had Mr. Kelly splashing about in a beautifully soggy tap dance to the music of "Singin' in the Rain." This number, it is agreed by everybody, was one of the all-time classics from musical films and is probably enshrined in the memory of all the millions who saw it throughout the world.

And, of course, it was melodious Debbie who was slipped in to provide the back-screen voice of the stubbornly insistent Miss Hagen when she was called on for a curtain speech at the film's premiere and was triumphantly revealed when the curtain was torn away. Needless to say, thereafter Miss Hagen was out, Miss Reynolds in.

That is the outline of the story. But, of course, there was much appropriate singing and dancing in the live-

liest Kelly style. Some of the numbers recalled early musical film clichés, such as fashion parades and pinwheel chorus groups of the sort that Busby Berkeley devised. There was a dancing duet with Mr. Kelly and Debbie to the old tune "You Were Meant for Me," and his dancing of "Broadway Ballet" was a rush of acrobatics, which was done to a medley of old songs from early Metro musicals—such honeys as "Broadway Rhythm," "Good Morning," and "The Wedding of the Painted Doll"—with Cyd Charisse stepping out of nowhere at the climax to do a lovely dream dance with Mr. K. And, I might add, they had the courage to kid Louella Parsons, the reigning queen of the Hollywood columnists, in a devastating takeoff by Madge Blake. Under the protocol of Hollywood, that was lese majesty!

But I must come back to that tap dance of Mr. Kelly's in the rain, a wild and joyous display of terpsichorean exuberance when he learned that he was in love. It was a superb exhibition of his volatile spirit and style, a blend of theatrical hoofing and graceful balletic élan. I don't think that any other dancer in movies, outside of Fred Astaire, could match Mr. Kelly in sheer vitality and grace. He was a master, a genius, and a brilliant screen personality. I pray there will always be available good, clean, uncut prints of *Singin' in the Rain*!

133

HIGH NOON

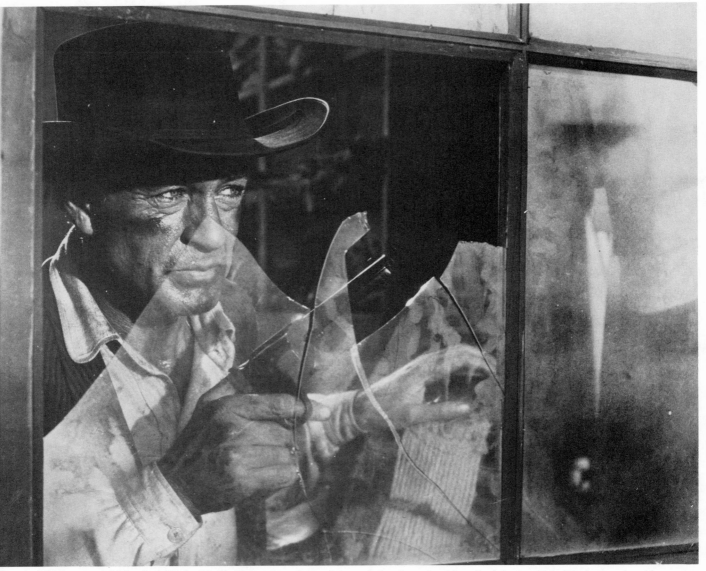

Beleaguered Marshal Kane (Gary Cooper) makes ready to fight alone for his principles and his life in the showdown gun battle in *High Noon*.

1952

Back in the years when Western movies were generally more concerned with the conflicts of good guys and bad guys—good and evil—than they have been in recent years, someone of taste and talent would occasionally grab a handful of clichés from the vast storehouse of Western legend and fuse them into a formidable work of art. Such rare and cherishable achievements may seem antique to some today, burdened as they were with clear moral precepts that may sound naïve in a cynical age. But they had the virtues of substance and unswerving sincerity. Such a film was Fred Zinnemann's *High Noon*, which was based on a tight, selective script by Carl Foreman and produced by Stanley Kramer with Gary Cooper as its star.

One last plea is made by Marshal Will Kane (Gary Cooper) to his Quaker wife (Grace Kelly) not to leave him on this their wedding day in the face of his impending encounter with a vengeful bandit returning to town on the noon train.

I rush to throw in those major credits because here was a celebrated case in which the high quality of the achievement was attributable to a team—a splendid collaboration of harmonious talents and intents. And what they produced was a movie that had not only a full dramatic thrust, a stating and resolution of a vital conflict that began and ended all within the running time of the film, but contained a moral issue and message that were particularly pertinent to its day. That was the need for heroes in a society that was complacent and morally slack.

Like most works of art, *High Noon* was simple—simple in the structure of its plot and comparatively simple in the layout of its fundamental issues and morals. It was the story of a marshal in a small Western town, possibly in northwestern Texas toward the close of the last century, on the day of his scheduled retirement and faced with a terrible ordeal. At 10:30 of a

Marshal Kane (Gary Cooper) fruitlessly beseeches help from the local minister (Morgan Farley) and townsfolk to confront the returning bandit and his henchmen.

Among other discouraging acts, Kane (Gary Cooper) has to punch out his resentful and obstructive deputy (Lloyd Bridges).

Sunday morning, just a few minutes after he had been wed to a prim Quaker miss and had handed over to the justice of the peace his marshal's badge, he learned that a desperado whom he had helped send away for life had been pardoned and would be returning to town on the noonday train with the avowed intention of squaring with him. Already three of his henchmen had ridden truculently through the town and set themselves up at the depot to await the arrival of the train.

Here arose the first big question: Should the marshal slip away as his new wife and several decent citizens reasonably urged him to do, leaving the field to a new marshal, who would be arriving the next day? Or should he face up to the responsibility which he strongly felt was his—that of defending the small town from the lawless tyrant who meant to get back in control. At first he opted for the former, and he and his wife rode away on a buckboard wagon toward a hopefully quiet and peaceful life. But clearly his conscience nagged him. "It's no good," he soon told his wife. "I've got to go back, Amy. They're making me run. I've never run from anybody before." And with that he pulled up the horses and drove back into town.

Now came the second larger question: How was he going to prepare for the inevitable face-off with the desperado? His wife had told him in the wagon that if he would not go away with her now, she would be leaving forever on the train that was passing through at noon. So he knew she was not behind him. Then he found the justice of the peace, who had also helped jail the desperado, hastily packing to leave. Candidly, the justice admitted, "I hope to live to be a judge again." And his deputy, a shifty fellow, turned in his badge in a rage because the marshal, named Kane, would not endorse him to be promoted to the job.

Still firm in his resolution, however, and confident in his belief that he would be able to recruit enough deputies from the town's citizenry to meet the threat, Kane went about getting his forces lined up in the hour he had before the train was due. This time span was made a major factor in the momentum and suspense of the film by frequent conspicuous reference to clocks ticking away on various walls and Kane repeating to those who urged him to leave, "There isn't *time* to get out."

First he went to see a Mexican lady whose favors he had briefly assumed from the desperado, Miller, after the latter was sent to jail, thus compounding the latter's thirst for vengeance, and urged her to get away. She didn't need any urging. She was already clearing

Left alone to face the bandits, Marshal Kane (Gary Cooper) watches his pacifist wife (Grace Kelly) and his former mistress (Katy Jurado) drive off in stony silence to leave town on the noon train.

The shootout begins between Marshal Kane (Gary Cooper), in background, and two of the returned bandits.

out. Then he picked up a handful of deputies' badges and went to the local saloon, which was doing a thriving business in expectation of a gala day. Nobody there would join him. Indeed, he had to hang a sleeper on the jaw of the disagreeable bartender who was willing to bet that five minutes after the train arrived, Kane would be dead. And a citizen from whom he evidently expected assistance was conveniently out when he called at his home.

Slowly Kane's confidence was ebbing as he went to the church, threw open the front doors, and called out bluntly to the assembled congregation, "I need help!" A few young fellows at the back responded bravely when the sudden peril to the community was explained—the peril of Frank Miller returning and taking over the town. But older men rose to counsel caution. This thing was being handled badly, they complained. One flabby reason after another was offered to discourage Kane.

The most respected elder launched into a pacifying speech in which he said that the town was just starting to boom, that it was being looked upon favorably by the big bankers "up north" and that a flare-up of shooting and killing would be bad publicity. Just go away quietly, he advised Kane. "It's better for you

Returning at the last moment to be with her husband, Mrs. Kane (Grace Kelly) finds herself momentarily caught and held as a shield by the bandit boss, Frank Miller (Ian MacDonald), as he moves to a showdown with the valiant marshal.

and better for us.'' Kane looked him up and down grimly, muttered "Thanks," and walked out.

Now came an episode which imaged Kane's mounting resolution and despair. He went to a nearby stable and started to saddle a horse. At that moment, his former deputy walked in and congratulated him (with a slight edge of taunt) for having the good sense to get away. A fight started, and the two men battled furiously (as they always did in old Westerns), until Kane knocked him out. This, in a sense, was the climax. Now there was no escape.

From here on, the movement was directed toward that 12 o'clock date with destiny, and Mr. Zinnemann (and his cutters) endowed it brilliantly with tension and suspense. Already he had been "cutting away" now and then to glimpse the henchmen waiting restlessly at the depot and looking down the tracks toward the horizon whence the train would come. Now, with the camera's contemplation fixed more and more often on that spot and on the clocks ticking off the seconds, a throbbing montage unrolled.

Kane in his office dismissing a final apologetic defector and starting to scribble his last will . . . the pendulum swinging slowly . . . the henchmen buckling on their pistols . . . the congregation sitting silent in the church . . . the barflies lined up tensely, expectantly in the saloon . . . again the pendulum swinging. . . .

Then, faintly, from a distance, came the long-drawn whistle of the train. A fast cut back to the depot caught the henchmen alert and looking off at a small puff of smoke approaching far down the arrow-straight track. The sound and the sight were electrifying. A look of weariness crossed Kane's face as he stepped into the back room and released a simpering drunk from a cell. Then out into the street, now deathly still, he went to stand forlornly alone while the buckboard with his wife and the Mexican lady on it silently passed him en route to the train.

The action thereafter was propulsive—and, I must add, familiar. Miller debarked and joined his henchmen to come stalking four abreast into the town, and Kane dropped into the shadow of a building, awaiting them. Suddenly he stepped out of the shadow, shouted "Miller!" and got off a shot, which dropped one of the henchmen. Now the battle was on. It ended, as always, with Kane, the good guy, gunning down the lot but with a crucial assist, quite unexpected, from his last-minute mind-changing wife.

I hardly need add the acting was superior on every count. Mr. Cooper was at top form as the stalwart, laconic Kane, and Lloyd Bridges was appropriately evil as his sharp-eyed and vicious deputy. Grace Kelly was pretty and pacifistic as the firm-jawed Quaker wife, and Katy Jurado played the Mexican lady with stubbornness and vitality. Thomas Mitchell, as the glibbest advocate of appeasement, Otto Kruger as the justice of the peace, and Lon Chaney as a cynical old marshal were outstanding among a host of small-town backers-out.

One further element of great importance to the effectiveness of the film was a fine musical score by Dmitri Tiomkin, which leaned heavily on a rolling ballad sung by the off-screen voice of the old cowboy star, Tex Ritter, as the credits unreeled. This ballad, later sung on records and radio by the then hugely popular Frankie Laine, went a long way toward attracting a tremendous audience for *High Noon*.

But the foremost appeal was that strong, moralistic account of one man's resolution to face danger in a just and honorable cause. This was a strongly pertinent message at that time when too many citizens were letting Senator Joseph McCarthy and his henchmen bully and frighten them with threats of repression by alleging that they were "Communists." Though, of course, the metaphor was apparent to only a comparative few, it gave to this powerful drama a lasting historical plus.

One further point should be noted: A cynical hint did creep in at the end when Kane, disgusted with the way the townspeople let him down, threw his marshal's badge at the feet of his joyful acclaimers and rode away with his wife. This gave a hint of the trend that Westerns would take in the next twenty-five years, but for the moment it was a cloud no bigger than—well, that puff of smoke from the approaching train.

Yup, this was the kind of movie that I, with regret, must say has generally faded out of fashion. They just don't make 'em like that anymore.

JULIUS CAESAR

1953

Considering the elevated standards that Laurence Olivier set with his British productions of *Henry V** and *Hamlet,* for doing Shakespeare's plays on the screen, one might have feared that an effort to turn the trick fairly in Hollywood was doomed to insignificance by comparison with the British. But not so, as Joseph L. Mankiewicz and John Houseman proved with their brilliant production of *Julius Caesar,* done for Metro-Goldwyn-Mayer in 1953. Their clear and incisive presentation of one of the more familiar and difficult of Shakespeare's plays shaped up most admirably alongside the best that the British achieved.

A mournful Mark Antony (Marlon Brando) stands over the body of Caesar while Brutus (James Mason), one of the conspirators in the assassination plot, attempts to justify the deed to the stunned Roman multitude from the steps of the Senate.

Caesar (Louis Calhern) and his wife, Calpurnia (Greer Garson), flank a solemn and worried Mark Antony (Marlon Brando) as they make their way toward the Senate.

Comparisons are dangerous where Shakespeare is concerned and where quality depends in some measure upon the material being played. Just as Olivier's brooding *Hamlet* was quite different in structure and style from the graphic and extroverted muscularity of his exalted *Henry V*, just so this American *Julius Caesar* was different from those other two—a difference that was forced upon it—and upon its makers—by the nature and contents of the play.

Of course, Shakespeare wrote all his dramas to be played within a modest theater and to be absorbed almost entirely through the channels of the ear. *Henry V* is essentially a compound of aural spectacle. *Hamlet* is a verbal introspection of a singularly complex character. *Julius Caesar* is a cold and caustic study of several men involved in a political assassination plot which is remarkably short on action and long on revealing talk. Its nature is not so evocative of rich images of movement and display such as spring from the vaulting poetry and the highly rhetorical *Henry V* and which came out so grandly through the medium of *motion* pictures and color in Olivier's film. Neither is it of a nature to provoke the kind of intellectual search that is provoked by *Hamlet,* and was also conveyed in the film.

Julius Caesar is a play of clashing interests, of contrasting moralities and ideas regarding man's attitudes toward tyrants as voiced by a handful of men. It is a play in which the characters spend more time making up their minds to do things—or trying to argue one another into action—than they spend implementing their plans. In short, it is a play in which the drama is almost wholly in the faces and mouths of men.

In fashioning the movie, Mr. Mankiewicz arranged that his camera stay close to the participants and to the clashes of personalities. That's where the tempest of ideas, interests, and passions raged. Although the concurrence of physical action was almost entirely confined to the actual assassination of Caesar, to the violent reactions of the mobs, and to the briefly shown, anticlimactic Battle of Philippi at the end, a feeling of turmoil and movement seemed to flow through the whole film.

It began in the opening sequence, with Caesar entering the stadium to receive the applause and adulation of the Roman multitudes, and Cassius and Brutus on the sidelines muttering dark, apprehensive thoughts as to Caesar's tyrannical ambitions and whether this boded ill for the state. It built through the several phases of their conspiracy to destroy the incipient tyrant while praises of him flowed from his partisans— and while an incidental nocturnal tempest symbolized the grave unrest in Rome.

The spirit of intrigue and tension grew when Cassius brought word to the conspirators that the Senate was going to give Caesar the crown, and the cabal led by Cassius and Brutus agreed that the time had come to strike. All of this ominous agitation was seen in the faces of the men and in the telltale groupings of the factions that Mr. Mankiewicz so artfully arranged. Even the plunging of the daggers into Caesar was seen only in the flurry of sudden movement on the edges of the frame and in the look of blank amazement and comprehension on Caesar's close-up face. His tumbling into the arms of Brutus, whom he trusted, and his gasping of the famous *"Et tu, Brute!"* was the image of the agony in his mind. The actual physical violence took place below the frame.

The climax of this play is the great funeral oration that Mark Antony delivers over the body of his slain friend, in which he eloquently arouses the multitudes to cries for revenge. And the unquestioned high point of the movie was the intensity with which this scene was staged and the brilliance with which Marlon Brando as Antony delivered the speech.

Before this film, Mr. Brando had drawn some heavy critical abuse for the calculated style of his acting and the way he mumbled his lines. But his Antony was an achievement of major proportions on the screen. Athletic and noble-browed, he looked the truest Roman of them all. His diction, clear and sharply spoken, cut with the precision of a sword. His performance was the surprise and delight of the film. By the force of it, the piety of Brutus was vindictively overwhelmed,

"Beware the Ides of March," an old soothsayer warns Julius Caesar (Louis Calhern) at the behest of the apprehensive Cassius (John Gielgud).

"Et tu, Brute!" The dying Caesar (Louis Calhern) clasps his treacherous friend (James Mason) at the climax of the brutal assassination plot.

and the subsequent defeat and deaths of Brutus and Cassius at the Battle of Philippi were rendered tediously inevitable.

However, I would say the best performance was that which John Gielgud gave as the lean and hungry Cassius. Perceptive, sarcastic, and intense, his Cassius was the perfect embodiment of the feverish rebel-liousness that Shakespeare put into words. But, then, of course, Cassius was the most clever and forthright realist in the play. If Brutus had followed his wishes at the outset, the play would have been over in Act 3.

As for the Brutus of James Mason, it had depth and authority but lacked a feeling of misguided conviction that would have attracted complete sympathy. Louis Calhern's Caesar was solemn, ponderous, and a bit overblown, conveying less a sense of a dangerous tyrant than of a spotlessly laundered stuffed shirt. Edmund O'Brien's Casca had the glibness of a smooth publicity man, and a dozen or so other good actors were convincing in the lesser roles.

Because of Shakespeare's design to do no more than introduce and allow the wives of Caesar and Brutus to speak a few anxious, wifely words, the appearances of Greer Garson as Calpurnia, great Caesar's historically prudent wife, and Deborah Kerr as Brutus' Portia were little more than ornamental in the film. Happily, Mr. Mankiewicz did not endeavor to fatten their supplementary roles. He properly presented *Julius Caesar* as a distinctly male chauvinist play.

Some critics objected to the use of black and white rather than the artful color of Mr. Olivier's productions. I did not subscribe to that objection. I felt the mood and somberness of black and white more aptly conveyed the essential contrasts of the play.

I don't know how much enthusiasm audiences have for Shakespeare these days. Indeed, I'm not even sure that *Julius Caesar* is studied in modern schools. But I promise that this screen rendering of it is as eloquent and powerful as one could wish, and, for students as well as entertainment seekers, it is worthy to be seen.

A STAR IS BORN

Vicki Lester (Judy Garland) sings ''Swanee'' in the memorable ''Born in a Trunk'' medley in the musical (1954) version of *A Star Is Born*.

1954

Countless film fans were very angry in 1954, when George Cukor's remade version of *A Star Is Born* came out, because this modernized musical drama with Judy Garland as its star was not a carbon copy, or even a reasonable facsimile, of the famous Janet Gaynor-Fredric March drama that was one of the great prewar films of Hollywood. Those who had lovingly committed their memories of the older film to a dim emotional shrine were aghast that this remake did not parallel the original story line, that its ascending star was a *singer,* and that it ran for more than three hours. Such desecration of a memory was regarded as something of a crime!

The resentment was understandable. The original *A Star Is Born* was, beyond any question, a moving and haunting drama in its time, and it called attention to the ironies of fame in films. Its story of a little Midwest farmgirl (Miss Gaynor) who went to Hollywood with the familiar but futile ambition of becoming a movie star and had the miraculous good fortune of catching the eye of a famous male star (Mr. March), who personally started her on the road to stardom, then fell in love with and married her, was one of those romantic fictions of which girlish fantasies were made. But the second part of it, which had her rocketing upward while he plummeted, a victim of his own mean disposition and his uncontrollable addiction to booze, was a sobering revelation of the fickleness of

143

The ever-loyal Vicki Lester (Janet Gaynor) goes through the humiliating experience of getting her drunken husband, Norman Main (Fredric March), released from jail in the original (1937) version of *A Star Is Born*.

fame in Hollywood. And in the end, when he saw the hopeless fracture that this reversal of prestige had caused in their private lives, he walked off into the ocean, with a scribbled endearment left behind.

Even in 1954 this story was distressingly dated, both in concept and in dramatic style. The romantic notion that an unknown, without any prior training or evident skill, could be suddenly catapulted to stardom by chance and intense publicity was a myth of the early days of movies that may have lingered in idealistic minds in 1937, when the original *A Star Is Born* was made. And the unrestrained sentimentality of that old William Wellman film may have worked with prewar moviegoers. But things were different in 1954.

Such stark and corrosive introspections of the natures and behavior of movie stars as were made in Billy Wilder's devastating *Sunset Boulevard** or in Vincente Minnelli's caustic *The Bad and the Beautiful* had got the public accustomed to a realistic and cynical approach. No longer were the younger moviegoers suckers for the old fan-magazine guff of stars being found on stools in drugstores. And the John Gilberts

Drunk and disorderly, the failing film star, Norman Main (James Mason), inadvertently strikes his wife, Vicki Lester (Judy Garland), in a humiliating interruption of an Academy Award celebration.

At a late-night private jam session, the still undiscovered Vicki Lester (Judy Garland) joins with members of her band in the second (1954) *A Star Is Born*, to sing the great torch song, "The Man That Got Away."

The moment of triumph and sadness in the original (1937) *A Star Is Born*, when Vicki Lester (Janet Gaynor) accepted an Academy Award under her married name, Mrs. Norman Main.

of the old days were dead. Further, the boy-meets-girl concoction of the original *A Star Is Born* had been obviously and cheerfully parodied in the opening sequence of *Singin' in the Rain*.

Therefore it was quite reasonable that Mr. Cukor and Warner Brothers should have chosen to do their new *A Star Is Born* as something different in structure and style, to make it a big show with music in which such a talented star-within-a-star as Miss Garland played in their picture could show how well she was able to perform.

To be sure, Moss Hart's rewritten version in which the heroine was a vocalist with a band when she caught the eye of the great male star who was already headed down the skids, was itself not as up-to-date or logical as it might have been. There were mushy areas in it as it traversed the old familiar ground of two mutually needful people being torn apart by their separate vanities, by the imbalance of their occupations, and by the public lives they were forced to live.

But the important thing was that Mr. Hart constructed the story so that emphasis was placed on the upswing of the wife, Vicki Lester, and not the downswing of her husband, Norman Main, who was played in this version by James Mason as a crabby, neurotic

introvert. Where Mr. March's original had been a pitiable but generally likable drunk, Mr. Mason's was devious and self-pitying.

Mr. Cukor, a master at this sort of sentimental story, got the maximum performances from both actors in their dual scenes. Such episodes as their meeting backstage at a Hollywood benefit show, their talking about marrying on a sound stage under an eavesdropping microphone, their bittersweet searching for each other in a million-dollar beach bungalow, their ordeal in a night court when Norman Main had been picked up as a dangerous drunk—these were moments of excellence in the picture. What did it matter that logic was not evident in everything they did, or that we never really fathomed the character of Norman Main? Theirs was a credible enactment of two people trying to grab a wisp of love in an environment and a business where they packaged the commodity.

What made this new picture potent and thoroughly valid in the postwar decade was the vividness of its presentation of a pop singer and her pursuit of her career. With a wonderful repertory of Harold Arlen-Ira Gershwin songs, Miss Garland enhanced this picture with bedazzling melody and, because of her own personal problems (she hadn't done a film in three years

145

before she was got into this one), made it the most mature and moving musical she ever did.

There was the ingenious rhythm number, "Gotta Have Me with You," with which she coaxed the drunken and obstreperous Norman off the benefit-show stage; the haunting torch song, "The Man That Got Away," done at an after-hours jam session in a dim café; "It's a New World," sung by Vicki to Norman on their wedding night in a modest motel (and echoed softly as background music in the suicide scene); "Here's What I'm Here For," sung in the marriage-proposal scene; and "Lose That Long Face," which underscored a sequence of painful anxiety and indecision in Vicki's career.

But, of course, the most fondly remembered of all the songs in the film was the superb "Born in a Trunk," an extensive compilation of the singer's dissertation on her theatrical upbringing, and a medley of old favorite songs such as "Swanee," "Melancholy Baby," and "I'll Get By." This was written by Leonard Gershe and belted out grandly by Miss Garland as a tour de force of singing-cum-pantomime.

And laced through it all were subtle traces of satire of Hollywood, though not as sharp as one might have expected or as apt in its day as the satire in the original *A Star Is Born*. Jack Carson's contentious press agent was not as vicious as was Lionel Stander in the earlier version, nor was Charles Bickford's producer as hard and deceitful as was Adolphe Menjou's subtle portrait of several well-known Hollywood snakes.

But the whole was so thoroughly satisfactory that I could not understand why anyone should have resented its resurrection. For me and for millions of others, a new "Star" *was* born.

P.S. Too late for comment in this volume is yet another musical remake of the yarn, starring Barbra Streisand and Kris Kristofferson, opening late in 1976. If there is still mileage in the bittersweet fable, as I rather suspect there is, it will only adorn with further luster the romantic sturdiness of this Hollywood fantasy.

REBEL WITHOUT A CAUSE

Fantasizing and caricaturing the conventional behavior of young married couples, the alienated Jason (James Dean) and Judy (Natalie Wood) embrace on the staircase of a deserted mansion into which they have broken.

1955

Two violent films recognizing the serious postwar problems of urban youth—an area that had not been invaded by movies up to then—came forth with smashing impact in 1955. They were Richard Brooks' *The Blackboard Jungle* and Nicholas Ray's *Rebel Without a Cause*. Of the two—both of which were impressive—I feel the latter merits citation here, primarily because its subject of deep psychological dis-

turbance and withdrawal among high-school-age children of well-to-do middle-class parents was treated more credibly than was the subject of hate and violence in a New York City ghetto high school described in *The Blackboard Jungle*.

Actually, both films were challenged, strongly at the time they were released, for misleading exaggeration. *The Blackboard Jungle* was felt to go so heavily toward showing the virtually uncontrolled rebelliousness and harassment of teachers in an all-boys' school

that it gave a much too alarming impression of conditions in such schools. Indeed, the American ambassador to Italy at the time, Clare Boothe Luce, refused to attend the Venice Film Festival if this film was shown as the selection from the United States, and it was thus withdrawn from competition on her pronouncement that it was unrepresentative of conditions in any American school.

Likewise, the critical reaction to *Rebel Without a Cause* tended strongly to object that the problems of disturbed and delinquent teen-agers were blamed more on the weaknesses, indifference, and general shortcomings of parents than on any inherent weaknesses in the youngsters. In fact, the parents portrayed in this account *were* such egregiously stupid or neurotic types that it *was* rather difficult to accept them as characteristic of American adults.

The mother and father of the principal character, Jason, who was played with remarkable versatility by James Dean, were exceedingly fatuous people—she a henpecking, domineering type and he a flabby, ineffectual cat's-paw who let himself be ruled by his

In a state of rage and frustration at his parents, Jason (James Dean) flings his father (Jim Backus) about as his terrified mother (Ann Doran) watches helplessly.

Jason (James Dean) pauses to sympathize with the lonely kid, Plato (Sal Mineo), as they are brought together in Night Court.

Alienated from their parents and their fellow high-school students, these three youngsters—Jason (James Dean), Plato (Sal Mineo), and Judy (Natalie Wood)—play out a fantasy ritual at the empty swimming pool of a deserted mansion near Los Angeles.

wife. Indeed, it was his subservience to her, his "chicken" nature, as his son complained, that contributed to Jason's agony. Such were the only indications of parental inadequacy shown. The son seemed to feel his parents were weaklings and that they blamed all their failures on him—their inability to stay settled in any one community, their shallowness in disciplining and directing him—and on his penchant to "get into trouble" and cause them social embarrassment and chagrin.

Likewise, the cause of the reckless living and running around with a bunch of wild kids by Judy, the second lead in the story—a pretty girl played by Natalie Wood—seemed to be simply her frustration in getting affection from her father, who would not let her kiss him, for instance, or show any interest in what she did, devoting himself excessively to her young-er brother, who appeared a spoiled and bratty kid.

And the third lead was a lonely lad, Plato, played by Sal Mineo, who had no companions (until the above two came along), whose parents were separated and who lived alone most of the time with a maid. In short, his cause of withdrawal was an empty, loveless, broken home.

The conjunction of these three youngsters came in the opening scene in a police station, where Jason had been brought for drunkenness, Judy for suspected streetwalking, and Plato for killing small dogs. Here the scope of their alienation and the limitations of their parents' concerns were laid out before the audience in conventional, uncomplicated terms.

So, too, were their individual problems on the opening day of school, when Jason was treated as an alien and severely bullied by a tight group of his peers, and Plato was ostracized until he found Jason friendly to him. Judy was, for the moment, attached to the leader of the bullying group.

An interesting frame of reference for the modern-day problems of these kids was then established with their attendance at a class in a nearby planetarium and hearing (and seeing) a lecture on the vastness and impersonality of the universe, which touched the minds of the more sensitive with an even greater awareness of their insignificance.

Immediately after this lecture, Jason was ambushed and hectored into fighting a furious knife duel with the leader of the gang. Blood was drawn on both sides, and the issue of superiority was then agreed to be transferred to the field of a "chicken run" that evening, when the two lads would test their nerve by driving stolen cars side by side toward a cliff overhanging the ocean and seeing which boy would be the last to leap out.

This contest was staged with extraordinary vividness and a mounting sense of peril by Mr. Ray, who packed into it a strong awareness of the isolation of all these kids in a vacuum of emptiness and self-destructiveness. For instance, just before they started their motors, Jason said to the other lad, "Why do we do this?" And the other, the aggressor, replied, "Well, you've got to do *something*." Then they shook hands, shared drags on a cigarette, and as they got into their cars, the bully said to Jason, "You know something: I like you." In short, a bond of respect and friendliness was formed in that fateful moment.

While racing toward the cliff, the jacket of the leader caught in the handle of his car door and he was unable to open the door and leap out, as Jason did close to the edge. The destruction of the leader in a blazing wreck at the bottom of the cliff—a harrowing parallel to the ultimate destruction of the earth as prophesied by the lecturer in the planetarium—deeply depressed the spirits of all the youngsters. Before leaving, however, Jason spoke to and reached out his hand to the badly shaken Judy, and in this conspicuous gesture of a symbolic bond of sympathy between two lonely, frightened youngsters, the essential theme of need for attachment was poignantly visualized.

From here on, the progression was fatalistic. Jason, returning to his home after significantly ditching the tag-along Plato, found his father doing petty household chores and unable to offer consolation or counsel to his son. The mother joined them, and a scene of despair and recrimination ensued, with Jason finally shouting, "We are *all* involved!"

This vague exchange of innuendos and the failure of the film to pinpoint the causes of conflict and tension may have seemed a weakness at first. But it was precisely this inability of children and parents in situations of this sort to articulate their problems that resulted in irremediable clash. So even though audiences may have felt frustrated and impatient at this point, it was precisely the condition of the characters. I feel sure this is what Mr. Ray meant the audience to feel.

Given no help by his parents, Jason tried to take his anguish to the police, but again he was frustrated by an attitude of do-nothingness. Warned by the bullies who tailed him not to say anything, he got hold of the equally shaken Judy and they sought sanctuary and solace together in the night-shrouded isolation of a deserted mansion near the planetarium. There they were joined by lonely Plato, who was likewise being tailed by the gang. And, in this symbolic vestige of adult waste and decay, they surrendered themselves to fantasizing and mockery, venting their youthful cynicism in parodying grown-up attitudes. But, ultimately discovered by the bullies and then by the police, poor little Plato was killed in a gun duel as Jason and Judy were brought to heel. The terminal scene, in which Jason was promised help by his father, neutralized the essence of the drama, but that could be charitably overlooked.

For all its now recognizable excesses, this film constituted a powerful breakthrough into an area of real social concern. The cover of phony fiction that Hollywood had traditionally drawn across the landscape of teen-age problems and parental inadequacies was ripped, and the topic was out in the open to be more thoroughly probed in subsequent films.

Further, Mr. Dean and Mr. Mineo were exploded into the status of cult heroes for the self-identifying delights of youth. Mr. Dean, with his strangely sullen manner and his defiant individuality, which was helped by his evident imitation of Marlon Brando's original coarse style, especially became the darling of the restless high-school crowd. And Miss Wood emerged as an actress who could give light and shade to serious roles. Unfortunately Jim Backus and Ann Doran were compelled to develop caricatures as the empty parents of Jason. But that was the fault of Mr. Ray, who never quite thereafter reached the heights that he did with this vastly popular film.

SMILES OF A SUMMER NIGHT

1955

Owing to the confusions of commerce, the first film of Ingmar Bergman that achieved a considerable circulation and made a strong impression on moviegoers in the United States was not at all in the vein of the profound and often morbid forays into the perversities of human nature that later became the wont of the director. His *Smiles of a Summer Night* was a delightful comedy that might be compared generically to some of the more sophisticated French comedies such as Jean Renoir's long-suppressed satire on the prewar aristocracy, *The Rules of the Game* (1939), and Max Ophuls' witty debunking of the myths of *l'amour, La Ronde* (1950). Mr. Bergman's marvelously mischievous film, made in Sweden in 1955, opened modestly in New York City in late 1957.

To be sure, it had been preceded by three minor Bergman works borne on the wave of rising interest in foreign-language films, but they were notably inconspicuous by comparison with some of the French and Italian hits. These three were the eclectic *Torment* (1947), for which Bergman wrote the bitter script; *Illicit Interlude* (1954), a wistful, poetic memory of a long-past love affair that was cheaply mistitled; and

The haughty and contemptuous Count Malcolm (Jarl Kulie) coaches his crafty wife, Charlotte (Margit Carlquist), in the aristocratic art of handling an ancient dueling pistol.

The Naked Night (1956), which did nothing to foretell the trend of Mr. Bergman's brilliant career. The last two films had been made by him in 1951 and 1953 respectively, and distributed in America for the sake of their erotic potential.

Following these, Mr. Bergman made two further films which, had they been released here in sequence, might have prepared us for *Smiles of a Summer Night.* They were *A Lesson in Love,* which was also in a distinctly comic vein, and *Dreams,* which bore a certain resemblance to some of the old Hollywood "women's films." But these were not released in this country until *Smiles of a Summer Night* had won for itself a preemptive visa by taking a prize at the 1956 festival in Cannes.

I cite this erratic history simply because it reveals the inadequate preparation we were given for Bergman's darkly philosophic and symbolic *The Seventh Seal**—and because it shows how we first got to know him not as a solemn Strindbergian legatee but as an arch, witty, uninhibited master of urbane comedy.

Shorn of its abundance of characterizations and delicious supplementary details, *Smiles of a Summer Night* was basically an old familiar staple, a delightfully postured bedroom farce, set in Sweden in the early 1900s and rich with comic contretemps. These came in a series of encounters, some solemn, some verging on burlesque, between the neat assortment of egregiously self-centered males and the several varieties of vigorous females who maneuvered to keep them under thumb. The action moved through the elegant chambers of city apartments and a stately country home, but the implicit channel of all maneuvering was toward the boudoirs and the beds.

But I don't want to give the impression that the picture was wholly designed to generate excitement and amusement over the difficulties of people having sex—although this ordinary vital impulse vibrated through the film and was the solvent of its frank eroticism and a lot of its ribald fun. The main thrust of Mr. Bergman's satire was to pillory the pompous Swedish male, full of conceit, extreme pretensions, jealousy

151

The rich and aromatic scene of family and guests assembled at the dinner table, presided over by the wise and all-knowing Madame Amfeld (Naima Wifstrand) in *Smiles of a Summer Night*.

Lawyer Egerman (Gunnar Bjornstrand) introduces his much younger second wife Anne (Ulla Jacobsson) to his former mistress, Desiree Armfeld (Eva Dahlbeck), while his sexually repressed son, Henrik (Bjors Bjelvenstam), inwardly writhes.

Admirers bring presents to the stage star, Desiree Armfeld (Eva Dahlbeck), as her former lover and continuing admirer, the lawyer Fredrik Egerman (Gunnar Bjornstrand), stands by stiffly.

An accomplished play of sexual allurement and patronizing forebearance is exercised by Charlotte Malcolm (Margit Carlquist) toward the pompous Fredrik (Gunnar Bjornstrand) in the beautiful gardens of a Swedish country house.

and hypocrisy, and to show an intense admiration for the wisdom and cleverness of his sexual counterpart, the Swedish wife and mistress (which he implied that all women were potentially).

The leading character was a lawyer, a stiff, seldom-smiling gentleman who had married a considerably younger woman after the death of his first wife. But balancing him in importance was a mature woman who had formerly been his mistress and to whom, in his puzzled anxiety about the unresponsiveness of his still virgin wife, he turned for professional advice. Of course it soon became apparent that he still had a yen for this old flame and would not be averse to indulging his passion and vanity with her again. Unfortunately, just as he was moving toward a sally while visiting in her apartment one night, her current lover appeared. He was even more pompous, being a grimly honor-conscious cavalryman.

The running game of tag between the sexes soon felicitously moved to a beautiful old house in the country where lived the actress' nimble-witted mother, herself an ancient courtesan. And here were further added to the collection: the cavalryman's cunning wife; the dowdy son of the lawyer, whose sexual urges were badly confused with a passion for theological studies; and a voluptuous chambermaid who tried her best to hook the son, but settled contentedly for the coachman in the end.

In the span of a summer weekend, these characters parried and thrust in what I now believe was the most urbane exercise in seduction that I have ever seen on the screen. Philosophical discussions, usually angled toward the exigencies of sex and the anomalies of inclinations restricted by conventions and codes, were deftly interspersed with encounters and confrontations of a purely physical sort that lightly relieved the intellectuality of the whole.

For instance, when the sad theology student, after a disquieting dinner-table debate about the etiquette of seduction and after despairing of his love for his father's wife, attempted to hang himself in his bedchamber, he accidentally pressed a button on the wall. Magically, a music box tinkled, the wall opened, and through it rolled a bed on which the sweet young wife was sleeping. Exit disquiet and despair. Later, in a jealous confrontation between the lawyer and the cavalryman, the latter insisted they salve their honor by a game of Russian roulette. The terrible tension of expecting an explosion each time the trigger of the pistol was pulled was ended with the farcical disclosure that there were no bullets in the gun.

There were no clear conclusions in this picture, no commonplace resolutions. The various characters were ultimately settled more or less in the beds they chose. The only axiom was that the male—at least, the chauvinistic Swedes depicted here, from lawyer to coachman—insisted upon maintaining his Dignity (meaning his male superiority) and that the female could slyly control him by not disturbing *this* fantasy.

There was one further aspect of this picture that could not be overlooked. That was an intensity of natural beauty and its concordant poetry. The shimmer of open country spaces and the mystery of the serene summer night gave appropriate framing to the old manor house and its inhabitants. Clearly, the small emotional hang-ups of the adult characters seemed tremendously childish and trivial in the gauzy half-light of the midnight sun which fell like an eternal blessing upon the ancient lawn. Mr. Bergman's great love for nature and his nostalgia for an atmosphere that embraced his own early memories were manifested here. And this subtly implied a final comment upon the pettiness of human beings who were seemingly insensitive to such beauty and to the wonder of life itself.

AROUND THE WORLD IN 80 DAYS

1956

The burning ambition to do something different, to break away from familiar movie patterns and make a bold try with a new sort of film, is an urge that has stirred moviemakers and producers since the first camera crank was turned. Among the most ambitious was a theatrical producer, Michael Todd, who had staged several kinds of mammoth tent shows and spectacular productions on Broadway before he turned his attention to movies and the inviting possibilities of the new giant screens. Having been involved in the promotion of Cinerama, the projection device that departed radically from the postage-stamp ratio that had been standard since Edison's Vitascope, Mr. Todd was emboldened to make a film that would fill this huge rectangular panel and overwhelm audiences. The vehicle he selected to carry his investment and his trust was the famous old Jules Verne novel *Around the World in 80 Days.*

It was a tale that more cautious moviemakers had passed up for fifty years for the simple and logical reason that it was obvious corn. It was also a much distended story that would call for considerable expense. But Mr. Todd attacked it with the confidence of a lion and the disposition of a carnival showman. He and his professionals produced a mammoth, extravagant, farfetched show that, fulfilling Mr. Todd's intentions, took the public by storm.

The only way to describe it was as a sprawling conglomeration of refined English comedy (at the outset), giant-screen travelogue, specialty acts by international artists, and slam-bang Keystone burlesque. It was noisy with sound effects and music. It was overwhelmingly large in the process akin to Cinerama which Mr. Todd modestly named Todd-AO. And it ran for just onto three hours, not counting intermission. Quite a show!

In a manner suspiciously imitative of the first Cinerama spectacle, it began with Ed Murrow, the popular television commentator, speaking a few well-chosen words and introducing a bit of the old Georges Méliés silent fantasy *A Trip to the Moon.* From this tiny black-and-white primitive, the frame expanded to that of the wide, curved screen and a dazzlingly brilliant color picture of a guided missile being whooshed away into space. This was explained by Mr. Murrow as evidence of how the world does move—all of which was by way of prologue to the nineteenth-century fable of Mr. Verne.

The eccentric pattern thus suggested, it continued expansively, with a rush of improvisation in the subse-

The manservant, Passepartout (Cantinflas), and his wagering employer, Phileas Fogg (David Niven), set off in a balloon for the first stage of their globe-circling adventure in *Around the World in 80 Days.*

Charles Boyer

quent adventures of Phileas Fogg. Once he and his comical valet, the nondescript Passepartout, were launched on their wagered endeavor to circumnavigate the globe in eighty days (remember, this was back in the 1880s, before the jets could do it in about two), anything could happen. And many things did.

In Paris, away from the Reform Club, where Mr. Fogg's audacious wager was made with a group of solemn London clubmen who looked a lot like familiar movie stars, the travelers did a bit of quick sightseeing and then embarked in a gaudy balloon which lifted them above a stunning layout of rural landscapes and chateaux to the surging music of the theme song, "Around the World." Crossing the Alps,

The balloon bearing Phileas Fogg and his servant Passepartout floats over a Spanish city in an early stage of their globe-circling adventure.

they scooped some snow from a handy peak to chill a bottle of champagne and, with a bit of geographical license, they landed their balloon in Spain.

This was a casual convenience which allowed Mr. Todd to introduce José Greco and his troupe of Spanish dancers in some handsome flamenco stomps. It also allowed the great Cantinflas, who played the absurd Passepartout, to enact his popular burlesque of bullfighting which he used to do perennially in his native Mexican films. Then the duo proceeded to Egypt where, on the sun-drenched banks of the Suez Canal, they encountered Fix, the archdetective, who became the comical nemesis of their further journeyings.

In India they met a princess in the form of Shirley MacLaine who thereafter became a companion in their adventures. They plunged through a studio jungle atop a rampaging elephant. In Siam they watched a magnificent myriad-oared royal barge moving upon a placid river. They rode ostriches through the streets of Hong Kong. In America they fought off whooping Indians from a rolling and rocking Western train, an experience that was made almost as dizzying as Cinera-

Red Skelton, George Raft, and Frank Sinatra

Marlene Dietrich and Frank Sinatra

Noel Coward

A GALLERY OF DISTINGUISHED PERFORMERS APPEARING IN CAMEO ROLES IN *AROUND THE WORLD IN 80 DAYS*

Beatrice Lillie

Buster Keaton (center)

The ever-adventurous Passepartout (Cantinflas) is barely dragged aboard a train in India by his considerate employer, Phileas Fogg (David Niven), in the fast-moving, wide-screen spectacle film, *Around the World in 80 Days*.

Noel Coward and John Gielgud.

A cheery game of cards is played by the wily detective, Fix (Robert Newton), Indian Princess Aouda (Shirley MacLaine) and the globe-circling Passepartout (Cantinflas) and his employer, Phileas Fogg (David Niven), as they ride across the American West.

Another redskin bites the dust as Indians attack the train bearing Phileas Fogg and his servant, Passepartout.

ma's famous roller-coaster ride. And, during a stormy crossing of the Atlantic in an antique ship, they stripped the old tub for firewood, in recollection of a Marx Brothers film.

Let it be said for Michael Anderson, the director, that he did a remarkable job in even keeping the picture going with some forty guests to be put up in cameo roles. Outside of Cantinflas and David Niven, who was charming as the punctual Mr. Fogg, and Miss MacLaine and Robert Newton, as the sneering, sinister Fix, there were such brief performances as those of the elegantly suave Noel Coward as a London employment agent, Charles Boyer as a Paris travel-office clerk, Ronald Colman as a pukka sahib, Marlene Dietrich as a dance hall hostess, and Buster Keaton as the conductor on the Western train.

There were and still are cinema purists who gravely questioned whether Mr. Todd succeeded in improving the breed of motion pictures with this extravaganza. The unities of content and structure were not detectable in its wildly sprawling form. But I feel sure that Mr. Todd's only intention was to entertain an audience for three hours. And he did that. In fact, there's still tremendous entertainment and novelty in this famous film, and it is too bad that it isn't shown in all its glory from time to time today.

To propel the ship of the globe-circlers across the North Atlantic, passengers and members of the crew, such as Victor McLaglen, Andy Devine, and the omnipresent Passepartout (Cantinflas) strip off all available wood to feed the boilers.

162

Passepartout (Cantinflas) tries to outrun a troop of Indians as they attack the train bearing Phileas Fogg across the American West.

The great flamenco dancer Jose Greco comes in for a lively interlude in the action-filled wide-screen spectacle, *Around the World in 80 Days*.

Colonel Nicholson (Alec Guinness) watches in disbelief as a young British commando (Geoffrey Horne), discovered in the act of attempting to dynamite the crucial bridge on the River Kwai, plunges a dagger into the Japanese commander, Colonel Saito (Sessue Hayakawa).

THE BRIDGE
ON THE RIVER KWAI

1957

Of the several exceptional motion pictures made about World War II after sufficient time had gone by to allow scholars and writers to ponder it philosophically, the most profound and powerful, not to mention engrossing, in my book was David Lean's *The Bridge on the River Kwai.* Not one of the several that hindsight may now deem worthy to compare with it—not Sam Wood's *Command Decision,* or William Wellman's *Battleground,* or Henry King's *Twelve O'Clock High,* or Billy Wilder's *Stalag 17*—had quite the scope and penetration of this amazingly comprehensive film, nor did they probe as many disturbing areas of military attitudes and minds.

There were actually two separate dramas in it (three if one chose to define the supplemental running adventures of an American sailor who early escaped from the focal prison camp and battled his way to freedom as a subsidiary drama all by itself). The first was a per-

An impatient Japanese prison camp commander, Colonel Saito (Sessue Hayakawa), strikes the British Colonel Nicholson (Alec Guinness) because he refuses to order his fellow officers in the camp to do manual labor in helping to build a crucial railway bridge.

Still defiant and unshakable after days of torture in the "sweat box" of a Japanese tropical prison camp, British Colonel Nicholson (Alec Guinness), is being taken for further brow-beating by the Japanese commander of the camp.

sonal drama of a conflict of wills between two men: the veteran Japanese commander of a miserable prisoner-of-war camp in the steaming Burmese jungle and a captured British colonel brought there with a batch of British prisoners to help the Japanese build a vital railway bridge.

The second was a tingling action thriller that dovetailed neatly with the climax of the first, concerning the adventures of a group of commandos sent to blow up the bridge when it was found by British Intelligence that the prisoners had almost completed it.

Such layering of drama upon drama in this almost three-hour-long film, projected on the wide screen in color for spectacular cinema effect, resulted in a towering entertainment of rich variety and revelation of the ways of men trained for and caught up in the tangles of a worldwide, unorthodox war.

Yet, significantly, there wasn't a scene of warfare in it, not in the ordinary sense of the word. Not a battle was fought, not an aerial dogfight, not even a clash between small forces of men. The only shots fired in anger were a few at escaping prisoners and a splattering fusillade that occurred at the climax of the second part when the Japanese discovered the commandos attacking and desperately tried to prevent them while the commandos effectively fired back.

That was because the picture was not about fighting as such or, indeed, about the problems and conflicts that occurred on the higher levels of command. It was about the fundamental nature of military commitment, discipline, and fortitude—about the anomalies of military training that prepared men to perform according to codes and resulted very often in reactions that might be expected from automatons. In short, it was about the hideous errors that might occur as the consequence of training men for waging war.

The foremost example of such confusion was the British colonel who, when he marched into the prison camp at the outset, leading a company of ragged men, disarmed and apparently exhausted but bravely whistling "The Colonel Bogey March," appeared a man of great bravery and resolution albeit a martinet—a legendary type of British officer. And when he stood up to the Japanese commander and firmly refused to order his officers to do manual work on the bridge because that would be a violation of the international Acts of War, he seemed magnificently heroic.

Likewise when he stood up to bullying, painful tortures, and even threats of death for refusing to do as

Colonel Saito (Sessue Hayakawa) prepares himself for the ritual of hara-kiri when he realizes he has been outwitted by the stubborn British Colonel Nicholson. He is spared that fate, however, when the latter allows him to save face.

The American Navy man, Shears (William Holden), and the British engineer, Major Warden (Jack Hawkins), are members of the commando team sent to blow up the bridge on the River Kwai.

demanded, he had our strong sympathy. This fellow appeared through all these ordeals (which were pictured most vividly by Mr. Lean) to be the stalwart upholder of his stated dictum, "This is where we must win through!"

But then, as the Japanese commander, who had seemed as rigid and determined as he, slowly capitulated because of the need of getting on with the bridge, called the British colonel into his quarters and began to bargain with him, the smell of a curious appeasement began to pervade the air. And as the crafty colo-

The British Colonel Nicholson (Alec Guinness) is brought from torture in the "sweat box" to confront the Japanese commander of a jungle prison camp, Colonel Saito (Sessue Hayakawa).

nel subtly assumed the upper hand in a series of shrewd negotiations, we saw his true mettle. He was not moved by resolution to obstruct the construction of the bridge and thus impede the Japanese war effort, which one assumed he was most determined to do; he was concerned with maintaining the letter of a professional military code. In short, he was shockingly uncovered as a "by the book" military man. He was willing to have his officers render their service for what *he* considered an "honorable" *quid pro quo*.

And once he had made that adjustment, he was quite as vigorous and efficient about building a bridge for the Japanese as he would have been about building one for his own country. He pitched happily into the project, strengthened the morale of his men, and even dragged some of them from hospital—to a variation on "The Colonel Bogey March"!

Meanwhile, at British headquarters in Ceylon, a small commando force was being trained and readied for the mission of going in and blowing up the bridge. Some information about its construction had been brought to them by the escaped American gob, who was "persuaded" by a bit of arm-twisting—another military ploy—to go along. The commandos began their mission all unwitting of the arrangement that had been made.

Their passage through the jungle, with many perils along the way but with a clutch of little Burmese girls to help transport their equipment and presumably minister to their personal needs, was recorded by Mr. Lean's cameras with superlative detail and suspense. When this group reached its destination and saw what was going on, they were as totally unprepared for the climax of the mission as was the audience.

167

Colonel Nicholson (Alec Guinness) struggles with a British commando (Geoffrey Horne) to prevent him from blowing up the crucial Japanese bridge on the River Kwai.

There on the bridge they saw the colonel, in full uniform and proudly ready to join the Japanese in a dedication ceremony. The night before, under cover of darkness and in anticipation of the opening, the commandos had set the dynamite charges and stretched the wires under water to the spot where one of them would plunge the detonator. Everything was properly arranged to blow up the bridge at the moment the ceremonial train started across.

But then, at almost the last moment, the colonel became alarmed. He saw exposed on the edge of the river those telltale wires. Scuttling down the bank to the river with the Japanese commander at his heels, he began to follow the wires to the spot where a young commando was waiting to explode the charge. Seeing him, and realizing that he was about to reveal the plot, the commando leaped out from cover, plunged a knife into the Japanese, and yelled to the British colonel, "I'm a British soldier! Commandos! We're going to blow up the bridge!"

Then the colonel saw the detonator and, realizing

what was afoot, shouted in absolute horror, "My God, you can't do that!" And, in an outraged frenzy, he violently attacked the lad. The British colonel had become so obsessed with building a bridge for the enemy—it could have been a bridge for anyone, so long as it was "regulation"—that he was ready to protect it with his life.

Thereafter the action was frenzied. The young commando tried to return to the detonator, with the colonel after him. Another commando, the American gob, came plunging across the river to kill the colonel, a sniper's bullet got the younger commando and then the American and the colonel were both blown up by a mortar shell shot from a commando post on the opposite hill. And the dying colonel, stumbling forward, ironically fell upon the plunger of the detonator and thus blew up the bridge himself.

Watching this horrendous shambles from another hilltop, a captive British medical man who had tried to discourage the colonel and then had removed himself from the whole thing, dumbfoundedly muttered, "Madness! Madness!"—a comment that obviously applied not only to this monstrous folly but to the madness of man in waging wars. And, on that echoing note, the picture closed.

In portraying the British colonel, Alec Guinness was superb, constructing a character of subtle psychological contradictions. For all the man's concern for his subordinates, you could see that he was essentially a snob; for all his sharp wit in contending with the Japanese commander, you could sense he was a fool. To him the vast magnitude of warfare was of no consequence or concern. His sole responsibility and interest was in preserving *his* authority and in getting on with his job.

This rigid militarist shown by Mr. Guinness stands memorably alongside the famous Prussian portrayed by Erich von Stroheim in *Grand Illusion.** He too was a stiff professional soldier who could not understand anything but living by the code. The thought of such inhuman men having sway over the lives of others is enough to turn one to stone.

As the counterpart to the British colonel, the Japanese commandant, played by the veteran actor Sessue Hayakawa, was even more ruthless in his nature. Jack Hawkins was tough and sardonic as the leader of the small commando band, and William Holden played the cynical and supercilious American gob. James Donald as the medical officer, Geoffrey Horne as the young commando, and Andre Morell as a British Intelligence colonel were fine in these lesser roles. And Carl Foreman deserved extensive credit for the script which he derived, anonymously, from the novel by Pierre Boulle.

A few of my readers protested, at the time the film came out, that I was unfair in perceiving the British colonel as a characteristic military type. "His action clearly revealed a mental disturbance quite apart from his army career," one of them wrote. Perhaps. But he was certainly representative of those weaker men whose personalities and doctrinaire training lead to militarism at its worst. And if one thinks such men vanished with World War II, just recall some of the horrible atrocities committed under the orders of rigidly disciplined American officers in Vietnam.

Yes, there is deathless drama and lasting meaning in *The Bridge on the River Kwai.*

GIGI

On the beach at Trouville, Gigi (Leslie Caron) and Gaston (Louis Jourdan) besport themselves on donkeys while Grandma Alvarez (Hermione Gingold) and the gay old boulevardier, Honoré (Maurice Chevalier), watch the flirtation approvingly.

Plagiarism of one sort or another, from clever cribbing to outright theft, has been so common in the making of movies that few people, aside from the victims, even tend to notice it. But there was one instance of "appropriation" so remarkable and adroit that I found it not only delightful but also eminently justified. It occurred in the making of *Gigi*, an outstanding and memorable musical film which Arthur Freed produced and Vincente Minnelli directed for Metro-Goldwyn-Mayer in 1958.

In this instance the act was committed by the very people who were the creators of the material by which they were inspired. They were Alan Jay Lerner and Frederick Loewe, the librettist and composer of the book and score of the brilliant Broadway musical *My Fair Lady,* which had been running in New York for three years when *Gigi* hit the screen. And their key collaborator on *Gigi* was Cecil Beaton, creator of the costumes, scenery, and production designs, which were remarkably recollective of those he had done for *My Fair Lady* just a few years back.

How could such a thing have happened? And how could it have resulted in a film of such felicities as *Gigi*, which thereby stole a march of six years on the film version of *My Fair Lady,* which in turn was thus made to look itself almost like a plagiarism when it finally came out? The story of that little complot is a saga all by itself.

My Fair Lady, which was based on the stage play *Pygmalion* by George Bernard Shaw, and had to do with the phenomenal transformation of a London Cockney flower girl into a lady of spectacular style and charm, had started its run on Broadway in 1955 and had instantly become a dazzling success. Indeed, so formidable was it as a stage production that the likelihood of its ever being made into a film within the lifetime of living people appeared slim. Screen rights were bought by Jack Warner with the understanding that the film could not be made until the stage show had played out, and no one could even guess when that would be.

It was under these circumstances that the clever and creative Mr. Freed had an inspiration. For years he had been enamored of a story by the French authoress

Gigi's crafty grandmother, Mme. Alvarez (Hermione Gingold), her intended paramour, Gaston (Louis Jourdan) and Gigi herself (Leslie Caron) get deliciously high in this playful scene celebrating "The Night They Invented Champagne" from the musical *Gigi*.

Gigi (Leslie Caron) is given her first lesson in the art of feminine grace and coquetry by her thoroughly accomplished great-aunt, Alicia (Isabel Jeans).

Colette about a little French girl named Gigi who lived in Paris with her grandmother at the turn of the century and was being raised by the grandmother and a great-aunt with the idea of her becoming a high-class courtesan. Does that sound somewhat similar to the story of the Cockney flower girl who was studiously transformed into a great lady? A pure coincidence, of course. Anyhow, Mr. Freed acquired the screen rights to *Gigi,* which had already been made as a French film and as a Broadway play (which, incidentally, had Audrey Hepburn in the title role—the same Miss Hepburn who later starred in the film version of *My Fair Lady*) and set out to make his musical film.

Again—we must assume by sheer coincidence—he got Mr. Lerner and Mr. Loewe to prepare the screenplay, the lyrics, and the musical score, and he got Mr. Beaton to follow closely with the production design and costumes. And, of course, we can only conjecture that it was by sheer accident that what they brought forth was material so similar to that of *My Fair Lady* that it must have surprised the gentlemen themselves.

This was apparent almost at the start of the film with the colorful introduction of the lively heroine. She was a bright little teen-age tomboy, athletic and lyrical, and highly resistant to the notion, insisted upon by her grandmother and her great-aunt, that she should grow up. Particularly was she resistant to their intention that she should dutifully acquire all the graces and accomplishments of a lady so she could take her place in the world as a courtesan. But the idea of "love" repelled her, and she let us know it early on in a lively song expressing her contempt for all the niceties of refined romance, "I Don't Understand the Parisians (making love any time they get a chance)."

In time, however, and with a great deal of artful pushing and tutoring by the great-aunt, who herself

Gaston (Louis Jourdan), Liane (Eva Gabor) and Honoré (Maurice Chevalier), celebrate in song at Maxim's in Paris.

had been a famous mistress in the years of *la belle Époque*, little Gigi began to catch the eye of an elegant and blasé young gentleman, a friend of the family, for whom her favors were tacitly being prepared. From looking upon her with emotional detachment as a merely amusing child, he suddenly realized that she was a young woman whom he incredibly adored. In short, he had become accustomed not only to her face but to all the other endearments that she had so delightfully acquired.

Well, that was the gossamer story, very similar to *My Fair Lady,* you must agree. But the story was only the beginning of the charm of the film. In the first place, the decor and the costumes, brilliant in color on the large screen, gave a delicious, idealized picture of Parisian elegance at the golden century's turn. The vividness and flash of all the places of which one had thrillingly heard—Maxim's, the Tuilleries Gardens, the Bois de Boulogne, the fashionable seaside resort of Trouville—were lusciously represented. And the extravagant costumes, of the gentlemen as well as the ladies, compounded awe and wonder on a geometrically accelerating scale.

And the cast—well, it's difficult to give you a fair description of the crispness and charm of every actor in it. Little Leslie Caron, who had made a major hit in the musical *Lili,* was superb as the mischievous Gigi, and brought a particular loveliness to those scenes wherein she conveyed the hesitation of the girl on the verge of womanhood. Louis Jourdan was handsome and tender as the gay blade, and Hermione Gingold

and Isabelle Jeans made a droll pair of artful schemers as the lusty grandmother and the aging, porcelained great-aunt.

But I suppose we must give honors equal to those herewith accorded Miss Caron to our old Gallic friend, Maurice Chevalier, as a cheerful old rip who got involved, as another good friend of the family, in the affair. Indeed, his smiling performance of an aging boulevardier who viewed the whole scene of shrewd connivance with delightful approval and joy, and who sang as his own observation the now classic "Thank Heaven for Little Girls," and also joined with the rococo Miss Gingold in the sardonic "I Remember It Well," was a richly appropriate capstone to his long cinematic career. It left us all with the feeling that M. Chevalier was still our old Parisian pal, despite the briefly muttered rumors he had been a cat's-paw of the Nazis in World War II.

Of the songs, Mr. Jourdan's soliloquy to Gigi ("Gigi, am I fool without a mind or have I merely been too blind . . .") was undoubtedly the loveliest and the best, a gracious love song full of romantic ardor. But I also loved the gay, effervescent number "The Night They Invented Champagne," sung by Miss Caron, Miss Gingold and Mr. Jourdan in a whirl of bibulous joy, and Mr. Jourdan's wistful torch song "She's Not Thinking of Me." Finally, M. Chevalier's reflective "I'm Glad I'm Not Young Anymore" appropriately rang down the curtain on this supremely stylish, happy film.

THE 400 BLOWS

1959

Whoever it was that invented the label *"la nouvelle vague"* ("the new wave") for the spate of markedly "different" movies that came from a group of virtually unknown French filmmakers in and around 1959 must have had a premonition of the purging effect these films would have not only upon traditional French film culture but upon the character of cinema throughout the world. Within the span of one year, the deadening conventionality that had been evident in the decreasing output of French movies since World War II (with three or four prominent exceptions) was smashed by this onrush of films which could be compared in the motion picture medium to the paintings of the French Impressionists and to the effect they had on the standards of the established Paris Salon.

Why such a development should have happened in an overwhelming rush was due to several circumstances, as well as to coincidence. The older, familiar French filmmakers—men such as René Clair, Marcel Carné, Jacques Becker, Jean Delannoy, and Jean Cocteau—were less and less able to get financing, largely because the expense of their ways of making pictures was too exorbitant. The French film market was declining to an alarming degree. Producers would not risk their money on extravagant, repetitious stuff.

Meanwhile, there had been burgeoning within numerous small film societies, and especially under the influence of the famous Cinémathèque Française, a horde of young film addicts with expansive and nonconformist tastes, yearning for films that would be reflective of the changing world in which they lived. Their Bible was *Cahiers du Cinéma,* a forthright publication for which some of them wrote aggressive and challenging critical reviews, and their sources of inspiration were in such diverse areas as the early and independent films of Alfred Hitchcock, Orson Welles, Howard Hawks, and the postwar Italian neorealists and the Free Cinema movement then waxing in England.

Foremost in the minds of these young people, some of whom were making attempts at their own short film productions, was to free French movies from conventionality, to bring them more in accord with the way

Antoine (Jean-Pierre Leaud) and his buddy René (Patrick Auffay) contemplate the seductive photos outside a Paris cinema while on a spree of playing hooky.

Antoine (Jean-Pierre Leaud) daydreams among his variously studious classmates in this scene from François Truffaut's *The 400 Blows.*

175

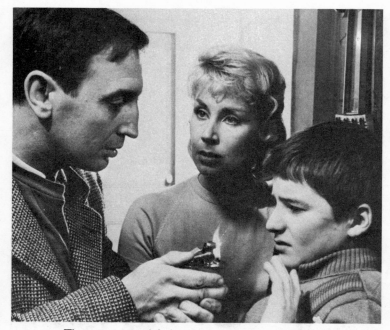

The exasperated father (Albert Remy) attempts to teach his son, Antoine (Jean-Pierre Leaud), a lesson on playing with fire, while the boy's mother (Claire Maurier) looks on.

An ill-used and bewildered Antoine (Jean-Pierre Leaud) looks out from behind the high enclosure of the reform school to which he has been sent in *The 400 Blows*.

people were thinking and living in a France full of problems, anxieties, and strife. Their cry was for realism—with style less important than substance, with story and character the chief concerns.

By coincidence and strokes of good fortune, several young hopefuls obtained the modest advancement to make pictures within the span of a few months, mainly because they offered to deliver feature films at limited costs. Stars were out of the question. They would use comparative unknowns. And expensive productions were precluded. They would shoot their films in the streets and in other natural settings, the way the Italians did after the war when they had little money for production but plenty of stories to tell.

That is why François Truffaut's superlative *The 400 Blows* opened in Paris within the same month as Alain Resnais' *Hiroshima, Mon Amour,* and both preceded by only a few months Jean-Luc Godard's *Breathless* (*A Bout de Souffle*) all of such varied distinction they merit recollection in this book. In addition, there was Claude Chabrol's *Le Beau Serge* and *The Cousins,* Louis Malle's candid *The Lovers,* and Marcel Camus' *Black Orpheus,* not to mention a cluster of others that were considered new wave entries within the year.

The 400 Blows is sometimes thought of as a juvenile tragedy, on the order of Vittorio de Sica's *Shoe Shine* or René Clement's classic *Forbidden Games.** I do not consider it tragic, as it details the haphazard drift of a thirteen-year-old Parisian youngster into a state bordering on delinquency because of neglect by his bourgeois parents and harassment by an obtuse teacher in his school, who moaned in exasperation at his pupils, ''I pity France in ten years!''

Actually, the first half of it was a delightfully roguish display of the freewheeling nature of this youngster as he larked among his classmates in school (calling down the wrath of his teacher), rambled with a like-natured pal through the redolent streets of Paris, went to the cinema, and rode on the whirling rotor in a cheap amusement arcade. Here his disposition toward freedom was that of any normal, healthy boy, and the spirit of it was complemented in these scenes of his perambulations by Jean Constatin's lyrical musical score.

Even when he entered the tiny and cluttered apartment where he lived with his parents, he was cheerful and mischievous so long as his elders were not there to nag him and he was free to let his boyish fancy roam. But when they came home with their vexations, especially the mother, and bore down on him with peevish complaints and household orders, his mood became stolid and subdued, and—for those who were keen enough to notice—the lyrical music expired.

Obviously these were not unusual or discouraging experiences for a boy who was born and brought up in a conventional and dull middle-class environment. And Truffaut made no effort to make it appear that they were. He detailed dispassionately the average monotony of a home where the table had to be set, the garbage taken out, and the greatest cultural stimulation was the father's supreme enthusiasm for his neighborhood auto club. These were, indeed, the honest details that made the ambience of the film so natural, unsentimental, parochial, and recognizable.

The first hint of unsettling discord came when the boy caught a glimpse of his mother surreptitiously kissing a strange man in the street, and when she came home late that evening and he heard her and his father quarreling in their room. This was a shock which Mr. Truffaut casually passed along, but it clearly disturbed and puzzled the laconic and sensitive boy. For, the next day at school, he told his teacher, as an excuse for having played hooky the day before, that his mother had died; and this initially amusing and characteristic boyish deceit led to distressing consequences. The parents were summoned to the school and, before the whole class, the father impulsively slapped the boy.

This was his first humiliation and the beginning of his emotional drift from dependence upon his parents to a bland sort of self-reliance. One runaway from home led to another, and eventually he was expelled from school because he lifted a whole passage from Balzac (his favorite author) for a homework theme. (The establishment of his passion for Balzac, incidentally, was one of the charming and significant bits in the film—a moment of comic confusion in the apartment when a candle the lad had lighted in a private shrine to the author set fire to some draperies.)

But the real shock and disillusion came when he was caught in the act of lifting a typewriter from his father's office (he was actually trying to return it when he was nabbed), and his father, now baffled and disgusted, took him to the police. This was the ultimate betrayal by those who should have been on his side, should have had sufficient insight into his nature to perceive and direct his growing up.

From here on the fate of the youngster was in the hands of the authorities, who obviously had no more knowledge of how to treat him than his parents or his teacher had. From a bleak, bewildering night in a police cell with a rabble of petty culprits and whores, the lad was passed on to a succession of correctional insti-

Final freeze shot of Antoine (Jean-Pierre Leaud) summarizes the poignancy of Truffaut's *The 400 Blows*.

tutions, so called, where the harshness and stupidities of the officials were roundly flayed by Truffaut. For instance, one scene in which the youngster was questioned by a psychiatrist was a classic synthesization of insight and subtle ridicule. It was done in one long set-up, with the lad squarely facing the camera and answering with magnificent equivocation the fatuous questions that were thrown at him by an off-screen woman's voice.

The final scene—or long sequence—was the peak

177

of the picture's irony. Here the boy, committed finally to a rigid and rather militaristic correction school, seized an opportunity to break away from a routine soccer game and run in desperation toward the sea—the great timeless symbol of freedom that he had previously expressed a longing to behold. Past farms, junkyards, and barren landscapes, he finally came to a wide, open beach, with the sound of the surf roaring loudly against a plaintive musical theme. And there, at the edge of the water, he looked seaward, hesitated, then turned back to face the camera (the audience) with bewilderment and pleading in his eyes. Upon that ambiguous image the camera closed in, froze—and the screen went blank.

The 400 Blows was a picture about a boy, yes—and what a boy, with a wonderfully firm and sensitive nature as revealed by the amazing new Jean-Pierre Léaud. But the lad was not the only one for whom compassion was realized. There were the shallow, ineffectual father (Albert Remy)—actually not his true father at all but the man who had generously married the mother when she found herself with child—who tried so hard to be good; the restless, attractive mother (Claire Maurier) who had evidently, at one time, been a prostitute and who now felt bitter and cheated by the life of drudgery she had to endure; the teacher (Guy Decomble), a middle-aged mediocrity who was tired and bored with his profession, and several others who were Parisians to the core.

As I've said, I had no feeling of tragedy at the end of the film—no hopelessness, as in *Shoe Shine*—only a feeling of sadness for the wrongs and mistakes that had occurred. And I think Truffaut felt the same way, for the story was acknowledged by him to be very much the story of his own haphazard boyhood. And certainly *he* wasn't plunged into a manhood of vengefulness and crime!

No, *The 400 Blows* was essentially a classic "true picture" of youth and a poignant lament for those poor adults who no longer knew what it was to be young.

BEN HUR

This scene of the chariot race in *Ben Hur* within a colosseum filled with thousands of extras was one of the most expensive and exciting screen spectacles ever made. It was staged on the lot of Rome's Cinecitta Studios.

1959

In most instances, "Bible movies," those elaborate spectacle films conveying more or less some hoked-up fiction based on Biblical lore, have been artistic fiascos but tremendous box-office hits in this country—especially when that old master of the epics, Cecil B. De Mille, was bringing them out in great bundles of Sunday school piety, pageantry, and sex. As a general rule, the sophisticated segment of the public regarded them with scorn while the mass audience flocked to see them.

But one had enough intelligence and restraint, along with dramatic excitement, to raise it to the realm of artistic respectability. That was William Wyler's expensive production of *Ben Hur,* based on a famous novel and equally famous silent film, made for M.G.M.

The novel, which was General Lew Wallace's *Ben-Hur: A Tale of the Christ,* published in 1880, was the *Gone with the Wind* of its day, and the silent film which was grandly made from it and released in 1926 was an equally sensational item, probably the biggest moneymaker of its time. But in doing a remake of it, Mr. Wyler projected a story of religious and political bigotry in brilliantly graphic fashion on the new giant-sized color screen. The all-too-familiar pattern of gaudy vulgarity was avoided, and a drama emerged that was visually exciting and meaningful.

Out of the literary claptrap of old General Wallace's tale, Mr. Wyler and his corps of writers, which included Karl Tunberg, Gore Vidal, Maxwell Anderson, S. N. Behrman and Christopher Fry, pulled a Christian-era story which they twisted around so that it had social and political innuendos that inevitably brought to mind memories of Jewish persecutions in the twentieth century.

It was the story of a prince of Judea, a stout, courageous fellow named Ben Hur, played by the muscular Charlton Heston, who opposed the autocratic designs of the pagan Roman conquerors and rulers to subju-

179

Ben Hur (Charlton Heston) receives the applause of the crowd after the spectacular chariot race in which he defeated his nemesis, Messala.

gate the Hebrew people of Judea. Marked as a troublemaker by Messala, his boyhood friend and now the Roman tribune, he was arrested for an alleged attempt to assassinate the tribune and sent into exile as a galley slave. His mother and sister were secretly imprisoned and ruin was brought on the House of Hur.

But Ben Hur escaped disaster. In a great naval battle in which his ship was sunk, he miraculously saved himself and managed to save the Roman admiral by hauling him onto a raft. For this timely deed he was honored by the admiral and taken to Rome, where he was allowed to dwell in freedom as the admiral's adopted son.

In time he returned to Judea in company with a powerful Arab sheikh who owned a team of splendid horses, and in a mammoth chariot race (held in a huge coliseum of a sort that certainly never existed in Jerusalem) Ben Hur drove these horses to victory against a team driven by Messala. This contest, in which the hateful rivalry of the two men was ferociously displayed by their slashing at each other as their chariots swept around the course, ended with Messala being crushed beneath his overturned vehicle and living only long enough to whisper, "The race is not yet over," to the vengeful Ben.

But this was far from the end of the picture. In the

180

second phase, Ben Hur went searching for his mother and his sister and finally located them in the hideous Valley of the Lepers, after passing on the way a great crowd of people gathered on a mountainside to hear a sermon by a saintly man called Jesus. But his heart was still full of bitterness and he said no other aim was possible for him "but to wash this land clean." His hatred was so strong that a young lady to whom he had become attached told him, "It's as though *you* had become Messala," but he was not deterred. Finally, he and his girlfriend did remove his mother and sister from the leper colony and took them to Jerusalem. And there they fortuitously arrived in time to witness the passage of Jesus paraded through the streets and staggering under the burden of the cross on the way to the crucifixion. So moved was Ben Hur that he attempted to give a cup of water to the agonized man, whom he recognized as the one who had previously given *him* a cup of water while he was being marched as a slave to the sea. And in an apocalyptic climax, a great thunderstorm occurred while Christ was being crucified, and Ben Hur's mother and sister were washed clean of their hideous disease—an obvious

Galley slave Ben Hur (Charlton Heston), miraculously escaped from chains in his sinking ship, has pulled the Roman admiral (Jack Hawkins) aboard a piece of wreckage and scans the horizon for a rescue ship.

A compassionate Ben Hur (Charlton Heston), his sister (Cathy O'Donnell), his mother (Martha Scott), and his girlfriend (Haya Harareet) behold the agonized Christ struggling through the streets of Jerusalem on the way to Calvary in this scene from *Ben Hur*.

Messala (Stephen Boyd) lashes at his hated rival Ben Hur (Charlton Heston) during their thundering chariot race in the spectacular *Ben Hur*.

Messala (Stephen Boyd), thrown from his overturned chariot and mortally injured, lies on the race course while the triumphant Ben Hur (Charlton Heston) thunders past.

symbol of the land being cleansed by the love of Christ.

It was notable, however, that no conversion of the hero to Christianity was implied, as it had been in the novel and in the silent film. Ben Hur remained devoutly a Jew, and he did not devote his regained fortune to the needs of the Christians under Nero. But in the example of Jesus and in Ben Hur's response to it, there was a sense of a genuine spiritual movement toward the ideal of the brotherhood of man. The moral, as in most Bible movies, was a generality, which at least had the virtue of reaching people all over the world.

The potency of this picture was in its superior achievement of vast melodramatic spectacle. From the outset there were many stunning scenes of life and activity in Judea at the beginning of the Christian era. The scene of the gathering of the multitudes to hear the Sermon on the Mount was literal, unpretentious, and moving, as was also the crucifixion scene, which was staged as a barbaric execution—an act of political vengeance—in what was recognized as a brutal, bloodthirsty age.

The great sea battle, which was staged with actual vessels for the silent film, was represented in this instance, alas, with unmistakable miniatures—that is, in the long shots—but the medium and close shots of on-deck fighting aboard the ship and of the hysterical turmoil and confusion among the drowning galley slaves were staggering in their magnitude. And the climactic chariot race was one of the all-time peak achievements of straight cinema action-spectacle. It ran for more than ten minutes and was staged in such a way (by the second-unit director, Andrew Marton, and the dean of stunt men, Yakima Canutt) that one sensed the vast

destruction among chariots, horses, and men. (Of course there were pious assurances that no animals or human beings were actually hurt, but that was hard to believe in view of the visible evidence and the fact that the film was made in lenient Italy.)

In every respect, material details and technical craftsmanship were excellent in this film, and the acting, on the whole, was much better than was customary when Hollywood actors enacted ancient Romans and Judeans. Mr. Heston was proud and mighty as the indomitable Ben Hur, and Stephen Boyd made his nemesis, Messala, an equally stalwart and resolute man. Jack Hawkins as the Roman admiral and Hugh Griffith as the impassioned Arab sheikh gave dignity and color to their well-integrated roles. Unfortunately, Ben Hur's loyal girlfriend was played lifelessly by Haya Harareet, and his sister and mother were more victims of gruesome makeup than of the stilted acting of Cathy O'Donnell and Martha Scott.

I do not suggest for one moment that this *Ben Hur* was a subtle film or that it offered new insights into complex characters. It blocked out a classic conflict and represented it in classic style. But from it one could hear echoes of the horrible holocaust in Nazi Germany more clearly than one could hear the clamor of conflict in Judea at the time of Christ, and one could sense more strongly the passions that moved people in modern Poland and Hungary than the fervor of those who actually struggled and suffered to bring a new religion to the world. But those were precisely the responses that I am sure Mr. Wyler wanted to generate with his film. And he did it with such artistry and compassion that it should be meaningful to large numbers of people for generations to come.

183

I'M ALL RIGHT, JACK

Erstwhile Private Stanley Windrush (Ian Carmichael), the memorable fall guy in the popular British service comedy, *Private's Progress*, attempts a hasty coverup when called out of temporary retirement to assume an active role in the Boulting brother's satiric sequel, *I'm All Right, Jack*. His father (Miles Malleson) is mildly surprised.

1960

Of all the forbidding subjects for successful satirizing on the screen—management versus trade unions in modern industry—the British Boulting brothers, John and Roy, had the audacity to take it on for a tentative go-round in their 1960 film *I'm All Right, Jack*. And, wonder of wonders, they produced a classic of high satiric farce!

Much of the credit for this achievement must go to newcomer Peter Sellers, who played the focal role of an overbearing shop steward in a British factory with such fierce and stubborn show of arrogance, lofty indignation, and ineptitude that he created an awesomely significant character.

But his was not the only fine performance or the only major asset of the film. He was joined by a brilliant cast of farceurs who had already done a stunning job in the Boultings' *Private's Progress* (1956), the outstanding British "service" comedy. And the film was blessed with a scathing screenplay and the wry direction of John Boulting.

Indeed, one of the reasons for the impact and popularity of the film when released was the fact that most of the characters—on the management "team," anyhow—were familiar and beloved extensions of the uniformed rogues in the service film. There was, first, lanky Ian Carmichael, who was the titular private in that film—the wide-eyed cat's-paw for a scheming uncle in the War Office who had a scandalous plan to use British soldiers to relieve the Nazis of a hoard of priceless art. Here he was still the wide-eyed nitwit, but a proper English gentleman, looking for a place to bestow his talents in postwar industry.

Next was Dennis Price, the shifty uncle, now the head of a missile factory and still moved by piratical inclinations—this time to swindle an unnamed Arab country in a massive armaments deal. Assisting him in this machination was Richard Attenborough, one of the uniformed schemers, now a sly businessman in a pinstriped suit. And last but far from least was Terry-Thomas, the snarling major in the previous film, now labor relations manager for his wartime associates-in-crime and stuck with the hopeless task of deal-

Top management of Missiles, Ltd.,—Richard Attenborough, Margaret Rutherford, and Dennis Price—instruct an innocent nephew (Ian Carmichael) on his expected duties as a new employee of the firm.

A union delegation, led by Kite (Peter Sellers), confront a member of the management team regarding the status of a new employee.

An astonished group of union pickets, led by Kite (Peter Sellers), protests vehemently against a management lockout.

Picture of a self-satisfied union leader (Peter Sellers) in his home with his wife (Irene Handl), a gentleman roomer (Ian Carmichael), and his daughter (Liz Fraser).

Kite (Peter Sellers) is compelled to take instructions from his angry wife (Irene Handl), while Stanley (Ian Carmichael) looks on.

ing with the recalcitrant and obstructive workers in their plant.

Up to the point where Mr. Sellers strode upon the scene, all was familiar tea and crumpets with this comfortable little gang. The Messrs. Price and Attenborough were deftly lining up an Arab ambassador to go along with them in their maneuver—the arrangement including a nice kickback to the wily ambassador, of course. And, as part of their complicated intrigue, they had given a minor factory job to the unlikely Mr. Carmichael, who had already failed in a few attempts (all amusingly pictured) to get into "soft" industries.

So here they were, launched very nicely on what appeared to be nothing more than a harmless little British exegesis on the suave deceptions of industrial management. Mr. Carmichael had been duly slotted to run a forklift, from which mobile point of vantage he might observe the activities of his fellow workers (not suspecting for a moment that he was put there to spy), and Mr. Terry-Thomas had cued us in precisely to the exasperations with which he had to contend.

"We've got men here," he hissed with dark repugnance through the yawning gap in his front teeth, "who can break out into a muck sweat merely by standing still!"

Then trouble surged into the picture. Suddenly onto the scene strode the pugnacious Mr. Sellers, authority graven on his face and outrage apparent in the firm strut with which he marched ahead of a mixed committee of factory workingmen. Hitler, turned out in civvies, could not have looked more adamant than he with his military haircut, his toothbrush mustache, his haughty manner, and his cold determination to oppose whatever maneuver management might be up to to screw the working class.

He wanted to know at the moment what the new man on the forklift was doing there, since he obviously wasn't a normal workman (having turned up on the job in a business suit and necktie) and then had clumsily used his forklift to expose a cozy group of card-playing workers behind a pile of crates.

"Is he," Mr. Sellers demanded, "one of these time-and-motion blokes?"—which happened to be a fair suspicion because there *was* one snooping around and Mr. Carmichael was unwittingly passing damaging information about the workers' slowdown tactics to him.

Mr. Terry-Thomas, all smiles and unction, assured

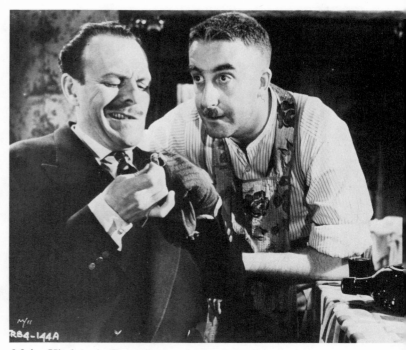

Major Hitchcock (Terry Thomas), the shifty labor-relations manager, discusses a delicate point in private with Fred Kite (Peter Sellers), the suspiciously pliable union shop steward, in the midst of an exhausting strike.

Fred Kite and Stanley Windrush watch helplessly as a gust of wind brings a sudden end to their climactic television debate in *I'm All Right, Jack.*

187

Mr. Sellers he didn't know. But he promised to look into the matter, and at the same time Mr. Sellers barked to the mystified forklift operator, "Don't you do nothing until your case has been gone into!"

When it was duly considered and Mr. Terry-Thomas had cheerfully agreed to fire the offending fellow, whom he reckoned incompetent, Mr. Sellers was doubly suspicious. Stepping outside the office to caucus with his attending committee, he soon returned to proclaim, "We cannot accept the principle that incompetence is justification for dismissal."

Clearly Mr. Terry-Thomas couldn't win.

Thus went this crisis-studded satire on the chicaneries of top management and the constant pettifogging and work-shirking of the union with which it had to deal. And eventually the whole controversy erupted into the shop steward's calling a strike, which boomed into a nationwide walkout when Mr. Carmichael refused to quit his job because his dear auntie, played by Margaret Rutherford, reminded him that "officers don't mutiny under fire," whereupon he became a major issue and the focus of a BBC debate during which he naïvely blew the whistle on management and labor alike. In this debate, Mr. Sellers humorously exposed the unrelenting pomposity and dull-wittedness of his man.

Obviously, organized labor, which is seldom represented on the screen, could not have been travestied more deftly than it was by this bumbling shop steward. Ideas and comprehension seemed to bog down completely in his head, which was evidently filled with nothing but trade-union cant and mush. Dreams of being able to visit Soviet Russia some day and "have a look at all them cornfields and ballet in the evening" were jumbled up with his notions that his mission in life was to march at the head of his workers and keep them from acting "like the Gadarene swine."

To complete the display of his incompetence was the scene in which his Cockney wife, played by Irene Handl, having walked out for her own private strike, left him in command of the family kitchen, amid piles of dirty dishes and pots. The totally stymied shop steward couldn't even dislodge a piece of toast from the heel of his shoe!

The others were also delicious in poking fun at their class. Mr. Carmichael's scorching of the scion of a stately family was very revealing, and Mr. Price was drolly suave and slippery in mouthing disarming platitudes while doing his self-serving mischief. "Between simple businessmen," he purred to the equally slippery Arab ambassador, "even peace is divisible." A chillingly foreboding joke!

Indeed, everything about this picture has a sharp, ironic ring today, in the light of what the British trade unions have done to the economy of their nation in the last decade. At the time it was released, and for some years after, the name of Mr. Sellers' character, Kite, was mockingly applied to any union leader who seemed to be using his power dictatorially. But now the gag is no longer funny. It is too ironically grim— and so might be the picture, if it weren't so humorous. It stands as a memorial to the irony of the old trades-union boast, borrowed from the army's goldbrickers and applied in the title of the film (minus the introductory exhortation), "Fuck you, *I'm* all right, Jack!"

L'AVVENTURA

1960

Add to the list of "puzzling pictures" that came from Sweden and France in the 1950s and 1960s Michelangelo Antonioni's *L'Avventura,* a strange and disturbing Italian film which I confess taxed my comprehension and patience when I first saw it at the 1960 Cannes Film Festival. It seemed to me on that occasion unconscionably long and disjointed, insufficient in providing information, and deliberately, annoyingly obscure.

But on further viewings of it, I began to perceive and realize what Antonioni was doing and my respect and admiration for the picture and for his unorthodox style increased. I saw that he had purposely bypassed the conventional narrative approach to dramatic storytelling, that he wasn't trying to *tell* a story at all but was trying to *show* the nature and intensity of the emotions of his characters in surrounding pictorial terms. He was out to suffuse the observer with such a flow of background images, environmental and architectural, natural and explicitly man-made, that a sense of what the characters were feeling would be suggested and enhanced by the cultural allusions, the symbolism, and the poetry of these images. The issue was not the story but how the characters felt. And I must say that with this understanding and with the experience of seeing all the artist's later works I now find *L'Avventura* a deeply moving and haunting film which has become more meaningful in our increasingly disturbed society.

Antonioni, as the author and director, helped confuse the audience with his curious laconism in the lengthy first phase of the film. After introducing a young woman who was concluding a moody love affair with a casually accommodating fellow in full view of her best girlfriend, Antonioni loaded these three cryptic people—Anna, Sandro, and Claudia, respectively—aboard a motor yacht with four or five other jaded worldlings and took them to a barren volcanic island off the north coast of Sicily. There they went ashore and wandered idly among the hideous volcanic rocks, not showing very much interest in anything, until Anna mysteriously disappeared. For a time she was wandering among them, then suddenly

Claudia (Monica Vitti) is trapped by her lover, Sandro (Gabriele Ferzetti), in *L'Avventura.*

Director Michelangelo Antonioni and his star, Monica Vitti, during a break in the filming of *L'Avventura.*

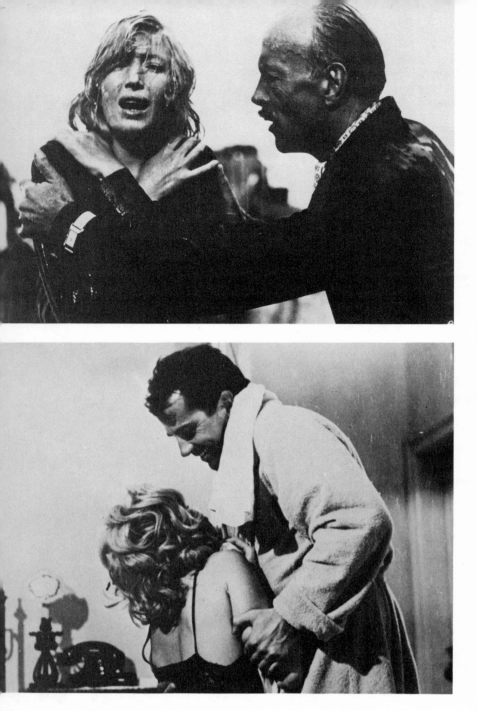

Claudia (Monica Vitti) is ineffectually comforted by Corrado (James Addams), an older member of the ill-fated yachting party in *L'Avventura,* after the mysterious disappearance of her friend, Anna, on a barren volcanic island off Sicily.

A confused and despairing Claudia (Monica Vitti) is humored by her erratic lover, Sandro (Gabriele Ferzetti), in a hotel room in *L'Avventura.*

she was not, and no amount of calling and searching succeeded in turning her up.

For anyone responsive to the signals of conventional narrative films, this seemed to be the introduction to a routine mystery. What had happened to the moody young woman? Had she fallen into a crevice in the rocks? Had her bored lover secretly pushed her into one of the treacherous caves that were endlessly filling and emptying with the wash from the powerful sea? Were there others on the island who might have done her in? Had she, in her evident desolation, committed suicide?

The ennui of all the characters, their petty bickerings (especially between a husband and his wife), the waspishness of Anna toward Sandro, the tense uneasiness of Claudia—all tended to cause the observer to feel vaguely annoyed with this group. Even the forbidding volcanic rock of this setting, vividly caught in the brilliant camerawork of Aldo Scararia, tended to generate a feeling of physical discomfort, restlessness,

Sandro has a troubled Claudia momentarily with her back literally to the wall in one of their disturbing confrontations in *L'Avventura*.

Barren rocks and the restless sea are background for Claudia's feelings of alienation and despair while fruitlessly hunting for her missing friend, Anna.

In happy mood, Claudia frolics with Sandro among the great bells and pull-ropes atop the basilica at Noto.

and dread. But this was the first intimation of the mood of Claudia (and probably Anna)—her feeling of loneliness, despair, isolation, and insecurity on this island. And with little exchange of conversation between her and Sandro as they pursued the fruitless search, Antonioni subtly communicated their mutual bewilderment and anxiety at this mystifying turn of events.

Thus Antonioni managed to build a feeling of exhaustion and boredom in this crucial phase. All things—the look of the island, the constant roar and menace of the sea, the discomfort and desolation of a lashing storm at night—interpreted the mood of Claudia to the audience and accounted for much of the impatience of those who saw the film for the first time.

As the search by Claudia, Sandro, and Anna's father (who had arrived with a boatload of police) continued, it was evident that the expected progress toward an unraveling was not being made and that this was far from a conventional plotted mystery. Eventually the whole party returned to Sicily and only Claudia and Sandro seemed bent on continuing the search. It grew clear that concern for the fate of Anna was being allowed to evaporate and the thrust of the film was redirected toward a search by Claudia and Sandro for themselves.

They did continue the pretense of seeking some clue to the disappearance of their friend as they cast about independently, then came together under the urge of a burgeoning love, but obviously their concern for Anna was but a deceptive, flimsy bond to support them in their sense of guilt and their hunger for sex. And so it appeared beyond question that the ultimate mystery in this film was the aims of these two people in their loneliness and cynical despair.

L'Avventura is a study of the spiritual torments and the emotional needs of lonely people—perhaps weak and inadequate people—in a rich but empty world. Obviously Claudia, like Anna, was frightened and insecure—alienated, as some critics put it—and tending to withdraw into herself. Conspicuously, Antonioni did not help us with any conventional clues to her background or previous conditioning. He picked her up at the point where the film began and confined her, including her friendships, within the circle of events he depicted. His interest was in her strong emotions and reactions within that span of time. And we had learned all we needed to know about her when the film came to an end.

The on-again, off-again passion of Claudia and Sandro is distinctly waxing at this point in their search for the missing Anna.

Giulia (Dominique Blanchar) joins Anna's father (Renzo Ricci) in the futile search for the young woman on the barren island off Sicily.

Likewise, the background of Sandro was characteristically vague. We knew of his affair with Anna, which evidently had been going on for some time, and the fact that he was a moderately competent but disillusioned architect. Indeed, in one of the sharpest and most revealing scenes in the film, after confessing to Claudia his weariness with being an architect, Sandro deliberately—even fiendishly—knocked over a bottle of ink upon an unfinished architectural design that a young student was doing on the terrace of a great baroque Sicilian church. The implication here of his humiliation at not having fulfilled the promise of his youth was supported by his stalking off thereafter and falling in behind a group of black-suited schoolboys spilling out of the church.

That episode had been preceded by a series of similarly strong "architectural" scenes in which Claudia and Sandro, motoring casually around Sicily, came to a weird, deserted community of dead-white modern buildings sitting starkly on the side of a hill, which depressed Claudia severely. Obviously this landscape was as symbolic of the barrenness of the modern age as the dead volcanic island was of the past.

The mood that this scene generated was erased, however, by an immediate cathartic sequel: Claudia and Sandro making love on a beautiful open hillside looking out over the sea. But the violence and rapture of their passion were suddenly interrupted by the deafening roar of a passing train within a few yards of them, a harsh intrusion on their intimacy by manmade machinery. Then the couple ascended to the rooftop of a convent looking out upon the baroque city of Noto, where they accidentally found to their delight that they could ring a whole peal of bells, thus signifying another shift in mood.

Eroticism was a strong element throughout the film, manifested in pleasurable, but also clumsy and bitter, episodes. Antonioni emphasized the transience of sex and love, as indicated in the experience of Anna and in the anxieties and hesitations of Claudia. Indeed, it was Claudia's insistence in the middle and final phases of the film that Sandro continue to tell her—and show her—how much he was in love with her that led to the ultimate disillusion and terminal compromise of the two.

They had rejoined some of the people who were on the yacht at a luxury hotel in the beautiful resort of Taormina. Claudia was afraid that Anna might reappear in this setting and destroy her now faltering affair. Torn by insecurity, she opted to go to bed one night instead of joining Sandro in the public rooms. When she awoke in the middle of the night and found he wasn't with her, she became deeply apprehensive. At dawn, she went looking for him through the empty, echoing halls of the hotel and, sure enough, she found him, not with Anna but with a notorious whore, twined together on a couch in one of the public rooms.

Shocked and chagrined by this encounter, Claudia ran from the room, roamed through the streets of the sleeping city, and apparently contemplated suicide, but the appearance of a passing workman evidently discouraged her. She saw she was being followed by Sandro, and fled to an empty terrace beside an old bell tower—a lovely, calm, poetic place of refuge in the dawn's half-light. She paused as he tentatively approached her, sat down on a bench, and began to weep. This silent display of his anguish and mortification humbled her. Slowly she moved to stand behind him, placed one tender hand on his head and, without facing each other, they remained thus as the film came to an end.

Much praise and credit for the bewitching quality of the picture have been given to honey-haired Monica Vitti in the role of Claudia. Her sultry nature combined with a chilling moodiness, which occasionally exploded in brief flashes of reckless gaiety, endowed this character with the essential instability and surprise. The fact that she was also exploited as a new sensation in Italian films helped sell the show. But Gabriele Ferzetti as Sandro was greatly contributive, too, making this seemingly cool worldling a very bundle of seething frustrations and needs. Both characters were haunting symbols of some of the corrosive hang-ups of our age.

Lea Massari as Anna was bitter and defiant in her short time on screen, and Dominique Blanchar, James Addams, and several others were appropriately chic and atmospheric in minor roles.

L'Avventura is perhaps Antonioni's best film, bearing in mind his *Blow-Up,** which was a totally different sort of thing. In the latter, his theme was illusion, the frightening thought that things aren't always what they seem, which was far from the theme of insecurity and isolation pursued in most of his other films.

THE LONELINESS OF THE LONG DISTANCE RUNNER

Colin (Tom Courtenay), No. 14, struggles to take the lead in the first phase of the cross-country race in the meet between his Borstal team and the team from an upper-class public school in *The Loneliness of the Long Distance Runner*.

1962

Coming late in the sequence of Britain's postwar "angry films," which because of their stress on slum backgrounds were sometimes known as the "kitchen-sink school," Tony Richardson's taut, uncompromising *The Loneliness of the Long Distance Runner* was

felt by some at the time it was released to have been generically anticlimactic and curiously vague as to what it meant to say. I admit to having been one of critics who initially felt that way.

Its story of a Nottingham slum boy sent to a Borstal school—the British term for a reform school—for participating in a petty robbery went over ground of grinding slum life that had already been realistically plowed by Mr. Richardson's earlier *Look Back in Anger* and by the *Saturday Night and Sunday Morning* of Karel Reisz. Further, it seemed to leave the hero hanging inconclusively at the end, frozen in a sort of social limbo that held nothing for society—or for him.

I gather that most of its viewers were likewise put off by it, because, in spite of some interesting criticisms, it never caught on commercially. Neither did it draw any interest when, a year or so later, its distributor brought it back for a second engagement, supported by a strong advertising campaign.

But the more I thought about it and reconsidered it in a second review, the more I realized why this picture baffled me and evidently most of its viewers. Its hero was more than a youngster who simply chafed and waxed angry at the bonds of poverty and inequality that kept him in lowly servitude, yet dreamed of some stroke of good fortune that would allow him to get free and move ahead. This lad was a congenital rebel, an individual who would simply not conform, a battered kid whose mistrust of the established system was so intense that he would do nothing to try to compromise with it.

He was, in the last analysis, an incipient anarchist—or a nihilist, if you'd rather—which was why he seemed so remote and mystifying to us viewers, who were thoroughly and traditionally schooled in the principle of the Judeo-Christian work ethic—if you do your job, you get ahead. This kid was without ambition. He was, to all our ways of viewing him, quite lost.

Yet here in Mr. Richardson's rendering of a screenplay by Alan Sillitoe and in Tom Courtenay's fine performance as the hard-bitten boy, there was conveyed such a poignant comprehension of the turmoil of anguish in the lad, such a sense of the hideousness and barrenness of the home and environment in which he lived, and such a feeling of freshness and freedom when he found an infinite release in the joy of long-distance running that this became a rare song of spiritual poetry.

A hint of the elevation of emotion that the film was going to reach was given at the very beginning with shots of the solitary lad running along a country road, away from the camera, in the early morning mists, while a wistful jazz tune played in the background and the voice of the lad tried to explain the feelings of a long-distance runner, the loneliness, yet freedom from

Colin (Tom Courtenay) is given a little lecture on the honor of representing his Borstal school—and, perhaps, eventually England—by the school's class-conscious governor (Michael Redgrave).

Colin (Tom Courtenay) races toward the finish in the elimination trials for a place on the cross-country team of his Borstal school.

restraint. This was behind the credits. And then the film opened abruptly on a van of manacled boys being rudely delivered at the entrance of a Borstal school.

Focal in this group of garrulous youngsters was our particular lad, grimly unsmiling, laconic, withdrawn from the capers of the rest, and coolly disdainful of the first instructions given them by the starchy governor and the arrogant head boy.

Colin (Tom Courtenay) in the center of an exercise class conducted by the physical training instructor (Joe Robinson) at the Borstal school.

"We are here to turn you into industrious and honest citizens," the governor explained, sounding the keynote of conformity. "If you'll play ball with us, we'll play ball with you."

He happened to be a keen sports-minded fellow, and only that morning before the van arrived, he had revealed with great pride to his associate that he had managed to arrange a track meet with a distinguished upper-class boys' school, the first meet of its sort in Borstal history. "This is a great day for us," he beamed. The prospect of his youngsters competing on such a level of traditional "sportsmanship" revealed him not only as a conformist but as a conventional, class-conscious snob.

And the additional word of advice from the head boy to the newcomers, "Always remember, they've got the whip hand," supported the precept that these youngsters were being disciplined by masters who expected them to learn to stay in line.

Such was the introduction of our hard-nut case to the school, and such was the environment of surveillance and regimentation into which he was now plunged. He faced it with a sort of cold obtuseness. When he was called before the house psychiatrist to

tell about himself and give some insights into his antisocial attitudes, he was caustic and craftily evasive, all with an impudent deadpan, to a point at which the unctuous psychiatrist finally had to give up. To effect "an emotional readjustment," a heavy schedule of football was prescribed, and it was in this pursuit that the governor and the athletic instructor discovered a glint of promise in the lad.

At first they thought he had the makings of a runner, a sprinter, when he outran all the football players in a scoring rundown, but then a "stayer" when the governor hopefully matched him in a practice run with the school's best long-distance runner, who happened to be the head boy. He won, much to the latter's vexation and jealousy, but to the surprise and delight of the governor, who saw this new boy as an excellent prospect for a winner in the upcoming interschool match. Thereupon he gave him permission to go out alone in the early mornings on training runs. And it was while he was out on these long circuits through silent woods and along empty roads, leaping and cavorting with pleasure, that we were allowed to know about him in a series of long flashbacks that represented his memories—the bitter thoughts that ran through his head.

We were shown him as the indifferent product of a factory-town, working-class home where he had been tyrannized over by a slowly dying father (who had evidently been as much of a hardhead as he) and the worry of a heavily burdened mother who had to take care of her husband, a job, and two small kids. Sullen in mood and manner, uninterested in doing anything except lying around the house in restless boredom and occasionally going larking with a chum, he appeared a completely stagnant youngster, one of those faceless fellows doomed to expire sooner or later in the heartless furnaces of Britain's postwar heavy industry.

He remembered how his mother and her boyfriend had gone on a spending spree with money from his father's meager insurance after the old man had died; how his mother had handed over to him a couple of crumpled bills and how he had gone into the old man's empty bedroom and calmly burned the money as a gesture of his disgust. He remembered how he and his buddy had taken a couple of girls to a cheap seaside place and he had wandered along the wide, empty beach and into the dunes with one of the girls, had screwed her, and how free but oddly uneasy and somehow trapped this made him feel.

The slum boy, Colin (Tom Courtenay), makes a pickup of one of the local factory-town girls (Julia Foster).

And then he recalled how he and his buddy, wanting money with which to treat the girls, impulsively broke into a bakery and stole a cashbox that contained a few bills, and how they tried to hide the money in a rainspout from which it was washed out, and how they were caught. These flashbacks, set against the openness and cleanness of those lonely practice runs, conveyed the jumble of emotions that darkly disturbed the boy.

Came the day, then, of the big track meet, with the team from the starchy public school getting out of their van and first encountering the Borstal boys in the dressing room, sizing up one another—the privileged lads and the pimply reprobates—obviously both sides aware of the class distinctions that kept them far apart. Then on to the field, where a weak show of class-school camaraderie was put on, with a band thumping out march music and well-dressed parents of the public school lads separated from the ranks of the Borstals, and wheezing, "Jolly good luck to you, boys."

Off went the race, the most important event of the meet, a five-mile run, with our lad and another from the public school very soon far out in front. Across hills, through woods, and over rivers the two were followed handsomely with thoughts couched in snatches of dialogue on the sound track again running through our youngster's mind. Most forcibly he recollected something the governor had said in suggesting to him what might happen if he became a champion: "I don't think there is any honor that would give a man more satisfaction than representing his country at the Olympic Games."

And then, as our boy's lonely figure was seen coming over a distant hill and running down toward the finish far ahead of the other lad, he was suddenly seen to slow to a jog trot, walk a few paces, and stop. Unheeding the shouts of the governor and the other spectators, "Run! Run! Run!" In a close-up of him, a tired expression of contempt and defiance crossed his face, as his rival caught up with him, passed him, and quickly sped on to win.

That was the way the picture ended, except for a last shot of the lad in the school's metal shop from which he had been previously sprung to a lighter detail when it was discovered he could run. Obviously he was slotted to a future of low-class drudgery.

Such a sudden, abrupt conclusion was like crashing into a stone wall. No wonder those who saw it felt stunned and incredulous. But it was, on due reflection, recognizable as the only way this lad could display his defiance of the system he abhorred. In the period of contemplation of his resentments while the race was being run, he yielded to his bitter, ingrown instinct to tell them all to go to hell. It was, as it seemed to us skeptics, an act of absurd self-sacrifice. But to the boy it was towering triumph. He had been true to himself.

I must say, feelings were divided—and still are— toward the boy, who was wrapped in a mood of mutinous defiance by Mr. Courtenay. At one moment, he was sensitive and pathetic, at another fractious and tough—a brilliant, subtle showing of his nature, but not one to elicit great sympathy. As the governor, Michael Redgrave was crisp, dogmatic, and obtuse, and Joe Robinson made the athletic director a ponderous, bull-necked brute. Alec McGowan as the psychiatrist, Avis Bunnage as the mother of the boy, and James Bolam as his chum were outstanding in a splendid cast.

The musical score was most appropriate, and the use of the old hymn "Jerusalem," with its message of hope to make England a "green and happy land," pouring from the throats of youngsters in a Borstal school, adding a thumping note of eloquence and echoing irony.

KNIFE IN THE WATER

1962

Of all the countries of Europe, Poland might have been least expected to produce movies of any consequence after World War II. Devastated by both the Nazis and the Russians, it was a nation which, indeed, had no tradition of great filmmaking even before the war. But the early postwar establishment of a small state-controlled film industry and a modern documentary film school at Lodz were the first modest indicators of Polish interest in postwar cinema. In the 1950s a spate of significant films emerged—nothing on the level of the great postwar films from Italy, but quite as good as the ones from Soviet Russia and much better than those from Germany.

Striking among these films from Poland were two grim works from director Andrezej Wajda, the first entitled *Kanal,* about a group of staunch resistance fighters who took to the Warsaw sewers toward the end of the war, and the other, *Ashes and Diamonds,* about social and political deterioration in the country after the war. While both were intensely realistic (reflecting the influence of the Lodz school), and revealed surprising candor in a Soviet satellite, their mood of defeat and cynicism limited their significance and possible popularity in a postwar world.

Then in 1958 there appeared in Warsaw a refreshingly incongruous satiric short entitled *Two Men and a Wardrobe,* which immediately brought attention to the young man who made it, Roman Polanski, as a writer and director to watch. Three years later he justified that hope by producing his *Knife in the Water,* which swiftly leaped to the front as a major international postwar film.

At the time, it was generally regarded as an uncommonly sharp and shrewd study of the competitive be-

An ominous face-off between Andrzei (Leon Niemczyk) and his young guest (Zygmunt Malanowicz) in their contention to possess the sexually symbolic knife in the Polish film, *Knife in the Water.*

The young man (Zygmunt Malanowicz) and Andrzei (Leon Niemczyk) at the moment before the latter tosses the knife of the younger man into the water.

198

The young man (Zygmunt Malanowicz) feigns drowning by hiding behind a marker buoy after being forced from the sailboat of his infuriated host.

The sexy young wife (Jolanta Umecka) poses not altogether unconsciously before the youthful hitchhiker (Zygmunt Malanowicz) aboard her husband's sailboat.

Andrzei (Leon Niemczyk) and the young hitchhiker (Zygmunt Malanowicz), whom he has taken for a weekend sail, fumble with the fateful knife to clear the grounded boat while Andrzei's wife, Christine (Jolanta Umecka), watches them from the cockpit.

havior of two isolated men, while the wife of the older man looked on. It seemed a remarkably perceptive and illustrative exposé of so many of the unspoken hangups of contemporary urban man that it surpassed what many older, more cosmopolitan filmmakers were trying to do. And with those as dramatic achievements, it deserved all the praise it received.

Today, with our heightened awareness of the neurotic aggressions of male chauvinists in an ultracompetitive social scheme, the insights of this solidly complex film render it even more interesting now. And its subtle intimations of the woman's participation in the scene fit very comfortably into the pattern of today's women's lib philosophy.

Mr. Polanski, in a deceptively simple way, moved his naturalistic camera as though it were an outsized microscope, minutely observing the behavior of these

The young man, wearing the bathrobe of his departed host, embraces and comforts the latter's wife in this climactic scene from the Polish film *Knife in the Water.*

three people isolated for twenty-four hours aboard a trim little sailing sloop. And within this controlled environment, as concentrated and confined for purposes of study and demonstration as a problem in geometry, he watched the snarling husband, his tidy and seemingly casual wife, and a sassy young student hitchhiker, whom they picked up in their auto en route to the boat, work out their smoldering aggressions and their sexual rivalries.

From the first harsh exchange between the two men on the road, when the younger one, carrying a rucksack, brashly thumbed for transportation and the older man, with alarming deliberation, almost ran him down, they testily taunted each other and childishly contended to display their superior skills and prowess, while the wife indifferently observed. The husband vaunted himself as a sailor and mocked the ignorance and clumsiness of the youth; the latter displayed his dexterity and agility with a murderous switchblade knife. The older man gave excessive orders; the younger one truculently obeyed, then exhibited his youthful vigor by shinnying up the mast.

Trifling and comical at the outset, when they first went aboard the little sloop and pushed off on an early Sunday morning for a day and a night on a lonely lake, the rivalry seemed no more than the jostling of two hostile boys daring each other to step over an imaginary line. And the casual goings and comings about the boat of the pretty young wife, innocently but seductively decked out in a tight two-piece bathing suit, did not seem pertinent.

But Mr. Polanski was subtle. The competition grew more vicious and the distraction of the woman more intense. From the husband admonishing the lad that he needed fast reflexes to be a sailor and the latter snapping back that sailing was "for kids," the clashes became more bitter, and the casual little peeks the camera took at the breasts and the crotch of the young woman indicated the surgings of lust.

At one point, when the wife and the husband were swimming off the boat, the boy suddenly grabbed the tiller and tried to sail off in it. But he could do no more than sail in circles, betraying his incompetence. Then, in a moment of inattention, the husband let the boat run aground.

Thus it went between these two archcontenders, on deck and in the cabin at night, when they carried their stupid competition even into a childish game of pick-up-sticks. Here again the boy paid his forfeit by throwing his knife with great accuracy into the wall, then followed that by reciting a bit of tender poetry, in reply to which the young woman sang a sad love song. It was evident that the boy and the woman were maneuvering toward some sort of involvement.

In the cool light of dawn, he found her musing alone on the deck and had a quiet talk with her, but then the husband came topside, with the knife, and again started giving orders. When the boy demanded the knife—which by now was fairly apparent as the symbol of the boy's sexual power—the older man snapped it at him, teased and taunted him with it, and then let it fall into the water, which infuriated the boy. He leaped at the man. There was a struggle, and then the older man pushed him overboard. In this sudden explosion of violence, the rivalry was glaringly revealed.

What followed was startling and pathetic. The boy did not come up, as the husband, thinking to "show" him, began to sail away. The wife, alarmed at this, dived into the water to hunt for the lad. The husband returned, and together they made a fruitless search. Now they were frightened and unsettled. The husband feared he had drowned the lad, and the wife, giving vent to her perturbance, angrily lashed out at him. Whereupon he, in utter distraction, struck out to swim

The young antagonist (Zygmunt Malanowicz) finally takes sexual possession of his older tormentor's wife (Jolanta Umecka).

ashore and the wife, incensed, remained aboard. What they didn't know was that the lad was hiding all the while behind a marker buoy that was not too far from the boat.

After things had quieted a little, the lad swam back to the boat, found the wife nude, and tried to soothe her, but she lashed out at him, slapped him hard, and charged him with being as stupid as her husband— indeed, "just like him!" Then the inevitable happened. The lad grabbed her in his arms and she yielded without too much resistance.

On the way back to the yacht club, she put the lad off upon a float of logs and she sailed on to the basin, where her husband awaited her. He didn't even rail at her when she hit the dock, but told her in deep contrition that he was going to inform the police. Silently they made the boat shipshape, piled the luggage in their car and started back for the city. Then she told

him the boy was alive—"so alive," she insisted, "that he made me unfaithful to you." That was the end of this exceptional exegesis on egotism and vanity.

There was a lot of keen discussion after the film was released as to what Mr. Polanski, who also wrote the screenplay, intended. Was he giving a modern connotation to the Oedipal rivalry, as one psychiatrist claimed? Was he dealing implicitly in symbols of castration and impotency? The director himself denied flatly that he had any such esoterica in mind. He was simply telling a story of two men in Poland and of the disturbing differences in economic status of the established one and the unemployed youth. Whatever one's own interpretation, it was a memorable movie, and Mr. Polanski has since forged ahead as one of the most brilliant innovators on the international film scene.

DR. STRANGELOVE, OR HOW I LEARNED TO STOP WORRYING AND LOVE THE BOMB

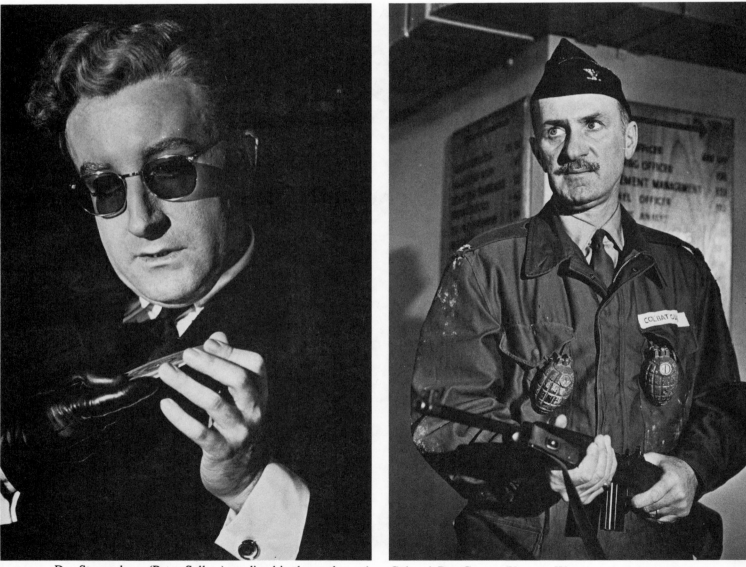

Dr. Strangelove (Peter Sellers) studies his doomsday calculator in *Dr. Strangelove, or How I Learned to Stop Worrying and Love the Bomb.*

Colonel Bat Guano (Keenan Wynn) moves in to capture General Jack D. Ripper.

There should be an Act of Congress or an amendment to the Constitution to compel that Stanley Kubrick's *Dr. Strangelove, or How I Learned to Stop Worrying and Love the Bomb* be shown annually to the President, the members of his Cabinet, the Joint Chiefs of Staff, and all high-ranking government officials who inhabit the Pentagon. For this famous black-humored satire on the American defense establishment, up to and including a caricatured Commander in Chief, and the bumbling behavior of his top war council during a hypothetical crisis over nuclear bombs is so creditably apprehensive about the kinds of narrow, biased military minds that *might* allow fear of Soviet Russia to trip this nation into all-out nuclear war that it should be a valuable reminder to all the gentlemen who have our safety in their hands.

When this film was released—please remember that was early in 1964 and the nation was still suffering trauma from the assassination of President Kennedy—I gravely questioned the discretion, not to mention the simple good taste, of joking so incisively and frighteningly about the competence of the highest council of the President of the United States. Despite my profound appreciation and howling enjoyment of the supreme wit and humor packed into this scalding film, I did think it was a highly dubious and dangerously sick kind of joke to be dropping on the body politic.

Now I feel different about it. I feel that all this picture had to say about the phobias of warmongering generals and the lies and misdeeds of high officials obsessed with paranoiac fears of the "Commies," plus concern for their own images, was shockingly borne out by the behavior of our Chief Executives and our bloated defense establishment in the Vietnam War. Further, I now feel that this picture, far from damaging the public's confidence in those who were responsible for our welfare and defense, had the effect of contributing to a mounting awareness and cynicism about the reliability of our leaders which finally helped force an end to the war.

What is more—and this was a bonus which came about by sheer coincidence, since I cannot believe that Mr. Kubrick was foreadvised by a soothsayer—the image of Dr. Strangelove, a sinister character who turned up late in the film as a national security consultant to the President, was such a conspicuous presentment of a man who later actually filled that job, with his heavy Germanic accent and his darkly Teutonic attitudes, that this person was often dubbed "Strangelove" by his critics.

And no wonder this curious resemblance caused misgivings in many sober minds. For the Dr. Strangelove in the picture, whom Peter Sellers played as one of the three roles he managed in various makeups but with equal skill and wit, was a frighteningly erratic "expert" with a crippled body, a fanatical brain, and a muscular tic that caused his right arm to shoot out every now and then in a Nazi salute. His cold-blooded calculations of the millions of people who would be killed in a nuclear face-off with Russia and the opportunity this would present to set up his ideal world society composed only of a salvaged elite was the sort of thing that caused viewers to squirm when they first saw the film.

But despite his titular preeminence, this character was not the key one in the film. That was a top-ranking

Air Force General "Buck" Turgidson (George C. Scott) imparts some profound military information in *Dr. Strangelove.*

Turgidson (in white shirt) and President Muffley (back to camera), surrounded by Pentagon brass, are given the doomsday data by the sinister security expert, gloating Dr. Strangelove (Peter Sellers), in this crisis scene from *Dr. Strangelove*.

Air Force General "Buck" Turgidson (George C. Scott) receives the alarming information that an American bombing plane has been directed to attack a Russian target while he is engaged in a private conference.

Howling with triumphant glee, Major T.J. King Kong (Slim Pickens) zeros in with his atom-bomb-loaded B-52 on a target in Soviet Russia.

General Jack D. Ripper (Sterling Hayden) reluctantly supported by RAF Group Captain Lionel Mandrake (Peter Sellers), prepares to stand off the Army detail sent to capture him in his own Strategic Air Command offices from which he has ordered a bombing attack on Soviet targets.

Air Force general, played by George C. Scott with such brash military machismo and such snarling and rasping volubility that he made one hoot with laughter while feeling one's blood run cold. He was one of those superexperts whose mind was so involved with military punctilio and programs, computer outputs, and inbred bigotry that he couldn't think straight in a crisis.

It was this unreliable commander who was most helplessly bewildered and paralyzed when word was flashed to the Pentagon one evening that a base general in the Strategic Air Command had assumed the authority of sending a wing of B-52 bombers on a mission to drop live nuclear bombs on targets inside Soviet Russia. Never mind that this general was a nut, fired by a wild, obsessive notion that the Russians were secretly polluting the water of the world so that everyone's "bodily fluids" (except the Russians', who "drink vodka") were being exhausted and that the time had come to make them stop. The point was that this wacky fellow had set a potential world calamity afoot, complicated by the peril that the Russians might retaliate with their own secret "doomsday device"; and it was up to the Air Force commander to tell the

Air Force General "Buck" Turgidson (George C. Scott) struggles frantically to prevent the Soviet Ambassador (Peter Bull) from glimpsing top secret information in the War Room of the Pentagon, while President Muffley (Peter Sellers) barely comprehends what's going on.

astonished President and his hastily assembled "war council" how such a fearful thing had happened and what might be done to head it off.

The action alternated in three areas—first in the office of the air base general where he ominously sealed himself off with a dumbfounded British liaison officer in order to resist arrest by an Army detail sent to stop him; second in the cabin of one of the bombers sent to destroy a Soviet base, with a cracky, trigger-happy Texas cowboy gleefully in command; and third in the Pentagon's huge War Room where the President and his large advisory staff gathered to try to do something in the precious minutes before the bombs were scheduled to fall.

It was in the War Room that the most chilling activity went on, mainly because it was the most realistic and therefore the most plausible. The stuff in the office of the base general, whom Sterling Hayden played with a beautiful balance of John Wayne toughness and sputtering insanity, and that in the cabin of the bomber, with Slim Pickens rallying his crew with a fantastic flow of ranchhand lingo pouring out from under his incongruously donned cowboy hat, was close to the line of pure farce clowning. It was grand, clever caricature. But the stuff in the shadowy War Room was all too credible.

Here the brash Air Force commander stalled to cover his inability and dismay with a bombastic flood of technical jargon under pressure from the pipsqueak President, whom Mr. Sellers (again) with a shiny, bald head made a symbol of bland ineptitude. Unbelievable inanities passed between them as the precious minutes ticked off and a now computer-triggered clash with Russia appeared inevitable.

One futile attempt at prevention was a hot line call from the President to the Soviet Premier in Moscow, but that turned—when the Premier was finally reached—into a dizzying tangle of euphemisms and typical telephone-conversation platitudes. One could fancy from the one-sided dialogue that the Premier was not amused.

The crunch finally came when the bomber, unable to be recalled, dropped its bomb on the Soviet base (with Mr. Pickens accidentally riding it down like a howling cowboy on a bucking bronco) and the President meekly telling the Premier, "We're all in this thing together, Dimitri. We're here behind you," as though consoling him about a rush-hour train delay. Now came the time for Dr. Strangelove's and the Air Force commander's unleashed glee over the prospect of all-out war and slaughter. "Boy, will we *clobber* them!" exulted Mr. Scott.

The picture closed with an aerial shot on the mushrooming cloud of an exploded nuclear bomb and the sound track sardonically serenading with "We'll Meet Again Some Sunny Day."

Mr. Kubrick, of course, got all the credit for the form and substance of this titanic thrust, which he and the famously irreverent Terry Southern concocted from a comparatively serious book, *Red Alert*, by Peter George. Certainly Mr. Kubrick's lethal humor and his skill at weaving it in with firmly simulated realism gave the unique texture to the film. But Mr. Scott, Mr. Hayden, and Mr. Sellers set the magnificent characterizations of more than just two-dimensional types. And Keenan Wynn also came in briefly with a picture of an Army knucklehead—the captain sent to capture Mr. Hayden—that was a gem of military ridicule.

Heaven protect us from ever having a national crisis occur on the order of the one experienced in this unforgettable film. But if it should—and I can't get over the niggling dread that it might—I only hope that we can all go with it as wildly and fatalistically as did Mr. Pickens, his cowboy hat waving, riding down on that kick-off bomb.

206

COOL HAND LUKE

George Kennedy and Paul Newman in a scene from Warner Brothers-Seven Arts' *Cool Hand Luke*, directed by Stuart Rosenberg.

1967

The so-called Prison Picture, a long-time staple of American films, just as the so-called Prison Ballad is a staple in our folk song and lore, came to its fruition with Stuart Rosenberg's *Cool Hand Luke*, a 1967 production which had Paul Newman in its title role. And that is no small compliment, for our screen has had some fine films in this genre, such as *I Am a Fugitive from a Chain Gang* (1932), with Paul Muni, and *Bird Man of Alcatraz* (1962), starring Burt Lancaster.

But this was one that went much deeper and said much more about the social condition and attitudes of the unusual, difficult jailbird than did the endless run of routine prison films, loaded with lumpish melodrama and fantasies of life inside the walls. This film was devoted not to mere exploitation of the cruel disciplines and brutalities of jailers; its principal interest was the psychic damage that came from the communal constriction and conditioning imposed on a convict by his fellow prisoners and the ultimate unbalancing of his ego and the destruction to which this led.

207

A riot of fun and frolic breaks out in a barracks of the convict camp in this scene from *Cool Hand Luke*.

The reticent young fellow who was picked up by police at the beginning of this film and sent off to a correctional work camp, obviously somewhere in the South, for the patently minor offense of being drunk and vandalizing parking meters, was more than a commonplace bum, more than a pathetic human being who was a "victim of society," as we say—which, of course, is what everybody who commits crime is regarded as today. He was a psychologically mixed-up and emotionally frustrated young man who was as much a silent sufferer from his own self-withdrawal and secret pride as he was from the ignorance and bullying of those among whom he was thrown.

He was a calculating loner, a terse and sarcastic misanthrope who treated his jailers with sullen defiance and his fellow prisoners with cool contempt. Grimly he endured the physical beatings and the verbal insults the guards heaped on him, and he mocked and smiled when his fellow convicts ridiculed and hazed him unmercifully. Clearly he was not a coward or weakling, and his air of detached dignity emerged (as we were later made to realize) from some unspecified boyhood hurt. So he continued in this pattern until finally a point was reached where he had to submit to or run from a showdown fight with the top-dog prisoner, whereupon he waded in gamely, defiantly, and ferociously until he dropped.

That was the turning point for him because, as juvenile men usually do, his fellow inmates considered him a hero and the topdog took him in tow, made him his boasted companion and, recognizing his superior wit and skill, backed him in surreptitious contests and used him in intraprisoner deals. Thus came a sharp dramatic juncture, a turning point in the film. It began with an interlude of levity that was relaxing and significant, and went on to more complicated changes that precipitated the tragic end.

In a grotesque and farcical encounter, the young champion won a bet, engineered by his patron, that he could eat fifty hard-boiled eggs at one unbroken sitting. It was a grossly amusing scene. And his comical triumphs at poker elevated him to heroic heights. But this elevation was fatal. Now he was Cool Hand Luke, the idol of the sycophantic prisoners and the growing concern of the guards. He began assuming bravura postures to demonstrate his contempt. And because it was expected of him, when he received word that his mother had died, he made a break for freedom, almost made it, but was caught and returned.

The inevitable commitment to this pattern—other

208

breaks other returns, other and cruel beatings and tortures until his pride and will were cracked—led to a sad and grisly climax for this congenital fugitive—a fugitive not only from the chain gang but from society and, indeed, from life.

What set this brutal picture above the rank of prison films and marked it as intelligent commentary upon the ironies of life were a sharp screenplay by Frank R. Pierson and Don Pearce, from a novel by Mr. Pearce, fine acting, and brilliant direction by Mr. Rosenberg, who came to theatrical films from television and hasn't again matched this vivid work.

The key to his style and visual impact was—in one word—proximity. Mr. Rosenberg worked his camera close when crucial action was going on or striking and vivid comprehensions of character and conditions were desired. Since his was essentially a story of the inner nature and spiritual torments of a man who suffered severe alienation (like the ''hairy ape'' of Eugene O'Neill), the closer he brought us to this character, the more enclosed in him he made us feel.

In the opening scene, for instance, when the drunken rebel was pointlessly knocking the tops off the parking meters, Mr. Rosenberg took us right in to see the sweat on his face and the anger and fury in his eyes. When he was standing in line to be instructed, along with other prisoners, as to how to behave in the work camp, or slugging it out with the bully, or painfully stuffing down those eggs, the camera was close, the blood was pulsing. We were one with Luke.

Likewise, Mr. Rosenberg got us close to the other characters when that was appropriate to the emotions being felt by the central character—to the big, bruising, canny bully played powerfully by George Kennedy; to the burly guards with their dark mirror-glasses; to other prisoners sweating in the work-camp fields. And especially he brought us close to Luke's mother in one critical scene in which she came to visit him in the work camp, propped up stiffly in the back of a flatbed truck. This scene, which was played superbly by Mr. Newman and Jo Van Fleet, told more by visual implications and guarded, metallic words about the likely background of the prisoner and the cast of his mother than might have been explained in a more explicit film.

Perhaps, for the sake of consistency in the realistic texture and the red-necked appearance, Mr. Newman was not the most appropriate actor for this role. He was too handsome, too clean-cut. But Mr. Newman was sensitive and revealing in projecting the anomaly of this man—the distortion and transformation that came about in him as a consequence of the inflation of his ego generated in abnormality by his peers.

This was, indeed, the underrunning theme and demonstration of *Cool Hand Luke*—that the vulnerable individual may be seized and destroyed by the mob in ways more subtle and pathetic than by beating with fists and clubs. Thus it endowed a prison picture with a universal theme that went well beyond the ordinary melodrama.

Cool Hand Luke did not reduce us to sentimental pity for this man. It left us with disquieting awareness that he was as much a victim of his weaknesses as King Lear. His fate might be that of anybody, inside a prison or out.

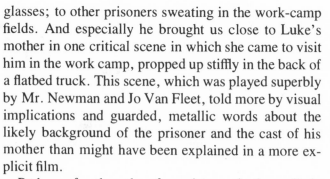

Luke (Paul Newman), the loner, is given an unmerciful drubbing by the bullying convict, Dragline (George Kennedy).

Mortally wounded after his breakout from the convict camp, Luke (Paul Newman) is supported and protected from vengeful guards by his convict friend, Dragline.

CABARET

1972

There are several powerful reasons why Bob Fosse's *Cabaret* should stand as one of the classic and cherishable films of the 1970s. Not least is the fact that it presented in a musical starring role the talented daughter of Judy Garland—Liza Minnelli—making her singing debut on the screen more than three decades after her famous mother clicked as a lass in *The Wizard of Oz.* This unprecedented continuity of a mother and daughter as singing stars was notable for cultural reasons other than sentiment. It brought into juxtaposition an awesome contrast in locales and styles that revealed how far the musical movie had

Sally Bowles (Liza Minnelli) and the mephitic Master of Ceremonies (Joel Grey) perform their satiric and cynical "Money!" number at the Kit Kat Klub in pre-Hitler Berlin.

come. And this was rendered more phenomenal by the coincidence that both performers were playing roles of little girls, as it were, in ambiences that were freakish and bizarre. But, oh, what grotesquely different ambiences they were!

Cabaret was a bitter, poignant exposure in a chin-up romantic style of a grim state of demoralization and degeneration in the early 1930s in Berlin—a place light-years away from the make-believe Land of Oz. It was a drama which intermingled innocence, optimism, and naïveté in a milieu of shameless cynicism, decadence, and despair. Sally Bowles was an American nightclub singer who was loose in the Berlin demimonde, dreaming of becoming a movie starlet while working in a third-rate cabaret. And the strange kind of hopefulness and bravery that this little spirit displayed among the hideous things that were happening within the orbit of the sordid cabaret placed in gruesome highlight the tragedy of a nation succumbing to Nazism.

Contrary to all the old conventions and expectations for the musical film, *Cabaret* was, in essence, serious and philosophical. It was several generations descended from a sketch by Christopher Isherwood, which appeared in his *Goodbye to Berlin,* published in 1939—a volume which today is painful history. In 1951 it was adapted by John van Druten into a play, *I Am a Camera,* which was poorly translated four years later into a middling film. This, considerably altered and stage-set in its titular cabaret, became a Broadway musical show in the 1960s, and *this,* considerably altered again, was the parent of *Cabaret.*

On the surface it seemed to dwell on Sally, a spontaneously combusting little singer who fell in love with Brian, a young English don who, without money or substantial prospects, was in Berlin to brush up on his *deutsch.* But their boarding-house affair (which, incidentally, freed him from a homosexual block) was shattered when Sally, pregnant by either Brian or a young German sport with whom she had a sidelines frolic, got an abortion even after Brian told her he wanted to marry her and take her to England to be a proper wife. Obviously she wasn't able to face up to this responsibility. She chose to remain in Berlin with her cabaret singing and her dreams.

And, as subplot, there was a poignant romance between two of their incidental friends—a poor, fortune-hunting German and a beautiful, wealthy Italian Jewess—which allowed for some tender moments and further pointing of the anti-Semitic theme.

But the fundamental focus of the picture was the stage of the Kit Kat cabaret and the turmoil of stygian intimations and dark emotions it generated. It was here that Sally's temporal being was captured and confined, isolated, yet not without submission, from her spiritual purity that never won the upperhand. And it was here that the deus ex machina of the film and its conception had command. He was the Mephistophelian master of ceremonies of the cabaret.

At first, this tiny creature with his ferretlike figure, his painted face, his frozen smile, and his chromium harmonizing that "life is a cabaret, old chum, so come to the cabaret," seemed no more than an agile puppet, a song-and-dance comedian of a sort that we'd seen without number in myriad Hollywood nightclub films. And his sprightly, mechanical marshaling of the jum-

Joel Grey as the Master of Ceremonies in *Cabaret.*

Brian (Michael York) and Sally (Liza Minnelli) celebrate a brief moment of euphoria in the poignant and prophetic musical drama, *Cabaret*.

Brian (Michael York) and Sally (Liza Minnelli), on an outing in the German countryside, find themselves wistfully contemplative in this scene from *Cabaret*.

The Master of Ceremonies (Joel Grey), accompanied by the corpulent chorus of Berlin's pre-Hitler Kit Kat Klub, sings and dances the satiric song, "Willkommen," in one of the flashy numbers in *Cabaret*.

ble of acts on the stage, from Sally's electrical performing early along of the title song to a sticky burlesque of transvestites that invited the usual guffaws, was uncomplicatedly amusing and moved the show along.

Likewise his dueting with Sally of a brilliantly satirical song, "Money, Money, Money," was one of the brightest things in the film, and his lone performing of a number with a coyly gowned caricature of an ape, to whom and of whom he sang poignantly, "If you could see her through my eyes, she wouldn't look Jewish at all," was funny, sardonic, embarrassing and, suddenly, toward its end, ineffably sad.

But as this character expanded in a stunning performance by Joel Grey, who seemed in his first screen performance to have been divinely created just for it, he took on disturbing dimensions. The glitter in his eyes became obscene. The lure of his repeated invitation to submerge oneself in the cabaret became, like the greasepaint and the spangles, to be a shoddy seduction to doom. Like Marlene Dietrich in the 1929 classic *The Blue Angel*,* a remarkably comparable film, he loomed as a sinister symbol of Germanic corruption and decay. Indeed, he became contrapuntal to the brown-shirted, swastika-labeled brutes who once or twice swarmed, with clubs swinging, into the

213

The little American singer, Sally Bowles (Liza Minnelli), belts out the song "Mein Herr" on the tiny stage of the Berlin Kit Kat Klub in *Cabaret*.

smoky cabaret and cracked the heads of innocent patrons in the nearby alleys and streets.

If Miss Minnelli's performance had not been a match for Mr. Grey's and if she hadn't had the advantage of magnetizing so much sympathy, she might have been outshone so badly that the balance of the show would have been lost and the fragile structure of a naturalistic play with music rather than a musical comedy would have collapsed.

As it was, Mr. Fosse kept the contours and the balance so perfectly aligned that the viewer was craftily entrapped by the verisimilitude. The cabaret and its characteristics were inherent dramatic elements just as were Sally and her lovers and the morbid atmosphere of Berlin. Indeed, only one song number took place outside the cabaret. That was a blood-chilling solo sung by a blond Hitler Youth in a *gemütlich* country beer-garden to which Sally and Brian had escaped—a grisly, ironic ballad, "Tomorrow Belongs to Me."

I could go on praising aspects of this picture—its superb photography, done by the Britisher Geoffrey Unsworth, who made the color as eloquent as words; the choreography by Mr. Fosse, the music by John Kander and Fred Ebb, and most of the minor character acting, excepting that of Michael York as a weak-tea Brian. But I haven't the space for itemizing—save, let me add, a personal word for Miss Minnelli's plaintive singing of the subdued torch song "Maybe This Time I'll Be Lucky," which reminded me so nostalgically of her mother's smoky rendering of "The Man That Got Away" in *A Star Is Born* that I choked up as much for Esther Blodgett as for poor little lost Sally Bowles.

There was cause for some criticism. The cabaret acts were not as shabby as they might have been; two or three of Sally's would have brightened the Las Vegas Thunderbird. The dismal confinement of the Kit Kat seemed low for such a talented girl. But something decidedly exceptional was done on the screen by *Cabaret*. It opened a whole new vista for the latter-day musical film. It showed that this kind of picture could have as much intelligence to convey as a tightly packed realistic drama. And it gave those of us who were living in those distant pre-Nazi years a feeling of reminiscent sadness for lots of things that are past and dead.

THE GODFATHER

Barzini (Richard Conte), head of one of the Mafia families, applauds solemnly as Don Vito Corleone (Marlon Brando) makes a gesture of friendship toward another at a strategy gathering of Mafia family heads.

1972/1974

For several extraordinary reasons, not least of which was the fact that they were both superior movies, *The Godfather* and *The Godfather II* constitute what I consider an unprecedented phenomenon in American films. Both films were made within the surprising span of two years—1972 and 1974—under the direction of Francis Ford Coppola, who also co-authored both scripts along with Mario Puzo, author of the popular novel on which they were based. Remarkably, they constitute the only instance where the

215

The aging Don Vito Corleone (Marlon Brando) privately and tacitly transfers his mantle and his power to the nervous and uncertain shoulders of his youngest son, Michael (Al Pacino).

sequel to a thoroughly successful film was equally if not more impressive than the original. Indeed, *The Godfather* and *The Godfather II* mesh so aptly and artfully that they appear to have been constructed as one long film. So conjunctive were they that I don't see how they could be separately contemplated now in a critical reappraisal and discussion. That is why I am considering them together in this book.

Another reason for their rare distinction is the fact that they placed a capstone on a major and characteristic genre of American sound motion pictures—that is, the gangster-crime films. This is a point that most critics noted and discussed in their reviews, more particularly of *The Godfather* but collaterally of *The Godfather II*. Critics tended to discover it, however, on the levels of complexity and techniques. Allowing those obvious distinctions, I feel the prime reason why these two films must be said to crown a major myth-generating genre is that they achieved the ultimate in fantasizing and romanticizing organized crime—and I use those two words with great discretion. The simple fact is that no matter how vivid and plausible a few top films about gangsters, mafiosi, members of the Cosa Nostra and all such twentieth-century criminals have been, including the two *Godfathers,* they have still been *romanticizations* of the true natures and deeds of big-time criminals, not literal portrayals. They have perforce been fabrications, based on research and evidence, it is true, but designed in the end to accord with the demands of a vast mythology.

Thus when the two *Godfathers* projected in most engaging ways a concept of postwar Mafia characters in the United States as privately loving, loyal, considerate, and even sentimental men, driven by traditional ambitions to achieve their cut of the American dream—wealth, power, social status, and respectability (for their children, at least)—they were but clinching for all time the public's illusions of the top-echelon mafioso, fostered by planted press stories, fiction, and films. Mr. Puzo himself acknowledged at the time *The Godfather* was released that it was a romantic story, and that Mafia members were "much worse guys than [these]."

The result was that this two-part saga of American organized crime, conceived in such rich, abundant detail and flow of dramatic events, wove a pictorial fabric of such immense and astonishing scope that it gave its audiences the feeling of being privileged and intimate voyeurs of the life-styles and business operations

Sonny Corleone (James Caan), hotheaded elder son of Don Vito, administers a disciplinary thrashing to his two-timing brother-in-law.

Don Vito Corleone (Marlon Brando) looks with anguish and anger upon the body of Sonny, slain by a rival Mafia family.

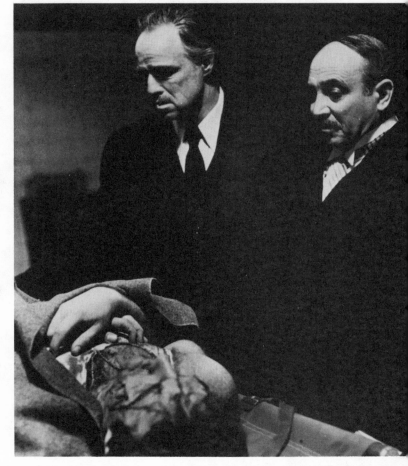

Michael Corleone (Al Pacino), the don's most reliable son, is drilled in the use of firearms by one of the family "soldiers" (Richard Castellano) to "hit" the enemies who have tried to murder the don.

Michael Corleone (Al Pacino) receives the homage of family members after he has been elevated to replace his dead parent as the new "Godfather" of the family.

Michael Corleone (Al Pacino) sits down serenely with the crooked police captain, McCluskey (Sterling Hayden) and the treacherous Mafia lieutenant Sollozzo (Al Lettieri) just before retrieving a hidden gun from the men's room and slaying both of them.

Robert De Niro, as the young Vito Corleone, kisses the hand of Guiseppe Sillato moments before stabbing the old Mafia Chieftan to avenge the death of his family in Sicily.

of one of the last great congeries of genuine adventurers and pirates in our complex industrial world.

These movies constituted a phenomenon because they also exposed more frankly and without question than any film of which I am aware the pattern of moral values, or lack of them, on which our capitalist society now operates. *The Godfathers* took the moral posture that what the members of this "family" did, so long as they were solid and loyal and acted according to the precepts of their code, was perfectly proper and acceptable, placing only themselves in physical peril. And this attitude was buttressed by the evidence that everyone here was working for the good of the family and the only evident harm that was being done was to their enemies and to rivals who were apparently much more reprehensible than they.

It was noticeable there was no statement of moral censure or judgment of what these characters did. We were not made to feel disgust or outrage at the mores of this clan. We may have been shocked by the examples of their ruthless arrogance and bold enterprise in pursuing their perilous line of work, but that was all. The philosophy implicit was "an eye for an eye and a tooth for a tooth" and "If you don't do it to somebody, somebody will do it to you." Ethical standards as we once knew them—or thought we knew them—did not prevail, nor did they even seem to enter the consciousness of the assorted members of this tribe. The justification for their expedients was "the bottom line." What was most important was that the expedients worked. And this seemed to be a conclusion with which audiences agreed.

Thus the things that these two pictures told us about ourselves through tacit implication and about the changes that have occurred in our moral conceptions of criminals since the days of the classic gangster films were astounding and challenging. The old law of "compensating moral values"—that criminals had to pay for their crimes—which always brought the wrongdoers to justice and usually violent deaths in the days of *Little Caesar* and *The Public Enemy* had obviously been stricken from the books. This was an awe-

Michael Corleone (Al Pacino), now ascended to the role of head of the family, discusses a new alliance with the independent gambling syndicate boss Hyman Roth (Lee Strasberg), in the sequential *The Godfather, Part II*.

At a hearing before a Senate committee on organized crime, Michael Corleone (Al Pacino) and the family lawyer, Tom Hagen (Robert Duval), coach an Italian-speaking witness (Salvatore Po) brought over from Italy.

some revelation that transcended entertainment as such and gave to these films the significance of a profound philosophical overview. In this respect, the *Godfathers* may have been frightening, but not hypocritical.

Considering the length of these two movies and the dramatic complexities of them, not to mention the wealth of detail, biographical and melodramatic, which they contained, I cannot attempt to do more than summarize them in broad terms. They told essen-

tially the story of the Corleone family, the head of which, Don Vito Corleone, had come to America from Sicily shortly after the century's turn, plunged into the ferment of New York's East Side melting pot, and had found himself through circumstances propelled into a career of crime.

The first *Godfather* found the family in 1945 at a major turning point in its fortunes. Don Vito had achieved wealth and power as the head of one of the five great Mafia families in the United States. He had well earned the status of godfather, boss and patriarch of his clan, but he was old and the necessity of finding a successor was at hand. This was more implied than stated in the opening phase of the film, in which all the family were gathered for the wedding of a daughter of the old man, and he punctuated his moments of pride and pleasure with interludes of attending to matters of "business" in an exclusive back room. To any reports of resistance from those with whom his people had to deal, he gave a simple instruction: "Make him an offer he can't refuse." Which, of course, was a guarded euphemism for putting on the screws.

Then, by chance, an attempt by an enemy to kill the old Don with a hit brought to the fore as a candidate for successor to him his youngest son, whom the old man had indicated he would prefer to see step away from the family business and go into government or some big corporate enterprise. But the need for someone to follow the ritual of exacting vengeance for the attempted killing fell upon this son, and his courage and skill in maneuvering the enemy into a trap and slaying him along with a crooked police lieutenant made this son the obvious choice. So, when Vito Corleone succumbed to a heart attack in his vegetable garden one peaceful day while playing with one of his grandchildren, this son, Michael, became the new godfather and gave every indication that he would be just as traditional and despotic as the old Don was.

The second *Godfather,* set ten years later, picked up the story with this son, now a seasoned Mafia leader and obviously a rich and coolly confident man, making a bid for respectability with a huge confirmation party for *his* son at his elaborate new home on Lake Tahoe in Nevada and, like his father, mixing business with pleasure at this baroque affair. But an attempt on Michael's life, as on his father's, sent him off on a surreptitious chase to try to pinpoint his intending killer. And the incidents of this chase—a meeting with Mafia heads in Cuba, a liaison with a Jewish lone wolf whose involvements in the rackets were most intriguing and mystifying, and other such—were intercut with lengthy flashbacks to the father's early life in New York and how he happened to join the Sicilian Black Hand, get married, and rise in the world of crime (with bootlegging notably unmentioned) to the point where we met him in the first film.

Thus, while the first film was mainly about the son and his ascent to power, the second was mainly about the father and *his* achievement. This reversal and juxtaposition of the main biographical developments in the two films was a fascinating aspect of their structures and a part of the whole phenomenon.

The conclusion of the second film was that the son did find his enemy (it turned out to be his own brother and Hyman Roth, the Jew), had them adroitly liquidated completely, lost the love of his wife, and ended up on the terrace of his Lake Tahoe home, alone and forlorn, looking grimly on the autumnal, windswept lake.

This does not begin to give a fair estimation of the flavor and excitement of the two films. Their distinctive generic features—the family parleys in back rooms, the dark and paunchy looks of the Mafia "soldiers," the killers stalking their prey, the high-level Mafia chiefs' gatherings, the blazing hits—were familiar from endless gangster pictures—superficially improved-upon clichés. But the great achievement in the *Godfathers* was the weaving of a tapestry of style. These were not two-bit Mafia people. These were characters with guts and criminal class, people we were introduced to and lived with through the chapters of their lives. We were guests at their ritualistic parties, their secret parleys, in their bedrooms and kitchens, at intimate scenes of illness and death. Mr. Puzo and Mr. Coppola gave them to us in full, with all their Sicilian emotions and all their singularly self-serving attitudes.

And the performers, with few exceptions, were superb. Although Marlon Brando as Don Vito Corleone in the first film received the most publicity and critical attention—and, indeed, gave a brilliant portrayal of a stiff, sullen, tired old chief, a believable survivor of punishing gangland wars—the star of both films was Al Pacino, who showed the upcoming son as deadpanned, dynamic, unrelenting, and as dangerous as a live high-voltage wire. (The father as a young man in the sequel was played excitingly by a new actor, Robert De Niro, but the slant he was directed to assume was that of a seriocomic "character," a young Italian immigrant just this side of a buffoon.)

James Caan as the oldest sibling was superb in the first film, a fellow charged with too much spirit, too erratic emotionally, unable to endure the discipline imposed by the family code. Mr. Caan was expressive and explosive in every scene he played. Alone, he was lost in a hail of bullets toward the end of the first film.

Others, too, were splendid: Sterling Hayden as the crooked cop, and his counterpart in the second picture, G. D. Spradin as a U.S. Senator on the take. Lee Strasberg was brilliantly acerbic and slippery as the lone wolf, Hyman Roth (a role clearly based on Meyer Lansky, the king of the big gambling mobs). And Robert Duval made something special and rare in gangster films of the role of the quiet, self-effacing, ever-loyal Irish lawyer of the Corleones.

Reflecting the old Sicilian custom of keeping women in their place, and these being largely men's pictures, the wives and daughters did not have major roles, but their presence and domestic relations with their menfolk were significant throughout, especially in the character of Michael's upper-class Protestant wife whom Diane Keaton made the singular exponent of revulsion and rectitude. It was her walkout in the second film, after she had almost been slaughtered in her bed by gunmen coming after Michael, that pegged the ultimate irony—the last sight of Michael alone and empty with his Pyrrhic victory.

There were certain things about these pictures that may have seemed weaknesses at first but become less important in the long view. For instance, there was a strange indefiniteness about what rackets the Corleones were involved in and how their lower-echelon machinery worked. These, we see now, were details that would have been redundant and routine. The creation of a frankly Jewish figure as a crafty and eventually treacherous sort may at first have seemed anti-Semitic and a clumsy attempt to stress that all organized criminals were not Italians. But to have avoided this would have been evasive and a show of hypocrisy. It was the abundance of arcana of this sort that helped make these such engrossing films.

Was it weakness to have failed explicitly to condemn the activities of the Corleones, the corruptions of organized crime, and the consummate cant of crime chieftains who could stand up in church and pray while their personally instructed henchmen were killing people in the streets? I can only say that such conventional moralizing would have seemed to me not only platitudinous but contrary to the very purpose and effect of these films.

The most powerful thrust of the *Godfathers* was to point through the ambience of crime and reveal the glaring dichotomy between preachment and performance in our "moral" society. The ruthless pursuit of their own interests by these people was convincingly condoned by deluding the audience with an eyewash of sentimentality and conveying the pragmatic notion that "others do it so why shouldn't we?" To have tried to discredit this pervasive attitude in our society, except by well-planted implications, would again have been hypocrisy.

The Corleones were no different, when you came right down to it, from any of the famous robber barons who worked our system and our economy for their own predatory advantage and now dwell in their own mythology.

This awesome saga of *The Godfathers* will live beside *Citizen Kane*.

LAST TANGO IN PARIS

1972

The vast attention that Bernardo Bertolucci's *Last Tango in Paris* received while it was several months in the making and when it opened in the fall of 1972 was not due to the prospect of its being a likely world-shaking film. It was because Marlon Brando was in it, and he was the hottest screen actor alive. With a long string of triumphs behind him, with a lurid reputation in his personal life, and because he had been a huge sensation in *The Godfather* earlier that year, there was every good reason why the public, not to mention "the industry," should have been insatiably curious about his next role and whether, as juicily rumored, *Last Tango* was going to be a superporno film.

Had the picture been no more than responsive to such a show of fan-audience idolatry, it would have happily fulfilled commercial interests and then gone

Paul (Marlon Brando) and Jeanne (Marie Schneider) dance the last tango in a cheap Paris dancehall toward the end of the film.

The initial encounter of Jeanne (Maria Schneider) and Paul (Marlon Brando) in a vacant apartment in *Last Tango in Paris*.

on down the road. But it was more than a mere box-office buster. It was a surprisingly powerful film—much more powerful and significant than many critics were willing to concede. It was not only vivid and engrossing in a cruelly sadistic way, but it said things that were important about human nature and the world in which we live.

The first thing to be made clear about it is that it was not—repeat NOT—pornography, not in any of the usual salacious senses of the word. Yes, it was full of candid explorations and brazen illustrations of sex. Sex was, indeed, the foremost factor in its deep psychological probe. But it was not an erotic picture of the sort that would agitate lust or serve an aphrodisia-

cal purpose, as every true porno picture should. It was the most devastating denigration of sheer lustfulness that I have seen. If it did anything to one's libido, man's or woman's, it was to turn it off!

It did explicitly tell the story of an aging American male, adrift and lately widowed in Paris, pursuing a young French girl, in a bath of sexual obsession. But it was about so many other things—the erosion of confidence and competence that occupational failure can bring, the tendencies to brutalize women that may surge in a true male chauvinist, the subconscious urge to self-destruction that lurks in today's frustrated men—that the sexual activity in the foreground was but a clue to the principal character's real concerns. And the groping of the girl in the story for some sort of discipline and stability was only betrayed by the abandon with which she surrendered herself to an older man.

The first big scene in the picture where the man,

Paul (Marlon Brando) and Jeanne (Maria Schneider) make a futile attempt to renew their old relationship in a tawdry dancehall.

Discontent and uncertainty disturb Jeanne (Maria Schneider) and her supposed fiancé, Tom (Jean -Pierre Leaud), who is more interested in making a documentary film than in her. This is the young man who made his debut as the boy in *The 400 Blows*.

Paul, and the girl, Jeanne, accidentally met in an empty apartment which they were separately considering whether to rent, was a crucial hint to the capriciousness and barrenness of their lives. He was obviously defeated and exhausted (though as yet we had not been told why) and she was erratic and restless, open to anything. Thus his sudden assault upon her, after they had barely exchanged a few tart words, and she had unprotestingly submitted to him sexually on the bare floor, was a classic indicator of the impulse of a frustrated man to rape, and her willingness to go along with it was a key to her disgust with herself. For him it was a thrust for a catharsis for what was eating on his mind; for her it was an act of flagellation to rid herself of some hidden sense of guilt.

Next we were given some inklings of their identities although they first agreed privately not to tell each other a thing about themselves ("We're going to forget everything," he told her)—again a clue to his impulse to isolate himself. He had been rendered a widower only a few hours before by his wife, the proprietress of a sleazy hotel, who mysteriously cut her throat. (There was, for a while, a slight suspicion that he might have killed her himself.) He, an ex-actor, ex-boxer, ex-journalist, and now expatriate, had been living off his wife for the past few years. And the girl, we were shown in a couple of sequences, was engaged to a young French filmmaker from whom she clearly craved intimate attention but only interested him as the subject of a documentary film. Later we were to learn

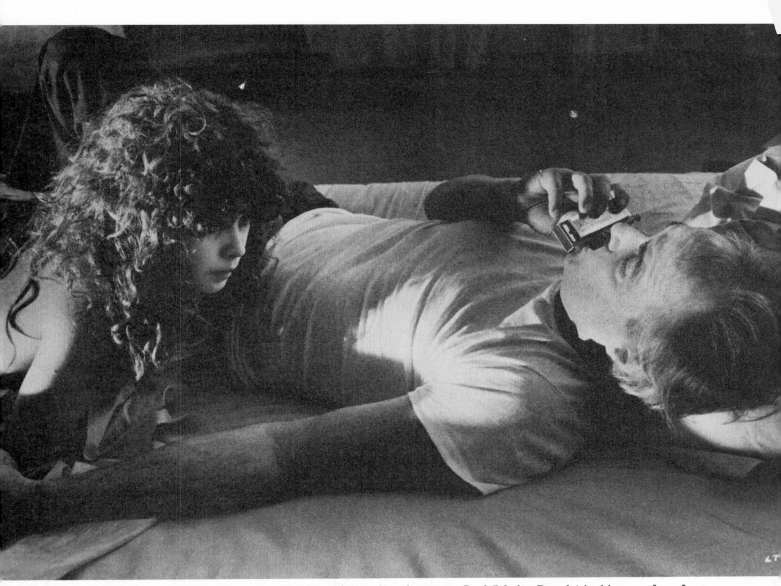

The youthful Jeanne submits to the gross seductions of the aging, degenerate Paul (Marlon Brando) in this scene from *Last Tango in Paris.*

that she had been devoted to her father, an army colonel killed in Algiers, and that his loss and the memories of her childhood were painfully on her mind.

But when she began to try to tell this to Paul in one of their continuing rendezvous, he cut her off sharply and rudely. "What a steaming pile of horseshit!" he exclaimed, but casually proceeded to tell her about his unhappy boyhood in the United States, thus revealing his passion for self-pity and his parallel lack of genuine interest in the girl.

And then, as their meetings grew more frequent and Jeanne seemed to be falling in love, he became pro-gressively more brutal, forced her to commit sodomy, and then reached the final humiliation of compelling her to stick her fingers up his ass, the while abusing her with filthy discourse, such as how he was going to get a pig to fuck her, vomit in her face, and such. She was totally repelled and tried to avoid him thence-forth.

Meanwhile, Paul, in his endeavor to fathom why his wife had killed herself, met with her lover, Marcel, and learned some fascinating things from him. He learned that she had given her lover a bathrobe exactly like one she had given him, that she supplied him with

Paul's brand of whiskey, and that once, in a mystifying fit, she had tried to strip the paper off the walls of Marcel's bedroom. Significantly, the walls of the bedroom of the wife and Paul were unpapered.

The ultimate revelation of the brutality and selfishness of Paul came in what I consider the most powerful scene in the film—that was when he, in evident anguish, kneeled alone beside the bier on which her body lay and vulgarly, hideously condemned her, calling her all sorts of vile names, demanding to know why she "did it," professing he didn't understand, and finally breaking down and weeping in another guilt-ridden display.

Many critics misread completely Paul's relation with his wife. They deduced from these encounters that he had been betrayed by her and that she, in assuming a lover, had shatteringly disillusioned him; I hold that his discussion with Marcel and his cursing of his wife exposed his contempt for this poor woman and the despair that caused her to turn to another man, to try to re-create her husband, then desolately kill herself. That last scene was for me the solution of the mounting mystery of Paul's nasty aggressiveness toward women that began in the first big scene.

From here on the course was conclusive. Paul happened to meet Jeanne in the street (at the same spot where he happened to see her the first time, by the way), tried desperately to persuade her to resume a relation with him and then, when she adamantly spurned him, got her to go with him to a cheap tango hall, plied her with champagne and repetitions of his old flashes of charm and wit, took her on the dance floor to tango, stumbled all over his feet, and then, in drunken derision, took down his pants and showed his ass.

A desperate Paul (Marlon Brando) chases the disgusted Jeanne (Maria Schneider) through the streets of Paris after she has refused his last attempt at reconciliation.

For all the despicable aspects of Paul that had been shown up to here, there was something tremendously touching and poignant about him in this long scene. Here he was, obviously beaten, a lonely loser at the end of his string, unable to make it with women, contemptuous of them and of himself, but pressing one final endeavor to make this "last tango" count—and failing.

As for Jeanne, the extent of her frustration and compassion was beautifully shown in this scene, too. Her patience with his banter, her efforts to humor him, and her ultimate condescension to take him to her home after his drunken exhibition were a token of what she may have hoped in her brief flush of love for this monster and her sadness at her loss. It was when he made one more endeavor to get her to have sex with him, put on her father's kepi and postured mockingly in this bourgeois apartment full of mementos of the dead military man, that Jeanne calmly fetched her father's pistol and put a shot into Paul's heart. Staggering out to a terrace overlooking the roofs of Paris, he fell dead.

A few critics felt this was a cop-out conclusion for the film. I felt it was brilliantly appropriate and penetratingly ironical. What more was there for this worn-out loser, still trying to work his hurtful pitch, but death and a blank-out explanation by his killer, "I don't know who he is. He tried to attack me. He was mad"? I feel that Jeanne did him a favor. She may even have been completing the vengeful job that she subconsciously felt like doing in their opening scene.

In light of the ambiguous reputation of Brando and the public's strong mixed feelings about him, it was no wonder that there were extreme reactions to his performance in this heavily antiheroic role. He was charged with all the weary resentments of his overacting, and so on, that have been heaped upon him ever since his first screen appearance in *A Streetcar Named Desire*. I thought his work here was excellent. His harboring of evil behind a mask of aging decay and degeneration was so expert, so accurate and intense, that I must say I've never seen a stronger symbolization of evil on the screen. Yet his skill at creating a feeling of pity and philosophical grief for this man, so clearly a creature of polluting forces, was irresistible.

And newcomer Maria Schneider was amazingly vibrant, too, in filling her freakish little hippie with all sorts of avid and tender nuances. Credit must go to Bertolucci, who assisted in writing the script and directed for tremendous implications—though it is known that Brando was vastly helpful in improvising many of his scenes, including the great one with the dead wife, and in spontaneously larding his dialogue with vivid Americanese.

The fact that this character was an American came about by chance. The role was originally intended for Jean-Louis Trintignant, until Brando agreed to play it, which was a stroke of fortune, because the American aspect added a startling new dimension to the film. Now this hideous creature became a withering metaphor for the ugly, uncouth, destructive American who has in many minds, especially in Europe, raped and corrupted the postwar world. To have wreaked his nationalized evil on a little French girl was the basest symbolic offense.

But I perceive in this character more than a symbol of the rapacious American. Paul was to me the epitome of a dying and disposable breed—the romantic soldier-of-fortune, the overglorified jock, the cavalier exploiter of women—yes, the male chauvinist pig. And it was interestingly symbolic and appropriate that Bertolucci chose Paris as the place to dispose of this spent image: Paris, the romantic City of Light, the focus of so many vain and foolish sexual fantasies!

Yes, *Last Tango in Paris* might be found, as time goes on, to mark ironically the fade-out of the Heroic Age of the entertainment screen.

INDEX

236

ACKNOWLEDGMENTS

For generous help and cooperation in making available to me the numerous—and essential—scene photographs that contribute much to this book, I am deeply grateful to the following organizations and individuals: Allied Artists Corporation (Ed Siegenfeld), Columbia Pictures (Mike Hutner and John Skouras), the French Film Office, Janus Films (Saul Turrell), Macmillan Audio-Brandon (Myron Bresnick), McGraw-Hill Films, Metro-Goldwyn-Mayer (Al Newman and Mary S. Ledding), the Film Stills Archive of the Museum of Modern Art (Mary Corliss and Valerie Hart), the Theater Collection of the New York Public Library (Paul Myers), Paramount Pictures Corporation (Charles Glenn), Roy Export Company Establishment, the Swedish Information Services, Twentieth Century-Fox Films (Jonas Rosenfield), the United Artists Corporation (Gabe Sumner and Mike Nickolay), Universal Pictures (David Lipton and Eric Naumann), the Walter Reade Organization (Sheldon Gunzburg) and Warner Brothers (George Nelson).

I am also particularly indebted to William Kenly, owner and custodian of the William Kenly Collection, who graciously provided many rare and valuable scene photographs as well as suggestions as to where others might be found; to Pare Lorentz for letting me have stills from his classic documentary film, *The River,* and allowing me to quote from his copyrighted narrative; to Donald L. Velde, Inc., and Charles Woerter, president, for providing photographs and helpful advice; to Fay Miske of Joseph Burstyn, Inc.; and to my old friend and fellow film enthusiast, John Lowe. Leo Dratfield of Films, Inc., and Myron Bresnick of Macmillan Audio-Brandon have generously helped with screenings of films from their companies' archives, and Lillian Gerard, Adrienne Mancia, Larry Kardish and Charles Silver of the Department of Films of the Museum of Modern Art have assisted with screenings and in many other ways. Likewise, Cinema V, the Avco Embassy Corporation, Richard Brandt and Jan Kadar have provided materials and aid for the volume that will be sequential to this.

I would further take this opportunity to state my lasting gratitude to my old employer, the New York *Times,* and its subsidiary, Arno Press, for their wisdom and foresight in publishing their multi-volume compilation of all film reviews printed in the New York *Times* between 1913 and 1973. The immediate availability of this collection for reference, not only to my own original reviews of most of the films discussed but to those of my fellow reviewers at the *Times,* has been a welcome convenience and invaluable aid.

Last but far from least, I am indebted beyond words to my enterprising and tireless research assistant, Harriet Dryden, who did the heavy job of assembling the stills with diligence and tact; to my dear and patient wife, Florence, who assumed the thankless task of typing the manuscript, along with many time-consuming chores; and to my loyal and helpful editor, William Targ, without whom . . .

PHOTOGRAPH CREDITS